# GAY RIGHTS

Other Books in the Current Controversies Series:

The Abortion Controversy
The AIDS Crisis
Alcoholism
The Disabled
Drug Trafficking
Energy Alternatives
Ethics
Europe
Family Violence
Free Speech
Gambling
Genetics and Intelligence
Gun Control
Hate Crimes
Hunger
Illegal Immigration
The Information Highway
Interventionism
Iraq
Nationalism and Ethnic Conflict
Police Brutality
Politicians and Ethics
Pollution
Reproductive Technologies
Sexual Harassment
Smoking
Teen Addiction
Urban Terrorism
Violence Against Women
Violence in the Media
Women in the Military
Youth Violence

# GAY RIGHTS

**David Bender**, *Publisher*
**Bruno Leone**, *Executive Editor*

**Scott Barbour**, *Managing Editor*
**Brenda Stalcup**, *Senior Editor*

**Tamara L. Roleff**, *Book Editor*

CURRENT CONTROVERSIES

Cover Photo: Donna Binder/Impact Visuals

Library of Congress Cataloging-in-Publication Data

Gay rights / Tamara L. Roleff, book editor.
    p. cm. — (Current controversies)
    Includes bibliographical references and index.
    ISBN 1-56510-532-X (lib. bdg. : alk. paper). —
ISBN 1-56510-531-1 (pbk. : alk. paper)
    1. Gay rights—United States. 2. Gays—United States. I. Roleff,
Tamara L., 1959–    . II. Series.
HQ76.3.U5G394   1997
306.76′6—dc20
                                                   96-36298
                                                        CIP

# Contents

Foreword                                                                    11

Introduction                                                               13

## Chapter 1: What Rights Should Gays and Lesbians Have?

Chapter Preface                                                            17

Gay and Lesbian Partners Should Receive Employment Benefits                18
*by Brian McNaught*
Providing domestic-partner benefits for gay and lesbian employees is
simply a matter of equal pay for equal work. To deny gay and lesbian employees domestic-partner benefits discriminates on the basis of marital
status and sexual orientation. By offering a domestic-partner benefits
package, companies can rectify these economic and social injustices and
validate the relationships of their gay and lesbian employees.

Homosexual Partners Should Not Receive Employment Benefits                 23
*by Jack Chambers*
Legal spouses are awarded social and economic benefits as a means of upholding marriage and the traditional family. Companies that offer benefits
packages to their employees' live-in companions—whether heterosexual
or homosexual—reward immoral behavior. Communities should not support companies that encourage immoral and deviant behavior in this way.

Limiting Domestic-Partner Benefits to Same-Sex Couples Is Justifiable      25
*by David Boaz*
Granting domestic-partner benefits to gay and lesbian couples while
denying them to heterosexual couples is justifiable because gay and lesbian couples do not have the option of legal marriage. Allowing heterosexual couples to receive domestic-partner benefits would undermine
marriage because the couple would receive all the legal benefits of marriage without having to make a commitment. However, domestic-partner
benefits for same-sex couples promote committed, stable relationships
and should therefore be encouraged.

Granting Domestic-Partner Benefits Only to Same-Sex Couples                27
Is Discriminatory *by Joseph Farah*
It is discriminatory to grant health benefits to homosexual domestic partners while excluding domestic partners who are heterosexual. This policy
cannot be justified on the grounds that homosexuals would marry if they
had that option: It is unlikely that most same-sex partners would choose
to marry if it were legal. Companies who promote same-sex-partner benefits are merely making a trendy political statement.

Gay and Lesbian Partners Should Be Legally Recognized as    30
Family Members *by Mary N. Cameli*
> Family members are accorded special rights and privileges that are not
> given to lovers and other nonfamily members. As a result, most gay and
> lesbian partners have been unfairly denied the benefits awarded to tradi-
> tional family members. Long-term gay and lesbian relationships should
> be legally recognized as nontraditional families and should be eligible to
> receive the same benefits and privileges as do traditional families.

Homosexual Partners Should Not Be Legally Recognized as    35
Family Members *by Frank S. Zepezauer*
> The gay or lesbian family must not be sanctioned as an official legal insti-
> tution. Recognizing homosexual families will lead to the destruction of
> the two-parent, opposite-sex family prevalent in every culture in human
> history. Society must stop the legitimization of the homosexual family.

Gay and Lesbian Foreigners Should Be Granted Asylum in the    39
United States *by David Tuller*
> Some foreign governments actively oppress gays and lesbians because of
> their sexual orientation. Many of these persecuted gays and lesbians have
> been granted asylum by several Western nations. The United States
> should join its allies in granting asylum to gay and lesbian refugees who
> have legitimate claims of persecution.

Foreign Homosexuals Should Not Be Granted Asylum in the    41
United States *by Lars-Erik Nelson*
> Although some homosexuals do face persecution in other countries, allow-
> ing them asylum in the United States because of their sexual orientation
> would lead to massive immigration fraud because of the difficulty in prov-
> ing a refugee's true sexual orientation. The policy of granting asylum be-
> cause of homosexuality is not consistent with other regulations for asylum
> and was only instituted because of political pressure from lobbying groups.

## Chapter 2: Should Society Legally Sanction Homosexual Families?

Gay Marriage: An Overview *by* Issues and Controversies on File    44
> A Hawaiian lawsuit may lead the way to legalizing homosexual mar-
> riages. Opponents argue that same-sex marriages will trivialize—or even
> destroy—the institution of marriage. However, advocates maintain that
> marriage is a fundamental right and that prohibiting gays and lesbians
> from marrying violates their civil rights.

### Yes: Society Should Legally Sanction Homosexual Families

Gays and Lesbians Should Be Allowed to Marry *by Andrew Sullivan*    53
> Marriage should be available to any two persons who want to formalize
> their commitment. Gays and lesbians have the same emotional need for the
> stability of marriage as heterosexuals do. There are many reasons—both
> conservative and liberal—to support gay marriage, and no reason to deny it.

Society Has a Compelling Interest in Allowing Gay Marriage    58
*by Jonathan Rauch*
> Marriage—whether heterosexual or homosexual—provides many benefits
> to society. Marriage tends to settle men down and reduce their promiscu-

ity, as well as ensuring that spouses will take care of each other in sickness and old age. Gay marriage should be sanctioned because it would have a positive influence on both the gay community and society at large.

Gays and Lesbians Have an Equal Right to Marriage                     66
*by Lambda Legal Defense and Education Fund, Inc.*
    Marriage is a fundamental right—not a special right—that should not be denied to gays and lesbians. Marriage confers many economic and social benefits that are not available to unmarried couples. Gays and lesbians should have the right to receive these benefits through legal marriage.

Gay and Lesbian Parents Can Raise Well-Adjusted Children              69
*by April Martin*
    Gays and lesbians make excellent parents because their children are planned for and truly wanted. Children of homosexual parents usually have no problem adjusting to their different lifestyle, and they are often more tolerant and open-minded than other children.

**No: Society Should Not Legally Sanction Homosexual Families**

Homosexuals Should Not Be Allowed to Marry *by James Q. Wilson*      72
    Granting homosexuals the right to marry would threaten marriage as an institution. Marriage is a sacred, life-long monogamous union between a man and a woman. Homosexual marriage would not have the same stabilizing influence of heterosexual marriage, nor would homosexual couples be as committed to monogamy as heterosexuals.

Gays and Lesbians Should Not Seek State-Sanctioned Marriage          80
*by Alisa Solomon*
    Gays and lesbians should not seek the right to legal marriage. Gay marriage will not reduce homophobia, but instead will further ostracize those gays and lesbians who choose not to marry. Moreover, the economic and social benefits conferred by marriage should be available to anyone, single or married.

Homosexual Parents Are Not in a Child's Best Interests               84
*by Robert H. Knight*
    Children raised in an openly homosexual environment are at a high risk of being unable to develop their own gender identities. Studies reveal that these children do not adjust well to their family situation and are more prone to social and psychological problems than are children raised in a traditional two-parent family.

# Chapter 3: Should Gays and Lesbians Be Allowed in the Military?

The "Don't Ask, Don't Tell" Ban: An Overview *by Craig Donegan*     91
    The "Don't Ask, Don't Tell" policy, which allows gays and lesbians to join the armed forces as long as they do not reveal their sexual orientation, faces intense opposition from the military. Critics of the policy charge that allowing gays and lesbians to serve will disrupt discipline, lower morale, and threaten combat readiness. Supporters maintain that such opposition is based on prejudice and that gays and lesbians have an equal right to serve in the military.

## No: Gays and Lesbians Should Not Be Allowed in the Military

Homosexuality Is Incompatible with Military Service      95
*by James A. Donovan*
> Homosexuals do not fit in with the standards of discipline and duty imposed by the military. Homosexual conduct is contrary to military ideals and will not promote mutual trust or respect among the ranks. Allowing homosexuals to serve in the armed forces will compel the military to provide special clubs, activities, and housing for gays and lesbians.

Allowing Gays and Lesbians in the Military Will Adversely Affect      100
Morale *by Mark E. Cantrell*
> Officially allowing homosexuals to serve in the military would demoralize heterosexual service members by forcing them to share accommodations with gay or lesbian roommates, to witness public displays of affection between homosexuals, or to contend with disruptions caused by romances between soldiers. Sensitivity training cannot eliminate service members' reasonable objections to these circumstances and will not result in a harmonious working relationship between gays and straights.

Homosexuals in the Military Present a Medical Risk *by Ronald D. Ray*    108
> The military requires healthy service members, and, as a group, homosexuals are not able-bodied. Studies reveal that most homosexuals regularly engage in promiscuous and unsafe sex, leading them to contract sexually transmitted diseases and AIDS at a significantly higher rate than heterosexuals. Allowing homosexuals in the military would increase the risk of heterosexual soldiers' contracting AIDS through contaminated blood supplies. The costs of caring for diseased homosexuals in military medical facilities would be very high as well.

## Yes: Gays and Lesbians Should Be Allowed in the Military

Gays and Lesbians Should Be Allowed to Serve in the Military      115
*by Barry M. Goldwater*
> Studies have shown that there is no valid reason to ban gays and lesbians from serving in the military. The armed forces once objected to the integration of blacks and women into the military, but history has proven that their concerns were unfounded. Likewise, lifting the gay ban will not harm America's military strength or readiness.

Homosexuals Can Enhance Military Effectiveness *by Richard H. Kohn*    118
> Homosexuals have fought well and honorably in the military for centuries. Continuing to resist the presence of gays and lesbians who serve openly in the armed forces will only undermine military effectiveness. When the military accurately reflects the diversity of society, its strength and effectiveness will be enhanced.

Homosexuals in the Military Are Not a Threat to National Security      121
*by Franklin D. Jones and Ronald J. Koshes*
> A historical review of the ban against homosexuals in the military reveals no evidence that homosexuals are a threat to national security nor that homosexuals in the military are poor workers. The data do not support the policy of excluding homosexuals from military service.

The Military Ban on Gays and Lesbians Is Based on Prejudice     126
  *by Alasdair Palmer*
> Critics argue that homosexuality is incompatible with military service be-
> cause it disrupts and undermines discipline. This view is misguided and is
> based on prejudice. There is no evidence that allowing gays and lesbians
> to serve openly in the military would be disruptive. Countries that have
> changed their policies to allow gays and lesbians to serve have noticed no
> negative effects on morale, efficiency, or discipline.

## Chapter 4: Do Gays and Lesbians Need Antidiscrimination Laws?

Antidiscrimination Laws for Gays and Lesbians: An Overview     133
  *by Richard L. Worsnop*
> Gay rights activists maintain that, as victims of abuse and discrimination,
> gays and lesbians need extra legal protection. They advocate laws protect-
> ing gays from discrimination as a means of leveling the playing field. Con-
> servatives claim that homosexuals already have the same civil rights as ev-
> eryone else; any additional protections would give them "special rights."

### Yes: Gays and Lesbians Need Antidiscrimination Laws

Gays and Lesbians Are Entitled to Protection Against Discrimination     136
  *by Michael Nava and Robert Dawidoff*
> Gays and lesbians are entitled to the same constitutional rights as other
> Americans. Their right to live their lives free of abuse and discrimination
> should be upheld by the force of the law.

Antidiscrimination Laws Protect Equal Rights for Gays and Lesbians     143
  *by American Civil Liberties Union*
> Several constitutional amendments, as well as numerous local, state, and
> federal laws, guarantee gays and lesbians equal protection under the law.
> Laws that permit discrimination against homosexuals oppress gays and
> lesbians and should be repealed. Laws that prohibit discrimination based
> on sexual orientation do not give homosexuals "special rights," but the
> right to be treated equally.

Discrimination Against Gays and Lesbians Should Be Stopped     149
  *by Richard Rorty*
> The heterosexual majority takes sadistic pleasure in persecuting gays and
> lesbians. In order to eradicate this mistreatment, society must do more
> than simply guarantee homosexuals' legal rights; heterosexuals must
> sympathize with gays and treat them accordingly.

Barring Antidiscrimination Laws for Gays and Lesbians Is     152
  Unconstitutional *by Anthony Kennedy et al.*
> Colorado voters approved an amendment to their state's constitution
> (Amendment 2) prohibiting laws that protect homosexuals from discrimi-
> nation. Because this amendment makes homosexuals a separate class with
> no right to seek legal protection from discrimination, it violates the Four-
> teenth Amendment to the U.S. Constitution, which guarantees all Ameri-
> cans equal protection under the law.

## No: Gays and Lesbians Do Not Need Antidiscrimination Laws

Homosexuals Should Not Be Granted Special Rights *by Tony Marco*    160
> Homosexuals are not an oppressed group that needs legal protection. As a group, gays and lesbians are economically well-off and politically powerful. Their calls for special legal protection are unfounded and should not be taken seriously.

Gay Rights Will Legitimize Homosexuality *by Hadley Arkes*    166
> The courts—including the U.S. Supreme Court—are increasingly willing to grant special rights to homosexuals. Gays and lesbians already receive the same legal protection as other people. The movement to give them additional rights is an attempt to establish homosexuality as a morally acceptable lifestyle.

Barring Antidiscrimination Laws for Gays and Lesbians Is    172
Constitutional  *by Antonin Scalia, William H. Rehnquist, and Clarence Thomas*
> Colorado's Amendment 2, which prohibits special treatment of homosexuals, is a democratic attempt by the majority of voters in a statewide referendum to reinforce their moral values and to prevent homosexuals from receiving special protections. The U.S. Supreme Court's majority decision striking down the Colorado amendment has no foundation in constitutional law.

Bibliography    182

Organizations to Contact    184

Index    187

# Foreword

By definition, controversies are "discussions of questions in which opposing opinions clash" (Webster's Twentieth Century Dictionary Unabridged). Few would deny that controversies are a pervasive part of the human condition and exist on virtually every level of human enterprise. Controversies transpire between individuals and among groups, within nations and between nations. Controversies supply the grist necessary for progress by providing challenges and challengers to the status quo. They also create atmospheres where strife and warfare can flourish. A world without controversies would be a peaceful world; but it also would be, by and large, static and prosaic.

## The Series' Purpose

The purpose of the Current Controversies series is to explore many of the social, political, and economic controversies dominating the national and international scenes today. Titles selected for inclusion in the series are highly focused and specific. For example, from the larger category of criminal justice, Current Controversies deals with specific topics such as police brutality, gun control, white collar crime, and others. The debates in Current Controversies also are presented in a useful, timeless fashion. Articles and book excerpts included in each title are selected if they contribute valuable, long-range ideas to the overall debate. And wherever possible, current information is enhanced with historical documents and other relevant materials. Thus, while individual titles are current in focus, every effort is made to ensure that they will not become quickly outdated. Books in the Current Controversies series will remain important resources for librarians, teachers, and students for many years.

In addition to keeping the titles focused and specific, great care is taken in the editorial format of each book in the series. Book introductions and chapter prefaces are offered to provide background material for readers. Chapters are organized around several key questions that are answered with diverse opinions representing all points on the political spectrum. Materials in each chapter include opinions in which authors clearly disagree as well as alternative opinions in which authors may agree on a broader issue but disagree on the possible solutions. In this way, the content of each volume in Current Controversies mirrors the mosaic of opinions encountered in society. Readers will quickly realize that there are many viable answers to these complex issues. By questioning each author's conclusions, students and casual readers can begin to develop the critical thinking skills so important to evaluating opinionated material.

Current Controversies is also ideal for controlled research. Each anthology in the series is composed of primary sources taken from a wide gamut of informational categories including periodicals, newspapers, books, United States and foreign government documents, and the publications of private and public organizations. Readers will find factual support for reports, debates, and research papers covering all areas of important issues. In addition, an annotated table of contents, an index, a book and periodical bibliography, and a list of organizations to contact are included in each book to expedite further research.

Perhaps more than ever before in history, people are confronted with diverse and contradictory information. During the Persian Gulf War, for example, the public was not only treated to minute-to-minute coverage of the war, it was also inundated with critiques of the coverage and countless analyses of the factors motivating U.S. involvement. Being able to sort through the plethora of opinions accompanying today's major issues, and to draw one's own conclusions, can be a complicated and frustrating struggle. It is the editors' hope that Current Controversies will help readers with this struggle.

*"The dispute over whether gay fathers and lesbian mothers are fit for custody of their children is becoming a key cause for gay-rights advocates."*

# Introduction

Tyler Doustou enjoyed playing with his parents like any other two-year-old. He loved to play catch with the parent he called "Da-Da." He was not shy about giving kisses to his mommy. But one day in 1993 his maternal grandmother, Kay Bottoms, sued for custody of Tyler, alleging that her daughter's lesbianism made her an unfit parent.

Henrico County (Virginia) Circuit Court judge Buford M. Parsons Jr. concurred. He ruled that Sharon Bottoms was a criminal because she "admitted in this court that she is living in an active homosexual relationship," an activity that violates Virginia's laws against sodomy. Explaining his decision to grant custody of Tyler to Kay Bottoms, Parson wrote that "the mother's conduct is illegal. . . . Her conduct is immoral and . . . renders her an unfit parent." Sharon Bottoms was allowed visitation rights two days a week, but Tyler was not allowed in his mother's home or to have any contact with his mother's partner, April Wade.

Sharon Bottoms appealed the circuit court's decision to the Virginia Court of Appeals. The three-judge panel of the Court of Appeals ruled unanimously that sexual orientation alone does not make a parent unfit. "The fact that a mother is a lesbian and has engaged in illegal sexual acts does not alone justify taking custody of a child from her and awarding the child to a nonparent," wrote Sam W. Coleman III in the June 21, 1994, ruling. The court cited case after case in which a parent who had committed a crime was not deemed unfit unless the criminal activity harmed the child.

Kay Bottoms appealed the ruling to the Virginia Supreme Court. In a 4-3 decision on April 21, 1995, the court ruled that Sharon Bottoms was an unfit mother whose homosexual relationship would bring "social condemnation" upon her child. Justice A. Christian Compton wrote for the majority opinion, "Living daily under conditions stemming from active lesbianism practiced in the home . . . will inevitably affect the child's relationship with its peers and with the community." Kay Bottoms retained custody of her grandson.

Many conservative groups applauded the Virginia Supreme Court's decision. These groups oppose gay parental rights, maintaining that homosexual parents can irretrievably influence a child to grow up to be gay or lesbian. Paul Cameron, chairman of the Family Research Institute in Colorado Springs, surveyed studies of children who were raised by gay or lesbian parents. He found that in adulthood, between 8 and 33 percent of the sons considered themselves to be gay or bisexual—a percentage well above the most recent national estimate that 1 to 2 percent of the general population is gay, lesbian, or bisexual.

Other opponents of gay families agree with the Virginia Supreme Court's opinion that children of gay or lesbian parents face social condemnation. Jaki Edwards, who during her adolescence was raised by her lesbian mother, maintains that she was devastated by her mother's lifestyle.

> I realize that homosexuals feel they can give a child love and support that even many straight families can't provide. But I've been there. I know the finger-pointing and the shame one carries. For years, you struggle with the thought that you might be a homosexual. People say "like mother, like daughter." Most of us become promiscuous to prove we're straight.

Edwards and other critics also question whether children who are raised by gay or lesbian parents will learn how to relate to members of the opposite sex. Edwards argues that the absence of an opposite-sex role model presents its own problems: "How will a man raised by two men know how to relate to a woman? A woman brought up like this doesn't know how to emotionally connect with men. I had to struggle for years to believe a man could really love me." Robert H. Knight, director of cultural studies at the Family Research Council in Washington, D.C., agrees, maintaining that these children miss out on seeing important relationships between men and women, mothers and fathers, and husbands and wives. Children need a parent of the same sex to learn their sexual identity, he contends, and a parent of the opposite sex to learn how to interact.

Gay-rights advocates, however, disagree with the gay-rights opponents' assessment of gay parents and their families. Family-law experts argue that homosexuality cannot be so awful a crime that a gay or lesbian parent's child should be taken away by the courts. They question the wisdom in such cases as the 1996 decision of the Escambia Circuit Court in Florida, which removed an eleven-year-old daughter from her lesbian mother and granted custody to her father, a heterosexual who had served nine years in prison for murdering his first wife. Columnist Carrie Nelle Moye asks:

> What kind of convoluted thinking determines that a person who has committed the ultimate crime, murder, is a better parent than a child's mother? Of course one would have to believe that the judge in this case would argue that murder is *not* the ultimate crime; it is at least second—perhaps further down?—than lesbianism.

The court's action in this case, Moye maintains, seems to imply that although the father is a murderer, at least he is a *heterosexual* murderer. According to supporters of gay rights, such cases prove that gay parents are unfairly discriminated against.

Gay-rights advocates and mental health experts argue that the emotional and sexual development of children raised by gay or lesbian parents is not significantly different from that of children raised by heterosexual parents. According to Michael E. Lamb, chief of the section on social and emotional development at the National Institute of Child Health and Human Development, early studies that suggested gays and lesbians made poor parents were based on individual cases of troubled children "by researchers with an ax to grind." Hannah Feldman, who lived with her lesbian mother between the ages of twelve and eighteen, asserts that her childhood was not much different than that of her friends who had heterosexual parents:

> I resented my mom for the same reasons my friends resented theirs—for making rules and curfews; for not accepting report-card B's; for grumping about the music I listened to, my reluctance to do dishes and how much time I spent on the phone. I loved her for the same reasons my friends loved their moms— for laughing with me, teaching me things, taking care of me when I was sick, understanding my various disappointments and frustrations.

Current research supports Feldman's assessment of her life with a lesbian mother, Lamb contends. "What evidence there is suggests there are no particular developmental or emotional deficits for children raised by gay or lesbian parents. . . . These kids look OK."

Gay and lesbian parents are raising between six and fourteen million children in at least four million households, according to the American Bar Association and other sources. The dispute over whether gay fathers and lesbian mothers are fit for custody of their children is becoming a key cause for gay-rights advocates. *Gay Rights: Current Controversies* examines the debates over what rights gays and lesbians should have, such as the right to marry and raise children, serve in the military, and be free of discrimination.

# Chapter 1

# What Rights Should Gays and Lesbians Have?

# Chapter Preface

In the 1980s, Alison D. and Virginia M., a lesbian couple who had lived together for three years in New York, decided to have a child. Together they chose the sperm donor, planned and participated in Virginia's impregnation, and contributed equally in the financial and emotional responsibilities of raising the child, a boy. The women underwent the process again two years later when Alison became pregnant and gave birth to a girl. Six months later, when Virginia's boy was 2½ years old, the women separated.

For the next few years, Virginia allowed Alison to visit her son. When the boy was 6 years old, however, Virginia, the biological mother, barred Alison, the nonbiological mother, from further visitation. Alison sued to regain the right to visit the child she considered to be her son. She claimed that she had to take her case to court solely because of her sexual orientation. A heterosexual parent, Alison contended, would automatically be allowed to visit her child. In her appellant brief to the court, Alison maintained that although she is not the biological mother, she is a "de facto" parent to the boy and therefore should retain some parental rights.

Nevertheless, the New York Court of Appeals rejected Alison's appeal. The court ruled that Alison did not have the right to request visitation with the boy:

> At issue in this case is whether petitioner, a biological stranger to a child who is properly in the custody of his biological mother, has standing to seek visitation with the child. . . . She is not the child's 'parent'; that is, she is not the biological mother of the child.

To support its decision, the court cited with approval a similar case in California, *Nancy S. v. Michele G.*, which had reached the same conclusion: A child's nonbiological parent is not entitled to demand visitation rights.

Whether same-sex couples should be legally considered coparents to their children is just one of the gay rights issues being debated in the courts. The authors in the following chapter examine whether gays and lesbians should receive employee or domestic partner benefits, whether same-sex couples should be legally recognized as family members, and how U.S. immigration laws should treat gay and lesbian immigrants.

# Gay and Lesbian Partners Should Receive Employment Benefits

## by Brian McNaught

**About the author:** *Brian McNaught is an educator, a corporate consultant, and the author of* On Being Gay *and* Gay Issues in the Workplace.

One of the biggest issues on the minds of most gay, lesbian, and bisexual employees, particularly those who are open about their sexual orientation, is that of receiving equal compensation for equal work. A good-faith effort to provide domestic-partner benefits for gay and lesbian employees is an essential ingredient in the company's mission to create an equal playing field where each employee feels valued.

### Equal Pay for Equal Work

Having domestic-partner benefits means that the partners of gay, lesbian, and bisexual employees would receive the same benefits from the company that are given to the married spouses of heterosexual employees. Beyond the obvious economic benefits represented here, there is an important symbolic value to gay employees. A commonly heard phrase in this discussion is "Equal pay for equal work."

When asked to explain the issue of domestic-partner benefits to employees in my workshop, I created the following scenario:

"Larry," I said to the executive sitting in the front row, "let's pretend that you and I went to the same university, pursued the same studies, graduated with the same grades and honors, and were recruited by the same corporation. We share an office. We do the same work. We are both hailed as the best and the brightest employees in the company. You get married. The next day your wife receives health-care benefits from the corporation. My partner, Ray, with whom I share my life, gets nothing. Because of all of the benefits your wife receives, you are getting paid more than I am to do the same job. I believe that is unfair. It is not fair to me. And it is not fair to our heterosexual co-workers who for whatever reason are not married to the person with whom they share their lives."

"You're right," agreed Larry. "It's not fair."

Same-sex couples cannot legally marry in the United States. (In some countries, such as Denmark, they are allowed to do so.) While a handful of cities, such as New York, permit gay and lesbian couples to register as partners, the gesture is without much substance. Despite how long, faithfully, and lovingly they have shared their lives with a person of the same sex, gay men and lesbian women are denied the legal protections and incentives associated

> *"When [a] company provides domestic-partner benefits to gay employees, it addresses the inequity in workplace compensation."*

with marriage. Because they cannot legally marry, gay and lesbian employees have not been able to qualify for the spousal benefits provided by their employer. When the company provides domestic-partner benefits to gay employees, it addresses the inequity in workplace compensation.

Some companies have decided to extend benefits to the domestic partners of all of their unmarried employees. Other companies have decided to extend benefits only to gay and lesbian employees who can not legally marry. These companies generally refer to this compensation as spousal-equivalent benefits.

Domestic-partner or spousal-equivalent compensation covers a broad range of benefits from medical and dental insurance to health-club membership. The medical and dental insurance, often referred to as "hard" benefits, can be more difficult to provide, particularly when the company is insured by an outside vendor. Some outside insurance vendors have balked at covering the domestic partners of gay employees because they fear it would be too expensive. (The experience of companies that provide "hard" benefits have shown those fears to be unsubstantiated.)

## "Soft" Benefits

Some domestic-partner benefits, such as bereavement and family leave, often referred to as "soft" benefits, require no outside negotiation with insurance vendors and can be implemented immediately. In 1988, for instance, the Attorney General of Massachusetts issued these inclusive parameters for state employees regarding family leave:

"Family leave is the time granted from work to employees upon the serious health condition of a dependent child, parent, spouse, named partner, parent of spouse or named partner, or any individual who fits the definition of a dependent under the IRS tax code."

The attorney general's guidelines for bereavement leave state: "Employees can take a leave of up to four calendar days with pay in the case of a death in their families (spouse or named partner, child, parent or parent of spouse or named partner, sibling, grandparent, grandchild) or person living in the employee's household."

Other domestic-partner or spousal-equivalent benefits that require no outside negotiation with insurance vendors include pension plans, relocation expense reimbursement, tuition, access to company facilities, discounts, health-club membership, and those other perquisites that are provided to the spouses of heterosexual employees.

> *"The cost to the company [of adding domestic-partner benefits] is no more than it would be to add the spouse of a heterosexual employee."*

Where companies are self-insured, they can also provide health insurance and dental insurance to the domestic partners of their gay, lesbian, bisexual, and unmarried heterosexual employees. Even when not self-insured, companies can find outside vendors who are willing to cover the domestic partners of "unmarried" employees. . . .

An ever-increasing number of corporations, organizations, and municipalities provide a range of domestic-partner benefits to their employees. Those corporations that provide both hard and soft benefits include Microsoft, Lotus Development, Apple Computer, Levi Strauss, MCA, Viacom, Sun Microsystems, Ben and Jerry's Homemade, and Montefiore Medical Center, to name only a few. The domestic partners of all gay employees of Boston, Seattle, and West Hollywood, among others, receive some form of domestic benefits. The American Friends Service Committee, the American Psychological Association, and the Episcopal Diocese of Newark, New Jersey, are among the many organizations that have such compensation.

## Low Cost to the Company

As these corporations and organizations have found, the cost to the company is no more than it would be to add the spouse of a heterosexual employee. In fact, since most gay and lesbian couples are two-income families, both generally insured by their own employers, only a small percentage of gay employees have actually signed up for domestic-partner benefits. Those who do are often without children, which also makes their benefits package less costly than that of the average married heterosexual worker.

A nationalized program of health care, as is provided in Canada, may make the issue of medical insurance for domestic partners moot. Much of the discussion today on medical benefits for the domestic partners of gay male employees has focused on the expense, often fanned by fear of AIDS. Some employers have worried aloud that covering the healthcare costs of more gay people would mean major AIDS-related expenses, yet those ill-founded fears have not been realized. Such fears betray a misunderstanding about AIDS, who gets AIDS, and how many people are HIV-positive. It also betrays misinformation about the cost of treating the disease. Should the domestic partner of a homosexual or heterosexual employee need HIV-related treatment, the cost to the insurer is less than it would be for chronic heart problems or cancer.

To qualify for domestic-partner benefits from their company, gay, lesbian, or bisexual employees generally must sign an affidavit testifying that they are involved in a committed relationship. The city of Berkeley, California, for instance, extends a variety of benefits to the domestic partners of all of their municipal employees, regardless of gender. To qualify, the employee must file an Affidavit of Domestic Partnership with the city. In the statement, they swear that:

> *"How does paying a gay person in a committed relationship the same as we pay a heterosexual person who is married undermine the value and need for marriage?"*

1. The two parties have resided together for at least six months and intend to do so indefinitely.
2. The two parties are not married, are at least eighteen years old, are not related by blood closer than would bar marriage in California, and are mentally competent to consent to the contract.
3. The two parties declare that they are each other's sole domestic partner and they are responsible for their common welfare.
4. The two parties agree to notify the employer if there is any change in the circumstances attested to in the affidavit.
5. The two parties affirm, under penalty of perjury, that the assertions in the affidavit are true to the best of their knowledge.

As explained in a memo from Lambda Legal Defense, a gay public-interest law group, the domestic partnership may be officially ended by one of the two parties upon filing with the Risk Management Office a statement, under penalty of perjury, that the partnership is terminated, and a copy of the termination statement will be mailed to the other partner unless both have signed the termination statement. After the termination of the partnership, the employee must wait six months before filing another Affidavit of Domestic Partnership.

Should the employer suffer a loss because of a false statement of domestic partnership or because of failure to notify of a change of circumstances, the employer may bring a civil action to recover losses and reasonable attorney fees.

## Rebutting the Argument Against Domestic-Partner Benefits

"Excuse me," said a workshop participant who waved his hand for attention after I had explained the reasoning behind domestic-partner benefits. "I believe that the company giving benefits to your gay partner puts your relationship at the same level as mine, and that's not right. Many of the problems we face today as a society are due to the breakdown of the family. We need to support heterosexual families. We need heterosexual families, or the world will end. Putting your relationship on a par with my family undermines heterosexuality, and I don't think this company ought to be endorsing the gay lifestyle. No offense intended."

"No offense taken," I said. "That's why we're here—to talk about these issues. I agree that the family needs to be supported. I agree that we need heterosexual unions. No gay person I know is arguing otherwise. But how does paying a gay person in a committed relationship the same as we pay a heterosexual person who is married undermine the value and the need for marriage? Are we assuming that if gay people are treated equitably that heterosexuals will decide not to marry? Do I need to be discriminated against in order for a heterosexual to feel his or her marriage is valued?

"You sometimes hear people say that by granting civil rights to homosexuals or by providing domestic-partner benefits the company is endorsing a lifestyle. To begin with, there is no one gay 'lifestyle,' any more than there is a heterosexual 'lifestyle.' It seems to me, though, that when you reward people for being heterosexually married by providing them with an assortment of benefits that unmarried heterosexuals do not receive and that gay people—who can't legally marry—do not receive, the company is discriminating on the basis of both marital status and sexual orientation. Furthermore, it's undermining the reasoning for providing benefits."

As explained to me, corporate benefits have two basic purposes: (1) to enhance the overall compensation package in order to attract and retain the very best employees, and (2) to cushion the impact of personal and family crises in order to reduce their adverse effect on an employee's job performance. By providing domestic-partner benefits to gay, lesbian, and bisexual employees, a company satisfies those two purposes. Such benefits make working for one company more attractive to talented gay people than working for another that has no benefits. Likewise, knowing that their savings will not be wiped out to pay for their partner's recovery from a possible illness reduces unnecessary stress and enables gay employees to focus on their work.

When MCA Inc., a unit of Matsushita Electric Industrial Co. and parent of Universal Studios, extended health-insurance coverage to the partners of its gay and lesbian employees, company president Sidney Sheinberg stated that the policy "underscores MCA's ongoing commitment to create a workplace free of discrimination by ensuring fair treatment of all employees regardless of sexual orientation."

Lotus Development issued a similar statement when they announced they would fully extend domestic-partner benefits. "Lotus recognizes that lesbian and gay employees do not have a choice to legalize permanent and exclusive relationships through marriage; thus they cannot legally share financial, health, and other benefits with their significant partners. For this reason, in the interest of fairness and diversity, Lotus will recognize the significance of such relationships by including them in our policies and benefits."

# Homosexual Partners Should Not Receive Employment Benefits

## by Jack Chambers

**About the author:** *Jack Chambers is a syndicated columnist in Austin, Texas.*

Ever since Adam and Eve were tempted in the garden of Eden, it has been difficult for people to say no to forbidden fruit. We should be encouraged, therefore, when someone demonstrates moral responsibility by resisting temptation. The folks in Williamson County, Texas, should be commended for refusing to take an "apple"—Apple Computer.

### No Tax-Incentive Package

In a 3-2 decision in December 1993, Williamson County commissioners voted against offering a tax-incentive package for Apple to build its $80-million customer support center in their community. The commissioners decided against offering the package because Apple provides so-called domestic partner benefits for its employees. These benefits, including health insurance, are offered to employees' live-in lovers, including homosexuals.

According to the *Austin American-Statesman*, Apple had estimated that the center would employ 1,400 people within a few years, and thousands more as it expanded from customer service into research, development and marketing. An economic impact study predicted that 4,500 jobs would be created by Apple's move, with $300 million, including $52.4 million in wages and salaries, pumped into the local economy by the year 2000. The county was considering tax breaks for Apple totaling $750,000 over the next seven years.

Since the vote not to extend the tax breaks, Williamson County has come under fire from business and political leaders and homosexuals, who view the decision as unfair governmental interference in a private company's personnel policies. This is ridiculous. Nobody is telling Apple what they can or can't do.

Jack Chambers, "A Texas County Refuses 'Forbidden Fruit,'" *Los Angeles Times*, December 16, 1993. Reprinted by permission of the author.

In fact, no one is preventing Apple from moving wherever they like.

A community simply decided not to give any extra enticement for a company to move there. That is their right.

I am philosophically opposed to the extension of such incentives. They amount to unfair subsidies for some companies over others. When newcomer corporations are given financial breaks by government officials, it is virtually impossible for "mom & pop" enterprises to compete with them. But if such packages are going to be offered, it is certainly justifiable for the decision-makers to take moral and social factors into consideration.

Bringing a company like Apple to a community could have a major negative impact. Extending benefits to live-in lovers is a way of rewarding immoral behavior. Our society has traditionally rewarded legal spouses with various benefits as a way of upholding the traditional institutions of marriage and family. When similar benefits are provided to people who simply "shack up," this only encourages people to "live in sin," as we used to call it.

If private companies want to extend such benefits to their employees, that's their prerogative. But local communities would be wise to refrain from offering these companies any special incentives. After all, when word gets out that a major employer offers financial benefits for people who participate in deviant behavior, those kinds of people are going to be attracted to live and work in the community. Local citizens shouldn't be chastised when they say, "We don't wish to offer any special attractions for homosexuals."

> *"When . . . a major employer offers financial benefits for people who participate in deviant behavior, those kinds of people are going to . . . live and work in the community."*

Commissioner David Hays, who had supported the tax-abatement package, surprised many people when he changed his vote. In a statement unfortunately atypical of elected officials, he said, "For me it boiled down to values."

Too many business and political decisions are based on a bottom-line mentality. So it is refreshing when government officials demonstrate that morality still counts. Perhaps we have learned something since the Garden of Eden. The folks in Williamson County showed us that you can refuse an Apple, no matter how good it looks. Other communities should follow their lead so that, unlike Adam and Eve, they just might maintain their innocence.

# Limiting Domestic-Partner Benefits to Same-Sex Couples Is Justifiable

**by David Boaz**

**About the author:** *David Boaz is the executive vice president of the Cato Institute, a libertarian public policy research organization that advocates limited government.*

New York's new Governor, George Pataki, plans to reverse [former governor] Mario Cuomo's policy of granting health benefits to the domestic partners of all unmarried state employees. Mr. Pataki is part of a rising political tide that includes Gov. Pete Wilson of California, who said in vetoing his state's domestic partnership bill that "government policy ought not to discount marriage by offering a substitute relationship that demands much less."

## Two Kinds of Domestic Partnerships

That's legitimate, but it overlooks that there are two kinds of domestic partnerships—heterosexual and same-sex. Although the most vocal opposition to domestic partnerships is aimed at gay couples, giving them benefits doesn't undermine marriage. Rather, it remedies the injustice that homosexuals can't marry the people with whom they share their lives, and it creates financial incentives for stable relationships. Is this not the goal we seek in encouraging marriage?

Giving domestic partnership benefits to unmarried heterosexual couples, on the other hand, does undermine marriage. They give people who can marry all the financial benefits of a legal union without demanding commitment. "If two heterosexuals are going to shack up together, then they ought to get married," said the Rev. Charles Bullock, who fought successfully to overturn a partnership law in Austin. "If they're not going to make that commitment to each other, why should the city?"

Although the voters' shift to the right in 1994 has imperiled domestic partnership laws, the trend toward giving benefits remains strong in the workplace—most recently at Microsoft, Time Inc. and Capital Cities/ABC. Even Coors, perhaps America's most famously conservative company, is studying the issue.

But many politicians, upset by rising illegitimacy and divorce rates, say that such policies fly in the face of concern about family stability. As Senator Trent Lott, Republican of Mississippi, said in seeking to overturn the District of Columbia's domestic partnership law, "We must begin to take a stand for the family."

> *"[Giving gay couples domestic partnership benefits] creates financial incentives for stable relationships."*

Gay leaders haven't helped themselves in this debate. They invariably urge that heterosexual couples be included in legislation and corporate policies. Many have even denounced the traditional family as a stifling, patriarchal institution, thereby fueling a middle-class backlash.

Gay leaders would be better off making a pro-family case, playing up their commitment to their partners and their desire for a legal union. This argument has found sympathy in the private sector. In 1992 Stanford University extended benefits to domestic partners of homosexuals (but not heterosexuals) because "their commitment to the partnership is analogous to that involved in contemporary marriage," said Barbara Butterfield, a university vice president.

Governments invariably get this wrong, while businesses usually get it right. Every city that has adopted domestic partnership laws has included both same-sex and heterosexual couples, and in almost every case more heterosexuals than homosexuals have filed for partnership status.

## Benefits Only for Same-Sex Couples

But many private organizations—including Stanford, Montefiore Medical Center, Lotus Development Corporation and the Public Broadcasting Service—have extended benefits only to same-sex couples. Most of these companies have said that if homosexual couples are allowed to legally marry, these policies would be ended—which is as it should be.

"This policy discriminates against heterosexuals who choose not to marry," an embittered heterosexual employee at Lotus said. Exactly. And that's a point that Governor Pataki and sensible gay activists ought to be able to agree on: commitment should be encouraged, while relationships without commitment should not expect social recognition or financial benefits.

# Granting Domestic-Partner Benefits Only to Same-Sex Couples Is Discriminatory

**by Joseph Farah**

**About the author:** *Joseph Farah is the author of* This Land Is Our Land *and editor of* Dispatches, *a biweekly cultural watchdog publication, and* Inside California, *a monthly political newsletter.*

Imagine you're a successful television writer. You've just signed a lucrative contract for a new fall series. Now you're eager for the Writers Guild of America West to extend your existing health insurance benefits to your live-in girlfriend.

Sorry, pal. No dice. Guild policies don't permit unmarried members to include their partners in health coverage. OK, fair enough, you say. This policy has probably been around for 40 years and predates the sexual revolution of the 1960s.

But wait a minute. It's not old. In fact, it's brand new. And there is a glaring exception to this policy. New rules expected to be adopted by the guild will permit extending health insurance coverage to domestic partners if—and only if—they are homosexuals.

Let me get this straight (no pun intended): If a male member of the Writers Guild shacks up with a woman, the woman is not eligible for health-insurance benefits. But if a male guild member shacks up with another man, that partner can be covered.

## Discrimination

Doesn't this represent a prima facie [self-evident] case of discrimination based on nothing more than sexual orientation? Isn't liberal Hollywood supposed to be against this kind of bias and double standard? And isn't this an example of granting special rights to homosexuals and lesbians? I thought liberals wanted only to guarantee equal rights for all.

Joseph Farah, "Bias for Gays: Hollywood's Dual Standard," *Los Angeles Times*, July 13, 1993. Reprinted by permission of the author.

These basic questions, if they have ever been raised over power lunches at Le Dome or Spago, don't seem to bother anyone in Hollywood. In fact, the hottest concept in the entertainment industry right now . . . seems to be extending health-insurance benefits to same-sex domestic partners.

The Writers Guild is about to do it. And Warner Bros. is the latest major entertainment company to announce such a move, effective August 1, 1993. MCA/Universal, HBO and Viacom have all adopted similar rules, most of which specifically exclude extending benefits to unmarried heterosexual couples. Sony, Disney and 20th Century Fox are reportedly considering jumping on the bandwagon.

*"[Granting domestic-partner benefits only to homosexual couples is] discrimination based on nothing more than sexual orientation."*

But let me pose a tough question to those in Hollywood who are implementing this policy: What intellectual or moral justification is there for providing special privileges to homosexual couples?

In 1992, you may recall, many of Hollywood's celebrity political activists called for a boycott of Colorado because that state's voters had the audacity to approve an initiative prohibiting special civil rights based on sexual orientation. Liberals, in Hollywood and elsewhere, scoffed at the notion that anyone was interested in extending special rights to homosexuals and ridiculed as bigots, homophobes and Neanderthals anyone who made such suggestions. Now Hollywood seems set on proving their case.

But why would the guild and these entertainment companies go out of their way to extend benefits to same-sex domestic partners to the exclusion of those of the opposite sex? Could it be they are just interested in making a trendy political statement?

Maybe this is the way would-be politicians in Hollywood attempt to legislate their own brave new morality on their own little captive culture. Considering the insular, homogeneous nature of the entertainment industry, there's an excellent chance that very little debate or discussion about these policies has even taken place.

## A Smoke Screen

The only plausible argument to emerge in support of this kind of blatant discrimination is that heterosexual partners have the right to marry while homosexuals do not. But this is no more than a smoke screen. The reasoning doesn't stand up to anything more than superficial scrutiny. For instance, does anyone who employs this logic really believe that all or even most homosexual couples would marry if they had the opportunity? Not likely.

A real cynic might suggest that the bean counters at the guild and major studios made a calculated decision to extend health benefits only to homosexuals because they represent such a tiny portion of the population. If benefits were extended to heterosexual domestic partners, the economic impact would be much higher. But Hollywood wouldn't allow the bottom line to intrude on issues of fairness and equality, would it? Nahhhhhhhhh.

You would think, however, that those crusading on behalf of gay rights would be the first ones to notice the stark duplicity in these policies. I haven't heard one word of dissent from those who have been most vociferous in condemning discrimination based on sexual orientation. Where are the sensitivity police now? Could it be their arguments were specious from the start?

# Gay and Lesbian Partners Should Be Legally Recognized as Family Members

by Mary N. Cameli

**About the author:** *Mary N. Cameli is an attorney in Chicago.*

The status of family, with all of its attendant benefits and burdens, is currently available only to persons related through blood or marriage. Providing opportunities to obtain family status to persons who live outside of traditional families is both equitable and worthwhile in advancing the goals traditionalists promote. For gay men and lesbian women, the problem of family status is exacerbated by public policy, and by statutes denying them marriage and criminalizing their sexual behavior. . . .

## Family Benefits

Family is a status given special accord in our society. Legal rights and responsibilities attach between family members. For example, rights of inheritance are spelled out in the law, and in the absence of a will, family members receive priority in inheritance. Certain family members are obliged to provide financial support for other family members, as in the case of parents and children.

Marriage is the vehicle by which otherwise unrelated adults create the family relationship. The Supreme Court has called marriage a fundamental liberty, "one of the basic civil rights of man." Typically, courts support the institution of marriage because it is "the foundation of the family and of society." In the context of gay and lesbian unions, though, courts quickly sidestep the fundamental rights issue and instead rely on a view of marriage that is centered around procreation. In *Singer v. Hara* (1974), it was noted, "[M]arriage exists as a protected legal institution primarily because of societal values associated with the propagation of the human race." This argument concludes that because marriage of a same-sex couple involves no possibility of children born of the union, a state is free to restrict marriage to male-female couples.

What these courts fail to recognize is that marriage has never been restricted to couples capable of reproducing. Furthermore, gays and lesbians are not any less fertile than the heterosexual population, and in fact are increasingly joining the ranks of parenthood. Many have children from previous unions and some become parents within the context of their gay or lesbian relationships. Finally, and most importantly, society favors the marital/family relationship for reasons other than procreation, and these reasons still exist in gay and lesbian relationships.

Generally, the family, with its economic interdependence, is seen as "the foundation of a strong society," according to E. Carrington Bogan et al. in *The Rights of Gay People: An American Civil Liberties Union Handbook*. Other groups of unrelated adults also form economically interdependent units that would both benefit and benefit from traditional family status. In fact, only 15% of Americans live in a traditional nuclear family, with a father providing financial support, and a mother tending to the home and child care. With only 15% of the population living in the basic, stable family unit as viewed by traditionalists, society could benefit from expanding the status of family to include others. Recognizing other configurations of adults who choose to be economically interdependent, and encouraging such reliances, could further the societal stability traditionalists seek to promote.

In addition to economic stability, families can provide emotional stability. Allowing competent adults who wish to form a family to do so increases personal choice, and allows people who are already living in these stable family units to enjoy the privileges and protections traditional families currently enjoy.

There is no reason to exclude persons who are not involved in a sexual relationship from forming family units. The key benefits provided to society by families are the economic and emotional benefits, and these benefits can be provided by any group of people who agree to live as a family for an indefinite period of time. However, many of the objections to allowing an expansion of the definition (and protections) of family status surround the gay and lesbian issue. These objections are largely based on false stereotypes of gays and lesbians, and on ideas about morality and sexuality.

## Benefits Denied to Nontraditional Families

The reluctance of courts and legislators to recognize an expanded definition of family has translated into an unwillingness to extend family rights and benefits to nontraditional families. These rights and benefits include employment benefits such as insurance and pensions, equal access to housing, status as next-of-kin in medical emergencies, guardianship preference for a disabled family member, preference in child custody and adoption, rights of inheritance, the power to make funeral arrangements for a family member, and the right to sue in tort for loss of consortium and mental duress upon injury of a family member.

For example, a lesbian sued her deceased lover's employer in 1990 for discrimination for refusing to pay her "death benefits" the company normally pays out to surviving spouses, children, and "other relatives who are dependent on the employee participant prior to his or her death who demonstrate financial need after death." For the most part, employee benefits such as insurance, pensions, funeral leave, and death benefits are not readily available to gay and lesbian partners of employees. Although a few government employers now extend employment benefits to nontraditional families, even fewer private employers have followed suit.

Housing benefits are another problem area for gay and lesbian couples. Some zoning ordinances restrict the relationships of persons living in single-family homes in a particular area. Courts have ruled such ordinances are valid and lesbian and gay couples can be excluded on this basis. Other problems exist in the rental context, where landlords can refuse to rent to unmarried couples, whether heterosexual, gay, or lesbian. In New York, where rent controlled apartments can be retained only by family members when the named tenant dies, gays and lesbians have only recently won the right to be considered "family" for the purposes of the rent control laws. Even in this context, though, the status of family is not presumed but must be demonstrated using several court-defined criteria.

> *"Providing opportunities to obtain family status to persons who live outside of traditional families is both equitable and worthwhile."*

Inheritance laws also favor traditional family members, even distant relatives, over a gay or lesbian partner if a gay man or lesbian woman dies intestate. Marriage laws, of course, give the married partners certain rights of inheritance in the absence of a will. Even when a gay man or lesbian woman has a will naming a partner, the will is more likely to be challenged and overturned than a will favoring traditional family members. The same holds true for life insurance claims where a lesbian woman or gay man has named a partner as beneficiary.

## One Lesbian Family's Predicament

In November 1983, a drunk driver struck Sharon Kowalski's car. As a result of the accident, Kowalski, then 27, suffered severe brain damage and other physical injuries, leaving her confined to a wheel chair. Kowalski was unable to act on her own behalf, creating the need for the appointment of a guardian. Kowalski had been living in a closeted lesbian relationship with Karen Thompson for four years before the accident. The two had exchanged rings, and each had named the other as beneficiary on their life insurance policies. Neither woman had revealed the nature of their relationship to their families.

Immediately after the accident, Thompson had difficulty visiting Kowalski in the hospital, or even getting information on her condition. Later, Thompson struggled to gain access to Kowalski to participate in her treatment, as Kowalski was repeatedly transferred from one facility to the next by her family. At each new juncture, Thompson met with opposition from the staff of the various facilities where Kowalski was placed and from Kowalski's parents.

Eventually, a legal battle ensued between Thompson and Kowalski's father, Donald, over the guardianship of Sharon Kowalski. Mr. Kowalski disputed Thompson's assertion that she and Sharon Kowalski were involved in a lesbian relationship, and the Minnesota trial court ruled that the relationship was "uncertain." The court named Mr. Kowalski guardian and gave him complete rights to determine his daughter's visitors. Mr. Kowalski promptly cut off Thompson's visitation, even though Sharon Kowalski expressed a consistent and reliable desire to continue the visits. Thompson battled Donald Kowalski in court for more than three years before visitation was reinstated. In the meantime, Mr. Kowalski had removed Sharon from a rehabilitation center, and placed her in a nursing home where her physical and mental capabilities regressed.

Eventually, Donald Kowalski asked the court to remove him as guardian, due to his own medical problems. Thompson again petitioned the court to name her as guardian. Instead, the court named as guardian Karen Tomberlin, a friend of Kowalski's parents who had not even filed a petition for guardianship. The court made the appointment without having a mandatory hearing to determine Tomberlin's fitness as a guardian.

## Overturning the Trial Court's Decision

On appeal, the court reversed and granted Thompson's petition for guardianship of Sharon Kowalski. In this unusually sharp opinion, the appellate court found that the court below abused its discretion when it denied Thompson's petition. The appellate court opinion was the first to reveal that the evidence overwhelmingly supported the appointment of Thompson. Sixteen of Kowalski's health care providers testified that Thompson had outstanding interaction with Kowalski, had extreme interest and commitment in promoting Kowalski's welfare, had an exceptional understanding of Kowalski's physical and mental needs, and was fully equipped to attend to Kowalski's social and emotional needs.

The appellate court detailed Thompson's frequent visits to Kowalski, and her unique ability to motivate Kowalski in physical therapy and personal hygiene, which Kowalski sometimes found painful. Thompson had built a fully handicap-accessible home in hopes of bringing Kowalski home to live with her. Tomberlin had testified that she was neither willing nor able to care for Kowalski in that manner and had hoped to supervise Kowalski's stay in institutions. Most compelling to the appellate court was that Kowalski had consistently expressed her desire to live with Thompson and have Thompson as her guardian. The appellate court was the first willing to believe this evidence from the health care providers.

Another important distinction the appellate court drew was that Thompson had not invaded Kowalski's privacy by revealing the nature of their relationship, and had not harmed Kowalski by bringing her to events in the women's community and the gay community, where they were both identified as lesbians. The appellate court ruled that this was all irrelevant because Kowalski herself had revealed the nature of the relationship to health care providers and others as soon as she was able to communicate. Further, it was in Kowalski's best interests for Thompson to reveal the nature of the relationship to the health care providers so that the doctors could be fully aware of who the patient was before she became disabled.

> *"Domestic partnership laws can be a bridge to greater inclusion in the law for gay men and lesbian women."*

The dispute over Sharon Kowalski's guardianship lasted seven years. The case demonstrates the magnitude of the problems suffered by nontraditional couples when the legal system fails to meet their needs. In the age of AIDS, when many gay couples face medical and legal battles, Karen Thompson and Sharon Kowalski represent the lack of legal protection afforded nontraditional families in medical emergencies and in long-term guardianship situations.

Because marriage is not available to lesbian and gay couples, many of the protections and benefits of marriage were unavailable to Thompson and Kowalski. As discussed earlier, the benefits that are difficult or impossible to obtain for lesbian and gay couples include employment benefits, housing benefits, next-of-kin status in medical emergencies, guardianship preference for disabled family members, preference in child custody cases, rights of inheritance, and the right to make funeral arrangements for family members. . . .

## Domestic Partnership Laws Are Needed

Lesbian women and gay men attempting to gain the benefits and protections of family status have few avenues available to that end. Currently, a combination of contractual and statutory provisions come closest to granting the same protections heterosexuals can obtain through marriage. Domestic partnership laws are a step in the right direction. In addition to the direct benefits of these laws, they can provide indirect benefits as well. A certificate of domestic partnership can provide proof to a court of the nature of a relationship for gay and lesbian couples. Domestic partnership laws can be a bridge to greater inclusion in the law for gay men and lesbian women.

Also, having such a law on the books evidences public policy in favor of such living arrangements. Overall, though, domestic partnership laws provide only a beginning to the solution of the problems for nontraditional families. Only inclusion in the marriage laws themselves will result in the same protections for gays and lesbians as their heterosexual counterparts.

# Homosexual Partners Should Not Be Legally Recognized as Family Members

## by Frank S. Zepezauer

**About the author:** *Frank S. Zepezauer is a freelance writer.*

Time is running out. The gay family must be stopped before it secures a permanent place in law and custom. Only a little time remains because the gay "alternative family" is already deeply institutionalized. And it might soon receive the sanction of marriage. The evidence surrounds us.

Many such "families," for example, already exist. In 1990, *Newsweek* estimated that between three and five million lesbians and gay parents had children in the context of a heterosexual relationship, that one-third of all lesbians were mothers, and that seven million children had gay parents. As far back as the 1970s, estimates on the number of lesbian mothers went as high as three million. It is now estimated that, nationwide, about 10,000 "families" have been established by lesbians. Of these, about 5,000 exist in the San Francisco Bay Area alone, part of a trend dubbed the "lesbian baby boom."

### An Extensive Support System

In the Bay Area, these "families" have acquired an extensive support system. Homosexual parents can, for example, consult the S.F. Bay Area Lawyers' Guild and the National Center for Lesbian Rights founded by Donna Hitchens and her law partner Roberta Achtenberg, formerly an assistant secretary at HUD [Department of Housing and Urban Development]. Also available, as Achtenberg reported, are "lesbian and gay legal and health care services, shared child care arrangements, [and] extended family relations. The Lesbian and Gay Parenting Project, based in San Francisco, hosts support groups, social events, workshops, and childbirth education classes. Congregation Sha'ar, a San Francisco synagogue founded by lesbians and gay men, now has a weekly religious

Frank S. Zepezauer, "Stopping the Gay Family: Now or Never," *Wanderer*, June 15, 1995. Reprinted by permission of the author.

school for its members' children." And in San Jose, children of such parents can join Gaybies while their parents seek support from the Gay and Lesbian Parents' Coalition International.

Such support networks appear across the nation. One book lists 47 groups, both national and local, which homosexual parents can consult for help. Among them: the NOW [National Organization for Women] Lesbian Task Force; the Gay Parents' Legal Research Group; the Lambda Legal Defense and Education Fund; and Dignity, the Catholic homosexual organization. Another book lists not only support groups but also sperm banks and services for children of homosexual parents, like Boys of Lesbian Mothers in Oregon. In 1990, the *Washington Blade* published a list of 260 gay/lesbian resources, including Children of Gays, Fathers' Coalition, and Lesbian Mothers with Young Children. At the top of the list was the ACLU [American Civil Liberties Union], just one of many liberal groups which have lined up behind the gay "alternative family."

## Homosexual Propaganda

These support networks have access to an extensive body of literature which has developed the theory and practice of homosexual parenting. It includes Adrienne Rich's influential *Of Woman Born*, which argues for the return of a mythical society based on a mother/child unit in which a father is, at best, tangential; Barbara Kritchevsky's "The Unmarried Woman's Right to Artificial Insemination: A Call for an Expanded Definition of Family"; and Cheri Pies' *Considering Parenthood, A Workbook for Lesbians*. Pies makes explicit homosexualism's revolutionary purpose: "We are challenging the traditional heterosexual nuclear family," she writes. "Having and raising children without men calls into question the heterosexual institution of marriage."

Another writer, Kath Weston, argues in *Families We Choose* that because the homosexual family is here to stay it needs to be integrated into our basic kinship system.

These books have been augmented by a steady flow of articles—authored by homosexuals and their liberal supporters—forming part of a still-growing collection of literature which reinforces the conviction homosexuals have in the propriety of their revolutionary family and propagandizes the heterosexual world into giving it approval.

> *"We . . . cannot tolerate the homosexual family, not as an officially sanctioned, legal institution."*

Such a conviction has been reinforced by a series of court decisions which serve as the precedents upon which homosexualists establish the legality of their "alternative family." As far back as 1978, an Oakland lesbian won custody of her four-year-old son despite her husband's legal protests. The judge ruled that the woman's lesbianism had no bearing on whether she should be granted custody.

This ruling, that homosexuality does not negate parental rights, would appear with increasing frequency in the next 15 years. In 1981, for example, a county judge in Florida declared unconstitutional a 14-year-old state law that prevented homosexuals from adopting children. In California in 1984, a lesbian "father" won visitation rights to a child born to her former lover. In 1989, a lesbian couple was granted the right to adopt a child afflicted with AIDS. In 1991, a Washington, D.C., judge allowed a lesbian couple jointly to adopt each other's children. Two years later, a Vermont judge ruled that a lesbian could adopt the children of her partner without either woman losing her parental rights. The same year, a New Jersey judge allowed the lover of a woman who gave birth via artificial insemination to adopt the child formally.

> *"[Homosexual marriage] will spell the doom of the father-required family as the fundamental kinship system of our society."*

Some setbacks have occurred, however, as was the case in 1995 in Virginia when, after protracted litigation, a lesbian lost custody of her child to her own mother. But the reality that the lesbian enjoyed extensive financial and legal support as well as generally sympathetic media coverage indicates a trend toward affirming the homosexual "family" both in custom and in law. It has been reinforced by a series of Supreme Court decisions, beginning with *Griswold v. Connecticut*, which have legitimized what was once known as "illegitimacy."

Judicial sanction has been complemented by political support, particularly from the liberal wing of the Democratic Party, which has for many years implicitly endorsed the "alternative family"—gay or "straight." This support was made explicit by the Clinton administration. It owed a heavy political debt to gay rights activists who, at the 1992 Democratic convention, revealed themselves as a major Democratic constituency. Homosexuals numbered over 100 delegates, playing a leading role in policy-making. Gay rights groups then donated more than $3 million to the Clinton campaign, putting them up—along with the Jewish community, the entertainment industry, and the environmentalists—among the party's big contributors. President Bill Clinton showed his gratitude by opening the military to homosexuals and by appointing to federal posts an unprecedented number of homosexuals, closeted and uncloseted.

Of these, the most conspicuous was Achtenberg who for years had campaigned for the legalization of homosexual parenting and had herself formed a mother/mother family with a lover who had been artificially impregnated. Her appointment as Assistant Secretary for Fair Housing and Equal Opportunity at the Department of Housing and Urban Development revealed that during a resurgence of family values centered on the father/mother/child unit, Democrats were endorsing a family form which banished the father—and sometimes the mother—from the family altogether.

These developments illuminate the central family values issue today: whether one of two basic kinship systems shall prevail. One is based on the father-required family. The other is based on the father-optional family.

The father-required family has formed the basic unit of nearly every known society in human history. No society until ours has ever sanctioned a father-optional family because, for all the talk about alternatives and options, the two cannot coexist. If the basic unit requires a father, then an option to reject a father destroys our fundamental kinship system. The father-required family cannot be an equal among a set of alternatives. It either binds everyone or binds no one.

We therefore cannot tolerate the homosexual family, not as an officially sanctioned, legal institution. There are fatherless families formed by heterosexuals and there are many heterosexuals who now endorse the "alternative family system"; and there have always been "broken" and "never formed" families brought about by chance or folly or wrongdoing. But we have never had a fatherless family recognized as a fundamental right.

For that reason, the crucial issue becomes the success of the homosexual family, because it would establish the father-optional—as well as the mother-optional—family in principle. Men and women could legally choose to deny a child the right to grow up with a mother and a father.

## What Must Be Done

This reality makes clear what we must do. We must deny single women access to sperm banks. We must deny single men access to surrogate mother contracts. We must reject domestic partner statutes. We must reject homosexual marriage and legally reaffirm the exclusive authority of heterosexual marriage in every state and in the United States in general.

We must do that now because time is running out. Homosexualists have already won widespread social and legal support for their "alternative family." They now occupy a major part of our cultural territory. They will win the rest if they can establish the legality of homosexual marriage. That could happen in Hawaii by 1996. If that happens, a rule of reciprocity may extend homosexual marriage to all the states. That will spell the doom of the father-required family as the fundamental kinship system of our society.

The heterosexual, two-parent family is being assaulted on many fronts. Of these, the most significant has been defined by the homosexualist drive to establish single-sex marriage.

It must be stopped.

# Gay and Lesbian Foreigners Should Be Granted Asylum in the United States

**by David Tuller**

**About the author:** *David Tuller is a San Francisco writer who covers gay and lesbian issues.*

My Russian friend Sergei is a lean and gentle man. But when he recounts the years he languished in prison for the crime of loving another of his own sex his soft voice hardens and his impish grin disappears. Sergei is staying in California now on a student visa, and is scared to go back home. Russia's brutal anti-sodomy law remains on the books, and hundreds of gays are still stashed away in labor camps and prisons. So my worried friend is considering an alternative legal strategy—applying for asylum based on his sexual orientation.

Until 1990, when Congress removed "sexual deviation" from the list of reasons for barring someone from the United States, the Immigration and Naturalization Service [I.N.S.] could prevent deserving individuals from entering or remaining in the country simply by citing their homosexuality. Now, in a twist that has immigration officials squirming, a handful of foreigners are clamoring for asylum or for suspension of their deportation proceedings *because* they are gay—arguing that their sexual orientation exposes them to deadly persecution back home.

## Well-Documented Persecution

Such persecution has been well documented. Although the international human rights community has been shamefully slow to take note, attacks on homosexuals by governments around the world are rampant. Gays are executed in Iran and "disappeared" by death squads in Colombia. China reportedly "treats" gays with electroshock and sends them to the countryside for "re-education."

In 1992, Nicaragua, our "democratic" ally, passed a law that calls for three-year jail terms for anyone who "promotes, propagandizes or practices" homo-

David Tuller, "Political Asylum for Gays?" *Nation*, April 19, 1993. Reprinted with permission from the *Nation* magazine; © The Nation Company, L.P.

sexuality in a "scandalous" manner. Lawyers say the phrasing is so ambiguous that the statute could be used to jail men or women for holding hands on the street, as well as journalists and others who write or speak sympathetically about gays and lesbians. The statute is being challenged in court.

To qualify for asylum here, gay immigrants must prove that they are part of a persecuted social group and that their fears of returning home are therefore "well founded." Organizations such as the International Gay and Lesbian Human Rights Commission in San Francisco estimate that there may be thousands of gay foreigners in the United States terrified to return home. Most of them probably don't realize that applying for legal status here is an option; others are frightened to come forward because they fear that if they do they could be deported.

So far only a dozen or so have mustered the courage to apply. Their applications make compelling, if horrifying, reading. "Many of my friends were killed during the time that I was there," wrote a Guatemalan man living in the Northwest whose appeal for asylum is pending. "There were a couple of places the bodies of homosexuals would be thrown by the police. . . . The last time . . . [I was arrested], they gave me a beating. Then they covered my head with a rubber hood, and they put in it that powder that you use to kill rodents."

Reagan and Bush minions at the I.N.S. routinely opposed gays seeking legal status here, but they were overruled in at least two cases by independent immigration authorities. In 1990 an immigration appeals board dismissed the government's energetic objections and found sufficient evidence of antigay persecution in Cuba to allow an immigrant to remain in the United States. A San Francisco immigration judge ruled similarly in the case of a man from Nicaragua in 1992, shortly after that country passed its new antigay statute.

On this issue, as with gays and lesbians in the military, the United States lags behind its Western allies. Germany, the Netherlands and Australia have all granted asylum to gay foreigners. In 1992, Canadian immigration authorities reached a similar decision in the case of an Argentine man who reported that he was repeatedly blackmailed, raped and tortured by police because of his sexual orientation.

So far, Bill Clinton's record on immigration-related issues is dismal. He has already abandoned a campaign pledge and opted to support the notorious Bush policy of forcing fleeing Haitians to return home without an asylum hearing. He also appears willing to give in to Congress's

> *"Attacks on homosexuals by governments around the world are rampant."*

meanspirited demand that HIV-infected foreigners continue to be barred from the United States. However, advocates for gays and immigrants will be closely monitoring whether [Attorney General] Janet Reno and her subordinates at the I.N.S. will not only seriously evaluate appeals from gays and lesbians but actively encourage those with legitimate claims to come forward without fear.

# Foreign Homosexuals Should Not Be Granted Asylum in the United States

## by Lars-Erik Nelson

**About the author:** *Lars-Erik Nelson is a syndicated columnist.*

On June 16, while Coast Guard cutters were stopping boatloads of desperate Haitians on the high seas, Attorney General Janet Reno established a new basis for claiming refuge in the United States: homosexuality.

In a directive to the U.S. Board of Immigration Appeals, Reno wrote that "an individual who has been identified as homosexual and persecuted by his or her government for that reason alone may be eligible for relief under the refugee laws on the basis of persecution because of membership in a social group."

Reno directed immigration appeals judges to use as a precedent the case of a Cuban refugee who had initially been turned down for asylum because of his criminal record—but then was granted a delay in deportation on the grounds that he was gay. He argued that Fidel Castro's government forced suspected homosexuals to undergo medical screening and inquiries about their sex lives.

His case—*In re Fidel Armando Toboso-Alfonso* (March 12, 1990)—is now to be the guideline for other asylum claims by homosexual aliens, Reno decreed.

Well, it was bound to happen sooner or later. We have long granted political and religious asylum to oppressed peoples from around the world. And there is even a precedent for sex-oriented asylum. Under the George Bush administration, we had a kind of heterosexual asylum: Chinese were granted refuge on the grounds that they opposed forced abortions. They simply had to say they feared persecution for wanting more than one child.

We have even seen such absurdities as musical asylum (Russian violinist Viktoria Mullova sought refuge here claiming that Communist authorities were giving her poor bookings) and acrobatic asylum (for two Ukrainian trapeze artists who wanted to join an American circus).

Many homosexuals can, in fact, demonstrate a more credible fear of persecution than some of the refugees who have already been admitted without much question. After all, Hitler targeted homosexuals along with Jews and Gypsies for extinction in the Holocaust. And in a few countries—most notably Iran—homosexuals face repression and possibly death at the hands of their government.

But still . . . homosexual asylum? This smacks more of special-interest lobbying than of any strategy to bring logic to America's changeable, chaotic rules on political asylum: All Cubans are welcome. No Irish need apply. Salvadorans—who knows this week? Vietnamese—not unless you can prove a relationship with a U.S. intelligence agency. Haitians—yes, no, yes, no, yes, no.

Like the since-repealed Bush policy on abortion foes, the new category for homosexuals is an invitation to massive immigration fraud.

"As an evidentiary matter, there is . . . no way to prove beyond a shadow of a doubt a person's true sexual preference," says an analysis by the Federation for American Immigration Reform, which argues that America cannot afford current levels of immigration. "Given the size of the homosexual population worldwide, the Attorney General here seems to be opening up a Pandora's box of possible claims—most fraudulent and self-serving—with no idea how many new and phony claims this precedent will attract."

According to the May 1994 issue of *Out* magazine, hundreds of homosexuals have already filed asylum claims on the grounds that they face persecution in such places as Brazil, Turkey, Colombia, Hong Kong, Iran and Russia.

Since there is already an asylum backlog of nearly 1 million people, a would-be immigrant could slip into the country by claiming homosexuality, getting a work permit and then waiting years before his or her claim is heard.

The Reno decision reinforces some politically damaging messages about the Clinton administration. First, that U.S. policy is based not on fairness but on political clout. The American gay community has lobbied heavily—with the help of Rep. Barney Frank (D-Mass.)—for recognition of the plight of gays and lesbians in oppressive countries.

Worse, the new rule comes at precisely the time when the Clinton administration has hardened its heart toward Haitian boat people. Special envoy William Gray announced Tuesday that even those Haitians who can prove legitimate claims of asylum will be turned away and offered safe havens in other countries. "They will not have resettlement possibilities in the United States," he said.

Not least, the new rules for homosexuals also give fresh ammunition to conservatives, especially the Christian right, who have worked up so much fury over Clinton's tolerance of gays and lesbians in the military. Now they see a President who would deny political asylum to Chinese opponents of abortion but would grant it to Chinese homosexuals. What fun the family-values folks will have with that!

# Chapter 2

# Should Society Legally Sanction Homosexual Families?

CURRENT CONTROVERSIES

# Gay Marriage:
# An Overview

**by *Issues and Controversies on File***

**About the author:** Issues and Controversies on File *is a semimonthly digest published by Facts On File.*

Almost unimaginable in the 1970s, legally sanctioned marriages between two people of the same sex have become a very real possibility as a result of a 1993 ruling by the Hawaii Supreme Court. In its controversial *Baehr v. Lewin* decision, the Hawaii court ruled that barring same-sex marriages was tantamount to sex discrimination. The case was sent back to a lower Hawaii court, which must decide if there is a compelling state interest in denying marriage licenses to same-sex couples. . . . The possibility that gays and lesbians could get married in Hawaii and have their marriages become legally recognized in every other state has alarmed many conservatives and galvanized gay-rights groups.

## The Arguments

Opponents of same-sex marriage include most social and religious conservatives, the hierarchy of the Roman Catholic Church and most Protestant denominations, and a majority of Americans as well. They say that giving marital recognition to gays and lesbians degrades the institution of marriage. Opponents argue the state should have the right to maintain what they claim is one of society's most fundamental institutions in the way it was designed—as a union between a man and woman. Many people find homosexual behavior immoral and do not want anything related to homosexuality to be accepted or endorsed in the U.S. The last thing the nation needs, say social conservatives, is for the institution of marriage to be further trivialized and moved away from its roots at a time when traditional family values are already under assault in contemporary culture.

But gay-rights advocates claim that marriage should be about love and commitment between two people, regardless of their sex or sexual orientation. They say that providing gay and lesbian couples with the same legal entitlements as heterosexual couples poses no risk to society or to heterosexuals.

They contend that civil marriage provides heterosexual couples and their recognized families with many legal and economic benefits that should not be denied to homosexual couples, many of whom also raise families together. Backers of same-sex marriage claim that society should define family and marriage in terms of people who care deeply about one another rather than use restrictive and outdated definitions of what families ought to look like. The government, they say, should encourage all kinds of committed, long-term relationships, including homosexual ones. . . .

## Domestic Partnerships

Over the last few years, private businesses have been at the vanguard in granting to homosexual partners and other unmarried couples at least some of the economic benefits that had formerly been extended only to married couples. In 1991, Cambridge, Mass.–based Lotus Development Corp. became the first major corporation to extend spousal benefits to same-sex partners of its employees. Smaller companies and organizations, such as the American Civil Liberties Union (ACLU) and Ben & Jerry's Homemade Inc., had recognized so-called domestic partnerships prior to 1991, but Lotus spearheaded the trend among large corporations.

Businesses with domestic-partnership policies generally extend benefits such as bereavement and illness leave and health and life insurance to unmarried but committed partners of their employees. Nearly 200 companies now recognize domestic partnerships to some degree. In some companies, a majority of domestic partnerships are filed between unmarried heterosexual couples. Other companies, including Lotus, extend the benefits only to homosexual couples, who cannot receive the benefits automatically by law since they cannot get married.

> *"Opponents of same-sex marriage . . . say that giving marital recognition to gays and lesbians degrades the institution of marriage."*

Some 30 municipalities, including New York City, Los Angeles and Atlanta, Ga., now offer domestic-partnership policies to their workers as well. The city of San Francisco, Calif., has gone one step further in recognizing same-sex unions. In March 1996, city officials began holding "marriage" ceremonies for same-sex couples. On the first day of the ceremonies, San Francisco Mayor Willie Brown, Jr. (D) presided over the rites, which joined some 175 same-sex couples in mass nuptials. The "marriages," which even come with a marriage license, carry no legal weight because same-sex couples cannot officially marry under California law. However, San Francisco, which has a large gay and lesbian population, is considered the first city to extend such a level of official acceptance and recognition to same-sex couples.

Domestic-partnership policies that seem to equate same-sex couples with heterosexual couples are seen by many as eliminating the need for same-sex marriages. But gay-rights advocates maintain that the benefits that ensue from civil marriage dwarf those of domestic partnerships. They say that besides having symbolic significance, civil marriage codifies unique rights, obligations and responsibilities between two people. Some of those benefits include inheritance rights, income-tax deductions, family health-care coverage, shared responsibilities for children and the right to authorize care for one's partner in medical emergencies.

Although some religious denominations will hold marriage ceremonies uniting same-sex couples, only the government can validate a civil marriage and extend its benefits. No U.S. state currently sanctions same-sex marriage, but that could soon change, depending on the outcome of the eagerly anticipated court decision in Hawaii.

Three same-sex couples—one gay male and two lesbian couples—sued the state of Hawaii in 1991 for denying them marriage licenses. The case, *Baehr v. Lewin*, eventually landed in the Hawaii Supreme Court. In May 1993, the court ruled that the state's marriage statute limits eligibility for marriage on the basis of the sex of the partners involved, and therefore violates the state's equal-protection clause against sex discrimination.

The state's law barring same-sex marriages could only be upheld, the court ruled, if a lower court could show a "compelling state interest" in keeping the ban. This so-called strict scrutiny standard is considered one of the most difficult standards to meet. A lower court is expected to begin hearings on the case in July 1996.

In response to the ruling, Hawaii Gov. Benjamin Cayetano (D) appointed a seven-member Commission on Sexual Orientation and the Law to study the issue. In December 1995, that commission issued its report and recommended that the state legislature should legalize same-sex marriage. "This is an equal-protection question, and they [same-sex couples] should not be denied this right on the basis of their gender," argued Thomas Gill, the chairman of the commission.

The *Baehr* decision has sent shock waves across Hawaii and the entire nation, where many states are considering laws to block recognition of same-sex marriages should Hawaii's lower court uphold them. Like drivers' licenses and other civil contracts, marriage licenses obtained in one state are generally honored in all other states. The U.S. Constitution (Article IV, Section I) provides that "full faith and credit shall be given in each state to the public acts, records and judicial proceedings of every other state." In effect, a same-sex marriage in Hawaii would automatically gain recognition in every other state.

> *"Gay-rights advocates claim that marriage should be about love and commitment between two people, regardless of their sex."*

That prospect prompted Utah to pass a law in 1995 that allows the state to deny recognition to out-of-state marriages that do not conform to Utah law. Three other states have passed laws to define marriage as a relationship that can exist only between a man and a woman. South Dakota, for example, updated its marriage statute to define marriage as "a personal relation, between a man and a woman, arising out of a civil contract to which the consent of parties capable of making it is necessary." As of April 2, 1996, some 14 other states had similar legislation pending, although such measures have already failed in nine states.

The Hawaii legislature also passed a law in 1994 that expressly defined marriages as "man-woman units." The amendment was mostly regarded as a symbolic gesture reflecting the legislature's opposition to same-sex marriage. In *Baehr*, the existing marriage statute was already interpreted as limiting marriage only to man-woman units, leading the state's supreme court to rule that such limits amounted to sex discrimination.

If Hawaii's courts do uphold same-sex marriage, it is unclear whether laws passed in other states would be able to withstand constitutional challenges based on the "full faith and credit" clause. States have generally recognized marriages and divorces performed in other states, even when state laws differ. The U.S. Supreme Court has never explicitly ruled how the clause applies to marriage. Some legal analysts maintain that the only way to avoid the "full faith and credit" clause and thereby ban same-sex marriages is to amend the Constitution, an arduous process that could take many years.

## Defining Marriage

Opponents of same-sex marriage claim that the Hawaii Supreme Court has created a nonexistent right and twisted the meaning of marriage. Hawaii legislator A. Leiomalama Solomon (D) says, "Same-sex marriage is a semantic, logical and legal impossibility. Marriage is unarguably defined as the state of two people of the opposite sex being united as husband and wife."

Noting that a majority of Americans disapprove of same-sex marriage, John Leo of *U.S. News & World* Report criticizes the "imaginative judges" who conjured up the right "without any input from the people." His point is backed by Melanie Kirkpatrick, who writes in a *Wall Street Journal* editorial that "gay-rights activists are asking for more than tolerance" on this issue. She says, "Marriage holds a preferred status under the law, and activists want that special legal status applied to same-sex relationships." She adds:

> Under our system of government, it is the people, not the courts, who are sovereign. The proper role of the courts is to limit themselves to enforcing rights actually protected in the Constitution. If we're going to tinker with a definition of marriage that has been around for about 6,000 years, let the people decide.

Such concerns also resonate among state legislatures, where conservative lawmakers feel that they should not be forced to comply with Hawaii's impending legitimization of same-sex marriages. As California Assemblyman William Knight (R) explains, "My concern is that a limited number of judges in Hawaii will be dictating public policy in California." Knight introduced a bill that passed the California Assembly in January 1996. Knight's bill would refuse recognition to "any marriage contracted outside this state between individuals of the same gender."

Conservatives are also worried that the legalization of gay marriages will lead society down a slippery slope to a point where states would have to recognize all kinds of currently banned practices that Americans do not favor.

> *"A same-sex marriage in Hawaii would automatically gain recognition in every other state."*

"If gay marriages become legal," asks Kirkpatrick, "what would be the constitutional bar to other voluntary relationships such as incest, polygamy or polyandry?" (Polygamy occurs when a man has more than one wife; polyandry is when a woman has more than one husband.)

## Equal Rights, Not Special Rights

Gay-rights advocates claim, however, that they are seeking equal civil rights, not special rights. "What we are asking for is our equal right to marry the one we love and care for, just as nongay Americans do," says Evan Wolfson, co-counsel attorney in *Baehr* and senior attorney at the Lambda Legal Defense and Education Fund (LLDEF), a gay-rights legal group. The substance of the debate is whether marriage *ought* to be defined by the state as only between a man and a woman, argue supporters of same-sex marriages.

Advocates of same-sex marriage stress the distinction between the civil aspects of marriage, which establish the legal and economic ties between two people, and the religious dimension of marriage, which is often bound up with different cultures' moral traditions. In the private domain, religious authorities can set their own standards, say some gay-rights activists, but as a body that represents a large diversity of peoples, the government should remain impartial with regard to administering its own civil policies.

They claim that it is unjust for the government to confer the economic and legal benefits of marriage only to opposite-sex couples. "We use marriage as a gateway for so many benefits in our society that, by forbidding us [gays and lesbians] the benefits that come with marriage, you are essentially discriminating economically against the whole community," contends Craig Fong, the former head of the Los Angeles chapter of the LLDEF.

Despite polls that show that nearly two-thirds of Americans disapprove of allowing gays and lesbians to marry each other, many people apparently support other homosexual rights, including some rights associated with civil marriage. A 1992 *Newsweek* poll found that 78% of Americans support equal rights for homosexuals in employment opportunities, 70% support inheritance rights for gay partners, and 58% support granting Social Security to gay partners. However, marriage is also entwined with moral and religious meanings that many people are unwilling to associate with homosexuality. Some 53% of Americans in the poll said that homosexuality is not an acceptable lifestyle.

To disentangle the government from the solemn dimensions of marriage, Cayetano sought a compromise on the issue. He suggested that the government could replace the word "marriage" in state statutes with references to domestic partnerships. "The state should leave the sanctioning of marriage to the religious organizations," he said. Some analysts have noted that in trying to extend marriage rights to gay and lesbian couples in Hawaii, Cayetano's proposal would end up eliminating marriage altogether.

## Gays See Bias in Marriage Laws

Supporters of same-sex marriage often compare their case to *Loving v. Virginia*, the landmark 1967 Supreme Court case that struck down state laws that prohibited interracial marriages. Despite popular support at that time for such laws in some states, the court held that laws against interracial marriages violated the equal-protection clause of the Constitution. The Court ruled:

> The freedom to marry has long been recognized as one of the vital personal rights essential to the orderly pursuit of happiness by free men. . . . To deny this fundamental freedom . . . [on the basis of race] . . . is surely to deprive all the State's citizens of liberty without due process of law.

According to Wolfson, "As with the same-race restriction, the different-sex restriction on marriage deprives gay people of a basic human right, promotes heterosexism, and brands us as inferior, second-class citizens."

Gay-rights supporters note that the Hawaii Supreme Court ruled that the ban on same-sex marriages was a breach of the state's own equal-protection clause. That clause forbids discrimination on the basis "of race, religion, sex or ancestry"—it does not mention sexual orientation. The court did not create any new rights for homosexuals, say gay-rights advocates, but merely affirmed its commitment to prevent the state from discriminating against people on account of their sex.

But opponents of same-sex marriage counter that the analogy to *Loving* is false since that case did not challenge the very definition of marriage. That blacks and whites should be able to marry does not contradict the meaning of marriage—a union between husband and wife—according to conservatives, but "same-sex" marriage is inherently contradictory. Furthermore, they contend that the ban against same-sex marriage affects men and women equally. Since same-sex mar-

*"Three . . . states have passed laws to define marriage as a relationship that can exist only between a man and a woman."*

riages are denied to both men and women, there are no grounds for claiming that the statute discriminates on the basis of sex, they argue.

Conservatives note that while the Supreme Court has repeatedly struck down state laws that are unfair to blacks, the high court has upheld laws that target homosexual behavior. They cite the 1986 case *Bowers v. Hardwick*, in which the Supreme Court upheld state laws that forbid consensual sodomy between adults—a kind of sex act primarily associated with homosexual men. The Supreme Court is also currently hearing a case, *Romer v. Evans*, in which it will decide if an amendment added in 1992 to Colorado's constitution violates the due-process rights of homosexuals. The measure, approved by 53% of the people of Colorado in a referendum, bans local statutes that specifically protect homosexuals from discrimination. [The Supreme Court struck down Colorado's amendment in May 1996.]

## Concern over Family Values

Opponents of same-sex marriage claim that homosexuality runs counter to widely supported efforts to preserve family values, a centerpiece of social conservatism. Marriage "is the building block of civilization," says Robert Knight, cultural studies director of the Washington, D.C.–based Family Research Council. "Equating a homosexual relationship with what Mom and Dad do devalues the whole concept of marriage," he contends.

Many conservatives view the push for same-sex marriage as just another blow to the already crumbling family unit—a trend they believe to be responsible for many of the social ills the nation currently faces. Lisa Schiffren, a speechwriter for former Vice President Dan Quayle (R), writes in the *New York Times* that same-sex marriage would usher in "a radical redefinition of society's most fundamental institution." She says, "A society struggling to recover from 30 years of weakened norms and broken families is not likely to respond gently to having an institution central to most people's lives altered."

Pope John Paul II, the leader of the world's Roman Catholics, issued a letter on family values in February 1994 in which he called proposed same-sex matrimony "a serious threat to the future of the family and society." The pope's comments were largely regarded as a reply to a vote taken two weeks earlier in the European Parliament, the legislative wing of the European Union. The parliament approved a nonbinding resolution that recommended that member nations support same-sex marriages and adoption rights by gays and lesbians.

Conservatives fear that same-sex marriage will legitimize homosexuality and will force educators and politicians to be "value-blind" to behavior that many find immoral. Robert Larimer Jr. of the conservative state organization Washington for Traditional Values, says, "It is hoped we will be wise enough, while tolerating differences, to reject the notion that homosexuality should be accepted as the legal and public health equal of heterosexuality."

Schiffren and others observe that many of the nation's cultural traditions, including its notions of the family, are based on Judeo-Christian religious ethics that have long considered homosexuality immoral. Since most Americans do not support same-sex marriages, why should they be forced to live with laws that affirm practices or views that are inimical to their own beliefs, they ask.

They say that in a democracy, people should have the right to maintain institutions that represent the values that are shared by the people, as well as those moral values that they want their children to inherit.

Some conservatives argue that the government's role in marriage is only for the purpose of protecting the welfare of children. Since same-sex couples cannot have biological children by their union, the government has no compelling reason to promote or uphold gay marriages, they say. According to Leo, "Society has a crucial stake in protecting the connection between sex, procreation and a commitment to raise children. If it didn't, why would the state be involved with marriage at all?"

A similar claim is made by Schiffren. "In traditional marriage, the tie that really binds for life is shared responsibility for the children." She asks, "What will keep gay marriages together when individuals tire of each other?"

But Andrew Koppelman, an assistant professor of politics at Princeton University in Princeton, N.J., calls that argument "weak on its face." Koppelman points to the *Baehr* case, among the parties to which is a lesbian couple raising a child after having raised foster children. Same-sex couples often raise children from their former heterosexual relationships, and sometimes from artificial insemination or adoption. Gay and lesbian parents criticize what they consider to be the restrictive definition of family put forward by conservatives. They contend that their families are just as deserving of the benefits that are granted to other families under the law.

The claim that procreation provides the only basis for the government's endorsement of marriage also riles many heterosexuals. Rosalyn Baker (D), a member of the Hawaii Senate, calls such reasoning "a slap in the face for people who choose not to have children, people who are older and get married, people who are disabled and get married."

Advocates of same-sex marriage contend that society should have an interest in promoting and supporting any form of committed, loving relationship and ending the social ostracism of gays and lesbians. "Same-sex marriages are not an assault on 'the family,' as is so often charged," said Rabbi Jerome Davidson in a letter to the *New York Times*. "They provide an option for gays other than a life of loneliness, of hiding, that is true to their real identities."

> **"Conservatives fear that same-sex marriage will legitimize homosexuality."**

Many gay-rights advocates claim that conservatives should champion rather than oppose same-sex marriage, which they claim would help stabilize the family. "It is an essentially conservative act to encourage couples, whether gay or straight, to settle down and take responsibility for each other," writes Bruce Bawer in a *New York Times* editorial. Bawer observes that gay men have often been criticized by conservatives for engaging in careless sex and are frequently blamed for spreading sexually transmitted diseases such as AIDS. "Isn't it wrong for the same right-wing activists who have decried gay promiscuity to now deny gay love and commitment?" asks Bawer.

Bawer and others say that same-sex marriage will likely have little impact on most heterosexuals. Bawer quotes Iowa legislator Ed Fallon (D) during debate in Iowa over a bill that would ban recognition of same-sex marriage. Fallon said, "There isn't a limited amount of love in Iowa. . . . Heterosexual couples don't have to rush out and claim marriage licenses now, before they are all snatched up by gay and lesbian couples." Gay-rights advocates say that, despite their opponents' claims, true traditional American values include tolerance, the protection of individual civil rights and the equal treatment of all people under the law.

> *"Gay and lesbian parents . . . contend that their families are just as deserving of the benefits that are granted to other families under the law."*

But marriage would make it easier for gay couples to adopt, which alarms many Americans. A February 1994 *Newsweek* poll found that 65% of respondents disapprove of adoption rights for gay partners. A 1993 *U.S. News & World Report* poll had found similar results, with 70% of respondents saying that they oppose allowing gays to adopt. Similar views are held in other countries. Since 1989, Denmark, Norway and Sweden have passed laws extending some marital rights to gay couples, with one large exception—a ban on allowing gay and lesbian couples to adopt.

## A National Debate

The debate over same-sex marriage has begun to reach beyond the states to the national level. In February 1996, conservatives held a "marriage protection" rally on the eve of the Iowa presidential caucuses to denounce the prospect of gay marriage. The rally received the support of several Republican presidential candidates, including Sen. Robert Dole (Kan.), Malcolm ("Steve") Forbes, Jr. and Lamar Alexander. Republican candidate Patrick Buchanan, who has never shied from speaking out against homosexual behavior, addressed the rally in person.

Conservatives in Congress have reportedly begun drafting a Defense of Marriage Act to define marriage as specifically between a man and woman. Such an act could receive widespread support among the American public. But gay-rights activists are also mounting a campaign to air their side of the issue, which they frame as a civil-rights debate for equality. A number of organizations that support gay rights, including the ACLU and the LLDEF, have come together to form the Freedom to Marry Coalition to counter what they view to be a premature backlash against same-sex marriage. With sharp divisions between gay-rights activists and conservatives, the debate is unlikely to fade any time soon.

# Gays and Lesbians Should Be Allowed to Marry

by Andrew Sullivan

**About the author:** *Andrew Sullivan is the author of* Virtually Normal: An Argument About Homosexuality *and the former editor of the* New Republic.

As with the military, [banning homosexual marriages] is a question of formal public discrimination, since only the state can grant and recognize marriage. If the military ban deals with the heart of what it means to be a citizen, marriage does even more so, since, in peace and war, it affects everyone. Marriage is not simply a private contract; it is a social and public recognition of a private commitment. As such, it is the highest public recognition of personal integrity. Denying it to homosexuals is the most public affront possible to their public equality.

This point may be the hardest for many heterosexuals to accept. Even those tolerant of homosexuals may find this institution so wedded to the notion of heterosexual commitment that to extend it would be to undo its very essence. And there may be religious reasons for resisting this that, within certain traditions, are unanswerable. But I am not here discussing what churches do in their private affairs. I am discussing what the allegedly neutral liberal state should do in public matters. For liberals, the case for homosexual marriage is overwhelming. As a classic public institution, it should be available to any two citizens.

## Extending the Definition of Marriage

Some might argue that marriage is by definition between a man and a woman; and it is difficult to argue with a definition. But if marriage is articulated beyond this circular fiat, then the argument for its exclusivity to one man and one woman disappears. The center of the public contract is an emotional, financial, and psychological bond between two people; in this respect, heterosexuals and homosexuals are identical. The heterosexuality of marriage is intrinsic only if it is understood to be intrinsically procreative; but that definition has long been abandoned in Western society. No civil marriage license is granted on the condition that the couple bear children; and the marriage is no less legal and no less defensible if it remains childless. In the contemporary West, marriage has become a way in which the state recognizes an emotional commitment by two people to each other for life. And within that definition, there is no public way, if one believes in equal rights under the law, in which it should legally be denied homosexuals.

> *"Denying [marriage] to homosexuals is the most public affront possible to their public equality."*

Of course, no public sanctioning of a contract should be given to people who cannot actually fulfill it. The state rightly, for example, withholds marriage from minors, or from one adult and a minor, since at least one party is unable to understand or live up to the contract. And the state has also rightly barred close family relatives from marriage because familial emotional ties are too strong and powerful to enable a marriage contract to be entered into freely by two autonomous, independent individuals; and because incest poses a uniquely dangerous threat to the trust and responsibility that the family needs to survive. But do homosexuals fall into a similar category? History and experience strongly suggest they don't. Of course, marriage is characterized by a kind of commitment that is rare—and perhaps declining—even among heterosexuals. But it isn't necessary to prove that homosexuals or lesbians are less—or more—able to form long-term relationships than straights for it to be clear that at least *some* are. Moreover, giving these people an equal right to affirm their commitment doesn't reduce the incentive for heterosexuals to do the same.

In some ways, the marriage issue is exactly parallel to the issue of the military. Few people deny that many homosexuals are capable of the sacrifice, the commitment, and the responsibilities of marriage. And indeed, for many homosexuals and lesbians, these responsibilities are already enjoined—as they have been enjoined for centuries. The issue is whether these identical relationships should be denied equal legal standing, not by virtue of anything to do with the relationships themselves but by virtue of the internal, involuntary nature of the homosexuals involved. Clearly, for liberals, the answer to this is clear. Such a denial is a classic case of unequal protection of the laws.

## The Conservative Argument for Gay Marriage

But perhaps surprisingly, one of the strongest arguments for gay marriage is a conservative one. It's perhaps best illustrated by a comparison with the alternative often offered by liberals . . . to legal gay marriage, the concept of "domestic partnership." Several cities in the United States have domestic partnership laws, which allow relationships that do not fit into the category of heterosexual marriage to be registered with the city and qualify for benefits that had previously been reserved for heterosexual married couples. In these cities, a variety of interpersonal arrangements qualify for health insurance, bereavement leave, in-

surance, annuity and pension rights, housing rights (such as rent-control apartments), adoption and inheritance rights. Eventually, the aim is to include federal income tax and veterans' benefits as well. Homosexuals are not the only
beneficiaries; heterosexual "live-togethers" also qualify.

The conservative's worries start with the ease of the relationship. To be sure,
potential domestic partners have to prove financial interdependence, shared living arrangements, and a commitment to mutual caring. But they don't need to
have a sexual relationship or even closely mirror old-style marriage. In principle, an elderly woman and her live-in nurse could qualify, or a pair of frat buddies. Left as it is, the concept of domestic partnership could open a Pandora's
box of litigation and subjective judicial decision making about who qualifies.
You either are or you're not married; it's not a complex question. Whether you
are in a domestic partnership is not so clear.

More important for conservatives, the concept of domestic partnership chips
away at the prestige of traditional relationships and undermines the priority we
give them. Society, after all, has good reasons to extend legal advantages to heterosexuals who choose the formal sanction of marriage over simply living together. They make a deeper commitment to one another and to society; in exchange, society extends certain benefits to them. Marriage provides an anchor,
if an arbitrary and often weak one, in
the maelstrom of sex and relationships to which we are all prone. It
provides a mechanism for emotional
stability and economic security. We
rig the law in its favor not because
we disparage all forms of relationship other than the nuclear family,

> *"Marriage has become a
> way in which the state
> recognizes an emotional
> commitment by two people
> to each other for life."*

but because we recognize that not to promote marriage would be to ask too
much of human virtue.

For conservatives, these are vital concerns. There are virtually no conservative arguments either for preferring no social incentives for gay relationships or
for preferring a second-class relationship, such as domestic partnership, which
really does provide an incentive for the decline of traditional marriage. Nor, if
conservatives are concerned by the collapse of stable family life, should they be
dismayed by the possibility of gay parents. There is no evidence that shows any
deleterious impact on a child brought up by two homosexual parents; and considerable evidence that such a parental structure is clearly preferable to single
parents (gay or straight) or no effective parents at all, which, alas, is the choice
many children now face. Conservatives should not balk at the apparent radical-
ism of the change involved, either. The introduction of gay marriage would not
be some sort of leap in the dark, a massive societal risk. Homosexual marriages
have always existed, in a variety of forms; they have just been euphemized. Increasingly they exist in every sense but the legal one. As it has become more ac-

ceptable for homosexuals to acknowledge their loves and commitments publicly, more and more have committed themselves to one another for life in full view of their families and friends. A law institutionalizing gay marriage would merely reinforce a healthy trend. . . .

## Providing Role Models

It would also be an unqualified social good for homosexuals. It provides role models for young gay people, who, after the exhilaration of coming out, can easily lapse into short-term relationships and insecurity with no tangible goal in sight. My own guess is that most homosexuals would embrace such a goal with as much (if not more) commitment as heterosexuals. Even in our society as it is, many lesbian and gay male relationships are virtual textbooks of monogamous commitment; and for many, "in sickness and in health" has become a vocation rather than a vow. Legal gay marriage could also help bridge the gulf often found between homosexuals and their parents. It could bring the essence of gay life—a gay couple—into the heart of the traditional family in a way the family can most understand and the gay offspring can most easily acknowledge. It could do more to heal the gay-straight rift than any amount of gay rights legislation.

More important, perhaps, as gay marriage sank into the subtle background consciousness of a culture, its influence would be felt quietly but deeply among gay children. For them, at last, there would be some kind of future; some older faces to apply to their unfolding lives, some language in which their identity could be properly discussed, some rubric by which it could be explained—not in terms of sex, or sexual practices, or bars, or subterranean activity, but in terms of their future life stories, their potential loves, their eventual chance at some kind of constructive happiness. They would be able to feel by the intimation of a myriad examples that in this respect their emotional orientation was not merely about pleasure, or sin, or shame, or otherness (although it might always be involved in many of those things), but about the ability to love and be loved as complete, imperfect human beings. Until gay marriage is legalized, this fundamental element of personal dignity will be denied a whole segment of humanity. No other change can achieve it.

Any heterosexual man who takes a few moments to consider what his life would be like if he were never allowed a formal institution to cement his relationships will see the truth of what I am saying. Imagine life without a recognized family; imagine dating without even the possibility of marriage. Any heterosexual woman who can imagine being told at a young age that her attraction to men was wrong, that her loves and crushes were illicit, that her destiny was single-hood and shame, will also appreciate the point. Gay marriage is not a radical step; it is a profoundly

> *"Giving [homosexuals] an equal right to affirm their commitment doesn't reduce the incentive for heterosexuals to do the same."*

humanizing, traditionalizing step. It is the first step in any resolution of the homosexual question—more important than any other institution, since it is the most central institution to the nature of the problem, which is to say, the emotional and sexual bond between one human being and another. If nothing else were done at all, and gay marriage were legalized, ninety percent of the political work necessary to achieve gay and lesbian equality would have been achieved. It is ultimately the only reform that truly matters.

## No Reason to Oppose Gay Marriage

So long as conservatives recognize, as they do, that homosexuals exist and that they have equivalent emotional needs and temptations as heterosexuals, then there is no conservative reason to oppose homosexual marriage and many conservative reasons to support it. So long as liberals recognize, as they do, that citizens deserve equal treatment under the law, then there is no liberal reason to oppose it and many liberal reasons to be in favor of it. So long as intelligent people understand that homosexuals are emotionally and sexually attracted to the same sex as heterosexuals are to the other sex, then there is no human reason on earth why it should be granted to one group and not the other.

These two measures—ending the military ban and lifting the marriage bar—are simple, direct, and require no change in heterosexual behavior and no sacrifice from heterosexuals.

> *"Homosexual marriages have always existed."*

They represent a politics that tackles the heart of prejudice against homosexuals while leaving bigots their freedom. This politics . . . makes a clear, public statement of equality while leaving all the inequalities of emotion and passion to the private sphere, where they belong. It does not legislate private tolerance; it declares public equality. It banishes the paradigm of victimology and replaces it with one of integrity.

# Society Has a Compelling Interest in Allowing Gay Marriage

**by Jonathan Rauch**

**About the author:** *Jonathan Rauch is a writer for the weekly London-based magazine the* Economist *and the author of* Kindly Inquisitors: The New Attacks on Free Thought.

Whatever else marriage may or may not be, it is certainly falling apart. Half of today's marriages end in divorce, and, far more costly, many never begin— leaving mothers poor, children fatherless and neighborhoods chaotic. . . . Homosexuals have chosen this moment to press for the right to marry. What's more, Hawaii's courts are moving toward letting them do so. I'll believe in gay marriage in America when I see it, but if Hawaii legalizes it, even temporarily, the uproar over this final insult to a besieged institution will be deafening.

## The Purpose of Marriage

Whether gay marriage makes sense—and whether straight marriage makes sense—depends on what marriage is actually for. Current secular thinking on this question is shockingly sketchy. Gay activists say: marriage is for love, and we love each other, therefore we should be able to marry. Traditionalists say: marriage is for children, and homosexuals do not (or should not) have children, therefore you should not be able to marry. That, unfortunately, pretty well covers the spectrum. I say "unfortunately" because both views are wrong. They misunderstand and impoverish the social meaning of marriage.

So what is marriage for? Modern marriage is, of course, based upon traditions that religion helped to codify and enforce. But religious doctrine has no special standing in the world of secular law and policy (the "Christian nation" crowd notwithstanding). If we want to know what and whom marriage is for in modern America, we need a sensible secular doctrine.

At one point, marriage in secular society was largely a matter of business: cementing family ties, providing social status for men and economic support for women, conferring dowries, and so on. Marriages were typically arranged, and "love" in the modern sense was no prerequisite. In Japan, remnants of this system remain, and it works surprisingly well. Couples stay together because they view their marriage as a partnership: an investment in social stability for themselves and their children. Because Japanese couples

> *"Today marriage is almost entirely a voluntary arrangement whose contents are up to the people making the deal."*

don't expect as much emotional fulfillment as we do, they are less inclined to break up. They also take a somewhat more relaxed attitude toward adultery. What's a little extracurricular love provided that each partner is fulfilling his or her many other marital duties?

In the West, of course, love is a defining element. The notion of lifelong love is charming, if ambitious, and certainly love is a desirable element of marriage. In society's eyes, however, it cannot be the defining element. You may or may not love your husband, but the two of you are just as married either way. You may love your mistress, but that certainly doesn't make her your spouse. Love helps make sense of marriage emotionally, but it is not terribly important in making sense of marriage from the point of view of social policy.

If love does not define the purpose of secular marriage, what does? Neither the law nor secular thinking provides a clear answer. Today marriage is almost entirely a voluntary arrangement whose contents are up to the people making the deal. There are few if any behaviors that automatically end a marriage. If a man beats his wife, which is about the worst thing he can do to her, he may be convicted of assault, but his marriage is not automatically dissolved. Couples can be adulterous ("open") yet remain married. They can be celibate, too; consummation is not required. All in all, it is an impressive and also rather astonishing victory for modern individualism that so important an institution should be so bereft of formal social instruction as to what should go on inside of it.

Secular society tells us only a few things about marriage. First, marriage depends on the consent of the parties. Second, the parties are not children. Third, the number of parties is two. Fourth, one is a man and the other a woman. Within those rules a marriage is whatever anyone says it is. . . .

## The Child-Centered View

So we turn to what has become the standard view of marriage's purpose. Its proponents would probably like to call it a child-centered view, but it is actually an anti-gay view, as will become clear. Whatever you call it, it is the view of marriage that is heard most often, and in the context of the debate over gay marriage it is heard almost exclusively. In its most straightforward form it goes as follows (I quote from James Q. Wilson's fine book *The Moral Sense*):

> A family is not an association of independent people; it is a human commitment designed to make possible the rearing of moral and healthy children. Governments care—or ought to care—about families for this reason, and scarcely for any other.

Wilson speaks about "family" rather than "marriage" as such, but one may, I think, read him as speaking of marriage without doing any injustice to his meaning. The resulting proposition—government ought to care about marriage almost entirely because of children—seems reasonable. But there are problems. The first, obviously, is that gay couples may have children, whether through adoption, prior marriage or (for lesbians) artificial insemination. Leaving aside the thorny issue of gay adoption, the point is that if the mere presence of children is the test, then homosexual relationships can certainly pass it.

You might note, correctly, that heterosexual marriages are more likely to produce children than homosexual ones. When granting marriage licenses to heterosexuals, however, we do not ask how likely the couple is to have children. We assume that they are entitled to get married whether or not they end up with children. Understanding this, conservatives often make an interesting move. In seeking to justify the state's interest in marriage, they shift from the actual presence of children to the anatomical possibility of making

> *"Children are not a trivial reason for marriage; they just cannot be the only reason."*

them. Hadley Arkes, a political science professor and prominent opponent of homosexual marriage, makes the case this way:

> The traditional understanding of marriage is grounded in the "natural teleology of the body"—in the inescapable fact that only a man and a woman, and only two people, not three, can generate a child. Once marriage is detached from that natural teleology of the body, what ground of principle would thereafter confine marriage to two people rather than some larger grouping? That is, on what ground of principle would the law reject the claim of a gay couple that their love is not confined to a coupling of two, but that they are woven into a larger ensemble with yet another person or two?

What he seems to be saying is that, where the possibility of natural children is nil, the meaning of marriage is nil. If marriage is allowed between members of the same sex, then the concept of marriage has been emptied of content except to ask whether the parties love each other. Then anything goes, including polygamy. This reasoning presumably is what those opposed to gay marriage have in mind when they claim that, once gay marriage is legal, marriage to pets will follow close behind.

But Arkes and his sympathizers make two mistakes. To see them, break down the claim into two components: (1) Two-person marriage derives its special status from the anatomical possibility that the partners can create natural children; and (2) Apart from (1), two-person marriage has no purpose sufficiently strong to justify its special status. That is, absent justification (1), anything goes.

The first proposition is wholly at odds with the way society actually views marriage. Leave aside the insistence that natural, as opposed to adopted, children define the importance of marriage. The deeper problem, apparent right away, is the issue of sterile heterosexual couples. Here the "anatomical possibility" crowd has a problem, for a homosexual union is, anatomically speaking, nothing but one variety of sterile union and no different even in principle: a woman without a uterus has no more potential for giving birth than a man without a vagina.

It may sound like carping to stress the case of barren heterosexual marriage: the vast majority of newlywed heterosexual couples, after all, can have children and probably will. But the point here is fundamental. There are far more sterile heterosexual unions in America than homosexual ones. The "anatomical possibility" crowd cannot have it both ways. If the possibility of children is what gives meaning to marriage, then a post-menopausal woman who applies for a marriage license should be turned away at the courthouse door. What's more, she should be hooted at and condemned for stretching the meaning of marriage beyond its natural basis and so reducing the institution to frivolity. People at the Family Research Council or Concerned Women for America should point at her and say, "If she can marry, why not polygamy?"

Obviously, the "anatomical" conservatives do not say this, because they are sane. They instead flail around, saying that sterile men and women were at least born with the right-shaped parts for making children, and so on. Their position is really a nonposition. It says that the "natural children" rationale defines marriage when homosexuals are involved but not when heterosexuals are involved. When the parties to union are sterile heterosexuals, the justification for marriage must be something else. But what?

Now arises the oddest part of the "anatomical" argument. Look at proposition (2) above. It says that, absent the anatomical justification for marriage, anything goes. In other words, it dismisses the idea that there might be other good reasons for society to sanctify marriage above other kinds of relationships. Why would anybody make this move? I'll hazard a guess: to exclude homosexuals. Any rationale that justifies sterile heterosexual marriages can also apply to homosexual ones.

> *"The two strongest [reasons for marriage] are these: domesticating men and providing reliable caregivers."*

For instance, marriage makes women more financially secure. Very nice, say the conservatives. But that rationale could be applied to lesbians, so it's definitely out.

The end result of this stratagem is perverse to the point of being funny. The attempt to ground marriage in children (or the anatomical possibility thereof) falls flat. But, having lost that reason for marriage, the anti-gay people can offer no other. In their fixation on excluding homosexuals, they leave themselves no consistent justification for the privileged status of *heterosexual* marriage. They thus tear away any coherent foundation that secular marriage might have, which is precisely the opposite of what they claim they want to do. If they have to undercut marriage to save it from homosexuals, so be it!

> *"If marriage . . . did nothing else, its power to settle men, to keep them at home and out of trouble, would be ample justification for its special status."*

For the record, I would be the last to deny that children are one central reason for the privileged status of marriage. When men and women get together, children are a likely outcome; and, as we are learning in ever more unpleasant ways, when children grow up without two parents, trouble ensues. Children are not a trivial reason for marriage; they just cannot be the only reason.

## Reasons for Marriage

What are the others? It seems to me that the two strongest candidates are these: domesticating men and providing reliable caregivers. Both purposes are critical to the functioning of a humane and stable society, and both are much better served by marriage—that is, by one-to-one lifelong commitment—than by any other institution.

Civilizing young males is one of any society's biggest problems. Wherever unattached males gather in packs, you see no end of trouble: wildings in Central Park, gangs in Los Angeles, soccer hooligans in Britain, skinheads in Germany, fraternity hazings in universities, grope-lines in the military and, in a different but ultimately no less tragic way, the bathhouses and wanton sex of gay San Francisco or New York in the 1970s.

For taming men, marriage is unmatched. "Of all the institutions through which men may pass—schools, factories, the military—marriage has the largest effect," Wilson writes in *The Moral Sense*. (A token of the casualness of current thinking about marriage is that the man who wrote those words could, later in the very same book, say that government should care about fostering families for "scarcely any other" reason than children.) If marriage—that is, the binding of men into couples—did nothing else, its power to settle men, to keep them at home and out of trouble, would be ample justification for its special status.

Of course, women and older men don't generally travel in marauding or orgiastic packs. But in their case the second rationale comes into play. A second enormous problem for society is what to do when someone is beset by some sort of burdensome contingency. It could be cancer, a broken back, unemployment or depression; it could be exhaustion from work or stress under pressure.

If marriage has any meaning at all, it is that, when you collapse from a stroke, there will be at least one other person whose "job" is to drop everything and come to your aid; or that when you come home after being fired by the postal service there will be someone to persuade you not to kill the supervisor.

Obviously, both rationales—the need to settle males and the need to have people looked after—apply to sterile people as well as fertile ones, and apply to childless couples as well as to ones with children. The first explains why everybody feels relieved when the town delinquent gets married, and the second explains why everybody feels happy when an aging widow takes a second husband. From a social point of view, it seems to me, both rationales are far more compelling as justifications of marriage's special status than, say, love. And both of them apply to homosexuals as well as to heterosexuals.

Take the matter of settling men. It is probably true that women and children, more than just the fact of marriage, help civilize men. But that hardly means that the settling effect of marriage on homosexual men is negligible. To the contrary, being tied to a committed relationship plainly helps stabilize gay men. Even without marriage, coupled gay men have steady sex partners and relationships that they value and therefore tend to be less wanton. Add marriage, and you bring a further array of stabilizing influences. One of the main benefits of publicly recognized marriage is that it binds couples together not only in their own eyes but also in the eyes of society at large. Around the partners is woven a web of expectations that they will spend nights together, go to parties together, take out mortgages together, buy furniture at Ikea together, and so on—all of which helps tie them together and keep them off the streets and at home. Surely that is a very good thing, especially as compared to the closet-gay culture of furtive sex with innumerable partners in parks and bathhouses.

> *"If marriage has any meaning at all, it is that . . . there will be at least one other person whose 'job' is to drop everything and come to your aid."*

## The Caretaking Benefit

The other benefit of marriage—caretaking—clearly applies to homosexuals. One of the first things many people worry about when coming to terms with their homosexuality is: Who will take care of me when I'm ailing or old? Society needs to care about this, too, as the AIDS crisis has made horribly clear. If that crisis has shown anything, it is that homosexuals can and will take care of each other, sometimes with breathtaking devotion—and that no institution can begin to match the care of a devoted partner. Legally speaking, marriage creates kin. Surely society's interest in kin-creation is strongest of all for people who are unlikely to be supported by children in old age and who may well be rejected by their own parents in youth.

Gay marriage, then, is far from being a mere exercise in political point-making or rights-mongering. On the contrary, it serves two of the three social purposes that make marriage so indispensable and irreplaceable for heterosexuals. Two out of three may not be the whole ball of wax, but it is more than enough to give society a compelling interest in marrying off homosexuals.

There is no substitute. Marriage is the *only* institution that adequately serves these purposes. The power of marriage is not just legal but social. It seals its promise with the smiles and tears of family, friends and neighbors. It shrewdly exploits ceremony (big, public weddings) and money (expensive gifts, dowries) to deter casual commitment and to make bailing out embarrassing. Stag parties and bridal showers signal that what is beginning is not just a legal arrangement but a whole new stage of life. "Domestic partner" laws do none of these things.

I'll go further: far from being a substitute for the real thing, marriage-lite may undermine it. Marriage is a deal between a couple and society, not just between two people: society recognizes the sanctity and autonomy of the pair-bond, and in exchange each spouse commits to being the other's nurse, social worker and policeman of first resort. Each marriage is its own little society within society. Any step that weakens the deal by granting the legal benefits of marriage without also requiring the public commitment is begging for trouble.

## Gay Marriage Makes Sense

So gay marriage makes sense for several of the same reasons that straight marriage makes sense. That would seem a natural place to stop. But the logic of the argument compels one to go a twist further. If it is good for society to have people attached, then it is not enough just to make marriage available. Marriage should also be *expected*. This, too, is just as true for homosexuals as for heterosexuals. So, if homosexuals are justified in expecting access to marriage, society is equally justified in expecting them to use it. I'm not saying that out-of-wedlock sex should be scandalous or that people should be coerced into marrying. The mechanisms of expectation are more subtle. When grandma cluck-clucks over a still-unmarried young man, or when mom says she wishes her little girl would settle down, she is expressing a strong and well-justified preference: one that is quietly echoed in a thousand ways throughout society and that produces subtle but important pressure to form and sustain unions. This is a good

> *"Being tied to a committed relationship plainly helps stabilize gay men."*

and necessary thing, and it will be as necessary for homosexuals as heterosexuals. If gay marriage is recognized, single gay people over a certain age should not be surprised when they are disapproved of or pitied. That is a vital part of what makes marriage work. It's stigma as social policy.

If marriage is to work it cannot be merely a "lifestyle option." It must be privileged. That is, it must be understood to be better, on average, than other ways of living. Not mandatory, not good where everything else is bad, but better: a general norm, rather than a personal taste. The biggest worry about gay marriage, I think, is that homosexuals might get it but then mostly not use it. Gay neglect of marriage wouldn't greatly erode the bonding power of heterosexual marriage (remember, homosexuals are only a tiny fraction of the population)—but it would certainly not help. And heterosexual society would rightly feel betrayed if, after legalization, homosexuals treated marriage as a minority taste rather than as a core institution of life. It is not enough, I think, for gay people to say we want the right to marry. If we do not use it, shame on us.

# Gays and Lesbians Have an Equal Right to Marriage

**by Lambda Legal Defense and Education Fund, Inc.**

**About the author:** *The Lambda Legal Defense and Education Fund, Inc. is a national organization that works to defend the rights of gays, lesbians, and people with HIV through litigation and public education.*

Thanks to a historic court case now underway [1996] in Hawaii, lesbians and gay men may be on the verge of winning the right to marry—a basic right still denied them in all fifty states. In the past, other people were refused the right to marry—for example, because of their race—until the law was changed to end this denial of a basic human right. Like non-gay people, gay people need and want the right to marry.

Even once gay men and lesbians finally win this fundamental right—a right central to true equality as well as a long list of important benefits—the battle will not be over. There may be a backlash to try to take away the right to marry, or to say that same-sex couples married in Hawaii are not married in other states. The battle may be a long one, with victories and setbacks over several years. To prepare for the struggle, we must gather true supporters of gay people's equal rights, and ask them to sign on to:

THE MARRIAGE RESOLUTION

> Because marriage is a fundamental right under our Constitution, and because the Constitution guarantees equal protection of the law,
>
> RESOLVED, the State should permit gay and lesbian couples to marry and share fully and equally in the rights and responsibilities of marriage.

Here are the answers to some questions people might have:

*Why do we need "gay marriage"?* We don't; we need *marriage*. The term "gay marriage" implies that same-sex couples are asking for rights or privileges that married couples do not have. What we are asking for is our equal right to marry the one we love and care for, just as non-gay Americans do.

# Gay Rights

*Isn't marriage traditionally defined as a union between men and women?*
Yes. But it is not right for the government to prevent gay people from sharing
the rights and responsibilities of marriage. What should matter is not the gender
or race of those marrying, but their commitment. After all, at different times
marriages were also "traditionally" defined as only unions between people of
the same race or religion, and as unions in which wives were the property of
their husbands. Those "traditional" elements of marriage changed to reflect
American constitutional values and everyone's basic right to equality.

*Do gay people really need the right to marry?* Absolutely. Many same-sex
couples share the same responsibilities as married couples. However, nowhere
in the United States do they receive the same recognition or benefits that married couples do. In fact, they face tremendous discrimination, and are treated as
second-class citizens. For example, lesbians and gay men who have been their
partner's primary caretaker are often turned away at the hospital when there's
been an accident or illness; refused "family" health coverage, taxation, and inheritance rights; and even denied protection in case the relationship ends.
Sometimes they see their children taken away, or their role as parents denied!
Regardless of the fact that they have taken responsibility for their partner's
well-being, both economically and emotionally, their legal status is, at best, that
of a roommate. Finally, lesbians and gay men are denied the emotional, social,
and even religious meaning that marriage has for many.

*What about domestic partnership?* In certain cities, municipalities, and companies, there is limited recognition of relationships between unmarried partners,
including same-sex couples. The benefits and responsibilities of such "domestic
partnerships" vary considerably. However, no domestic partnership plan can
confer the same set of benefits and responsibilities that marriage does. Domestic partnership is of limited help to some unmarried couples, but is no substitute
for the equal right to marry.

*What's happening in Hawaii?* The case began in 1991, when the state clerk refused marriage licenses to three couples (two lesbian couples, one gay male couple). In 1993, the state Supreme Court
ruled that the refusal violated the state
Constitution, which guarantees equality and prohibits sex discrimination.
The case is now back in the lower
court, where, unless the state can
come up with a "compelling" reason

> *"What we are asking for is our
> equal right to marry the one
> we love and care for, just as
> non-gay Americans do."*

for discriminating, it must stop. The state legislature passed a law again trying to
restrict marriage, but gave only one reason (procreation) for the discrimination.
Because this is not a good reason for refusing to allow these couples to marry,
lawyers are optimistic. But this equal rights battle cannot be left just to lawyers,
nor is it just about Hawaii.

*Isn't marriage really about procreation?* No. Many non-gay people marry, and cannot or do not have children. And many gay men and lesbians do have children, but are so far denied the right to raise those children within a marital relationship. Legally and in reality, marriage is best understood as a relationship of emotional and financial interdependence between two people who make a public commitment. Many of them—gay or non-gay—wish to be parents; many others do not. The choice belongs to the couple, not the state.

*Do all lesbian and gay men want the right to marry?* No, gay people are as diverse as non-gay people; many would not choose to marry

> *"It is not right for the government to prevent gay people from sharing the rights and responsibilities of marriage."*

even if they could. However, virtually all gay people want the right to decide for themselves whether and whom to marry, just as non-gay people do.

*Don't some religions oppose lesbian and gay relationships?* Yes, but this is not a fight to force any religious institution to perform or extend religious recognition to any marriages it doesn't want to. This is about the right to the civil marriage license issued by the state. Just as the state should not interfere with religious ceremonies one way or the other, so religious groups should not control who gets a civil marriage license. Of course, many lesbians and gay men are active in their respective religions, many of which do recognize and support their loving unions and commitments.

*Isn't this a bad time to fight for the right to marry?* To some, there is never a good time to fight any battle for equal rights. But here we have no choice. In this particular battle, the timeline centers on the lawsuit. When and if the Hawaii Supreme Court hands down a final ruling affirming the right of same-sex couples to marry, many people in Hawaii and elsewhere will get married there. When they return home to other states, the nationwide validity of their legally contracted marriages may be challenged. Although there are powerful legal and practical reasons why a couple's lawful marriage in one state must be recognized throughout the country (this is, after all, one country, and if you're married, you're married), there will undoubtedly be an effort in some states and possibly in the federal government to block this recognition. As always in the struggle for human rights, the outcome will depend in part on how well those committed to equal rights have prepared for the state-by-state and national legal and political battles.

Just a generation ago, a similar "same-race" restriction was in place, and state governments denied interracial couples the right to marry. Under slavery, African-Americans were not even permitted to marry at all, which was one of the ways they were legally dehumanized! Today we realize that this was wrong, and the choice of a marriage partner belongs to each man or woman, not the state. The same is true for lesbians and gay men. It's a matter of basic fairness, social responsibility, civic equality, and human dignity.

# Gay and Lesbian Parents Can Raise Well-Adjusted Children

**by April Martin**

**About the author:** *April Martin is a psychologist in private practice.*

As lesbian and gay prospective parents we do an extraordinarily thorough and responsible job of exploring our concerns and evaluating our suitability for parenthood. The children of lesbians and gay men are the most considered and planned-for children on earth. There is virtually no such thing as an unwanted child among us. We go to support groups and workshops on considering parenthood. We talk to our friends and lovers and family. We talk to our therapists. We read books. Many years may go into the planning process. We do an impressively careful job of weighing our needs, our resources, and our expectations. . . .

We live in a society which pressures heterosexuals to raise children and pressures lesbians and gay men not to raise children. The desire to become a parent, however, recognizes no distinctions based on sexual orientation. If we could remove the effects of all that pressure, we would undoubtedly find that heterosexuals want children a good deal less of the time than they have them, and that lesbians and gay men want them more. As a community of lesbians and gay men, we are just beginning to open ourselves to those desires. In the 1980s, only rarely did one of my gay or lesbian clients mention the question of children. Today, the issue of whether or not a life's plan will include parenting comes up with a great many of the gay men and lesbians I see. . . .

## Raising Healthy Children

One tired lesbian mother of a very assertive child bemoaned, "I think we made her *too* secure." Barring such outcomes, however, there is a large body of research which supports the fact that our children are at least as healthy as anyone else's. (A few studies show that children raised by lesbians are *better* adjusted than children from straight families.) The studies have examined the children's social functioning, self-esteem, ability to express feelings, intelligence, and tendencies toward one or another sexual orientation. Though the courts and even the mental health profession are slow to catch on, the data is there and irrefutable. What we have to offer in our lesbian and gay families is exactly what children need to grow into healthy, happy, and well-adjusted children.

Many of us found growing up as lesbians or gay men to be painful, isolating, shameful, and frightening. If we endured teasing or rejection from others because we were different, we undoubtedly suffered a lot. We may imagine that our children will have to go through a similarly hurtful social ostracism, and will grow up feeling bad about themselves. We may worry that they will be angry with us for thrusting them into such a difficult life.

> *"The children of lesbians and gay men are the most considered and planned-for children on earth."*

The reality is not like this, however. People's worst fears—that our children will be harmed by teasing, shaming, or social ostracism for coming from a gay family—do not seem to be coming to pass. On the contrary, the pride we feel in our families gives our children the tools to deal with prejudice. As in any family that contains a member of an oppressed minority, our children learn to understand the problems of ignorance and bias. Depending on where they live and who they are, they make decisions about whom to tell and whom not to tell. In general, our children only rarely encounter any significant homophobic treatment. In instances when they do, they are prepared to handle it.

One young man, now thirteen, made a statement that echoed the sentiments of many other children I spoke with. He said, "I think growing up with lesbian parents taught me about how people can be different. And being different is just different, it isn't better or worse. I feel good about myself for understanding some things that a lot of other kids don't know. My moms have helped me a lot."

For some children, this means there aren't even any difficult feelings to contend with about coming from a different kind of family. Other children, though, do go through some sad feelings about not having a father, for example, or feel some frustration about explaining their families to schoolmates. *The fact of their having some negative feelings does not mean that they are psychologically damaged by them.* This is an important distinction. The truth is that everyone, from whatever kind of family, wishes that some things about their family were different. Our task as parents is to listen to our children's feelings with compassion, and without guilt or defensiveness in response. For children, coming to terms with the disappointments in life is part of growing up. Ultimately it is feeling loved and understood that helps all of us overcome life's imperfections. We are giving our children love of the very best quality, and they will feel it.

Paula's personal history affected her beliefs about what a child would need. "I thought my child would grow up and want a daddy or be angry with me for not providing one. My father had died when I was young and I knew the feelings I had had were painful. I was worried, even though I knew I had *lost* my father, and this child would never know a father."

Gloria was also raised without a father, and her experience led her to the opposite conclusion. "I never missed having a father. I grew up in a family of women, my mother, my aunt, and my grandmother. My father was never involved with the family. I had male cousins, and other male relatives, and that seemed just fine to me. I felt that even if I had a boy, I could do everything with him that a father would do, and he wouldn't be missing anything. And I have men friends who would be close to him."

The world consists of two genders, and our children, whether boys or girls, need to grow up having relationships with both men and women, but those relationships can be with people other than parents. No parent can give a child everything. Nor can we predict which things our children will miss most. However, your pride and confidence about your family structure will be communicated to your child. Your willingness to listen to your child's changing needs, and to whatever wishes or longings there may be, will make it possible for any family configuration, with or without a father or a mother, to be a healthy environment.

> *"A few studies show that children raised by lesbians are better adjusted than children from straight families."*

We are all concerned about how our children will handle the world's response to their families. Will they be stigmatized for their parents' sexuality? Will they suffer the discomforts of prejudice that many of us have felt? Some of the answers have to do with how open we are able to be about our family structure in our neighborhoods, families, and communities. The degree of openness we are able to maintain, and the amount of community support we have for our openness, will have a great influence on how comfortable our children are able to be with their friends and schoolmates. The easier it is for our children to discuss their families, the less stress they will experience. Even when children feel a need to be evasive with some people about their families, they manage to find close relationships in which they can be open. Our children are doing a fine job of developing social circles, fitting in, and living quite healthy lives.

# Homosexuals Should Not Be Allowed to Marry

**by James Q. Wilson**

**About the author:** *James Q. Wilson is the author of* The Moral Sense *and the Collins professor of management and public policy at the University of California at Los Angeles.*

Our courts, which have mishandled abortion, may be on the verge of mishandling homosexuality. As a consequence of a pending decision, we may be about to accept homosexual marriage.

## Hawaii and Same-Sex Marriages

In 1993 the supreme court of Hawaii ruled that, under the equal-protection clause of that state's constitution, any law based on distinctions of sex was suspect, and thus subject to strict judicial scrutiny. Accordingly, it reversed the denial of a marriage permit to a same-sex couple, unless the state could first demonstrate a "compelling state interest" that would justify limiting marriages to men and women. A new trial is set for summer 1996. But in the meantime, the executive branch of Hawaii appointed a commission to examine the question of same-sex marriages; its report, by a vote of five to two, supports them. The legislature, for its part, holds a different view of the matter, having responded to the court's decision by passing a law unambiguously reaffirming the limitation of marriage to male-female couples.

No one knows what will happen in the coming trial, but the odds are that the Hawaiian version of the equal-rights amendment may control the outcome. If so, since the United States Constitution has a clause requiring that "full faith and credit shall be given to the public acts, records, and judicial proceedings of every other state," a homosexual couple in a state like Texas, where the population is overwhelmingly opposed to such unions, may soon be able to fly to Hawaii, get married, and then return to live in Texas as lawfully wedded. A few scholars believe that states may be able to impose public-policy objections to such out-of-state marriages—Utah has already voted one in, and other states may follow—but only at the price of endless litigation. . . .

Contemporaneous with these events, an important book has appeared under the title *Virtually Normal*. In it, Andrew Sullivan, the editor of the *New Republic*, makes a strong case for a new policy toward homosexuals. He argues that

> *"Homosexual uses of the reproductive organs violate the condition that sex serve solely as the basis of heterosexual marriage."*

"all *public* (as opposed to private) discrimination against homosexuals be ended. . . . *And that is all.*" The two key areas where this change is necessary are the military and marriage law. Lifting bans in those areas, while also disallowing anti-sodomy laws and providing information about homosexuality in publicly supported schools, would put an end to the harm that gays have endured. Beyond these changes, Sullivan writes, American society would need no "cures [of homophobia] or reeducations, no wrenching private litigation, no political imposition of tolerance."

It is hard to imagine how Sullivan's proposals would, in fact, end efforts to change private behavior toward homosexuals, or why the next, inevitable, step would not involve attempts to accomplish just that purpose by using cures and reeducations, private litigation, and the political imposition of tolerance. But apart from this, Sullivan—an English Catholic, a homosexual, and someone who has on occasion referred to himself as a conservative—has given us the most sensible and coherent view of a program to put homosexuals and heterosexuals on the same public footing. His analysis is based on a careful reading of serious opinions and his book is written quietly, clearly, and thoughtfully. In her review of it in *First Things* (January 1996), Elizabeth Kristol asks us to try to answer the following question: what would life be like if we were not allowed to marry? To most of us, the thought is unimaginable; to Sullivan, it is the daily existence of declared homosexuals. His response is to let homosexual couples marry.

## The Arguments

Sullivan recounts three main arguments concerning homosexual marriage, two against and one for. He labels them prohibitionist, conservative, and liberal. (A fourth camp, the "liberationist," which advocates abolishing all distinctions between heterosexuals and homosexuals, is also described—and scorched for its "strange confluence of political abdication and psychological violence.") I think it easier to grasp the origins of the three main arguments by referring to the principles on which they are based.

The prohibitionist argument is in fact a biblical one; the heart of it was stated by Dennis Prager in an essay in the *Public Interest* ("Homosexuality, the Bible, and Us," Summer 1993). When the first books of the Bible were written, and for a long time thereafter, heterosexual love is what seemed at risk. In many cultures—not only in Egypt or among the Canaanite tribes surrounding ancient Israel but later in Greece, Rome, and the Arab world, to say nothing of large parts of China, Japan, and elsewhere—homosexual practices were common and widely tolerated or even exalted. The Torah reversed this, making the family the central unit of life, the obligation to marry one of the first responsibilities of man, and the linkage of sex to procreation the highest standard by which to judge sexual relations. Leviticus puts the matter sharply and apparently beyond quibble:

> Thou shalt not live with mankind as with womankind; it is an abomination. . . .
> If a man also lie with mankind, as he lieth with a woman, both of them have committed an abomination; they shall surely be put to death; their blood shall be upon them.

Sullivan acknowledges the power of Leviticus but deals with it by placing it in a relative context. What is the nature of this "abomination"? Is it like killing your mother or stealing a neighbor's bread, or is it more like refusing to eat shellfish or having sex during menstruation? Sullivan suggests that all of these injunctions were written on the same moral level and hence can be accepted or ignored *as a whole*. He does not fully sustain this view, and in fact a refutation of it can be found in Prager's essay. In Prager's opinion and mine, people at the time of Moses, and for centuries before him, understood that there was a fundamental difference between whom you killed and what you ate, and in all likelihood people then and for centuries earlier linked whom you could marry closer to the principles that defined life than they did to the rules that defined diets.

> *"Gay or lesbian marriage . . . [would] question the role of marriage at a time when the threats to it . . . have hit record highs."*

The New Testament contains an equally vigorous attack on homosexuality by St. Paul. Sullivan partially deflects it by noting Paul's conviction that the earth was about to end and the Second Coming was near; under these conditions, all forms of sex were suspect. But Sullivan cannot deny that Paul singled out homosexuality as deserving of special criticism. He seems to pass over this obstacle without effective retort.

Instead, he takes up a different theme, namely, that on grounds of consistency many heterosexual practices—adultery, sodomy, premarital sex, and divorce, among others—should be outlawed equally with homosexual acts of the same character. The difficulty with this is that it mistakes the distinction alive in most people's minds between marriage as an institution and marriage as a practice. As an institution, it deserves unqualified support; as a practice, we recognize that married people are as imperfect as anyone else. Sullivan's understanding of the prohibitionist argument suffers from his unwillingness to acknowledge this distinction.

## Natural Law and Homosexual Marriage

The second argument against homosexual marriage—Sullivan's conservative category—is based on natural law as originally set forth by Aristotle and Thomas Aquinas and more recently restated by Hadley Arkes, John Finnis, Robert George, Harry V. Jaffa, and others. How it is phrased varies a bit, but in general its advocates support a position like the following: man cannot live without the care and support of other people; natural law is the distillation of what thoughtful people have learned about the conditions of that care. The first thing they have learned is the supreme importance of marriage, for without it the newborn infant is unlikely to survive or, if he survives, to prosper. The necessary conditions of a decent family life are the acknowledgment by its members that a man will not sleep with his daughter or a woman with her son and that neither will openly choose sex outside marriage.

Now, some of these conditions are violated, but there is a penalty in each case that is supported by the moral convictions of almost all who witness the violation. On simple utilitarian grounds it may be hard to object to incest or adultery; if both parties to such an act welcome it and if it is secret, what differences does it make? But very few people, and then only ones among the overeducated, seem to care much about mounting a utilitarian assault on the family. To this assault, natural-law theorists respond much as would the average citizen— never mind "utility," what counts is what is right. In particular, homosexual uses of the reproductive organs violate the condition that sex serve solely as the basis of heterosexual marriage.

To Sullivan, what is defective about the natural-law thesis is that it assumes different purposes in heterosexual and homosexual love: moral consummation in the first case and pure utility or pleasure alone in the second. But in fact, Sullivan suggests, homosexual love can be as consummatory as heterosexual. He notes that as the Roman Catholic Church has deepened its understanding of the involuntary—that is, in some sense genetic—basis of homosexuality, it has attempted to keep homosexuals in the church as objects of affection and nurture, while banning homosexual acts as perverse.

But this, though better than nothing, will not work, Sullivan writes. To show why, he adduces an analogy to a sterile person. Such a person is permitted to serve in the military or enter an unproductive marriage; why not homosexuals? If homosexuals marry without procreation, they are no different (he suggests) from a sterile man or woman who marries without hope of procreation. Yet people, I think, want the form observed even when the practice varies; a sterile marriage, whether from choice or necessity, remains a marriage of a man and a woman. To this Sullivan offers essentially an aesthetic response.

> *"Homosexual marriage . . . could further weaken an already strained institution."*

Just as albinos remind us of the brilliance of color and genius teaches us about moderation, homosexuals are a "natural foil" to the heterosexual union, "a variation that does not eclipse the theme." Moreover, the threat posed by the foil to the theme is slight as compared to the threats posed by adultery, divorce, and prostitution. To be consistent, Sullivan once again reminds us, society would have to ban adulterers from the military as it now bans confessed homosexuals.

> *"Marriage is a union, sacred to most, that unites a man and woman together for life."*

## Missing the Point

But again this misses the point. It would make more sense to ask why an alternative to marriage should be invented and praised when we are having enough trouble maintaining the institution at all. Suppose that gay or lesbian marriage were authorized; rather than producing a "natural foil" that would "not eclipse the theme," I suspect such a move would call even more seriously into question the role of marriage at a time when the threats to it, ranging from single-parent families to common divorces, have hit record highs. Kenneth Minogue recently wrote of Sullivan's book that support for homosexual marriage would strike most people as "mere parody," one that could further weaken an already strained institution.

To me, the chief limitation of Sullivan's view is that it presupposes that marriage would have the same, domesticating, effect on homosexual members as it has on heterosexuals, while leaving the latter largely unaffected. Those are very large assumptions that no modern society has ever tested.

Nor does it seem plausible to me that a modern society resists homosexual marriages entirely out of irrational prejudice. Marriage is a union, sacred to most, that unites a man and woman together for life. It is a sacrament of the Catholic Church and central to every other faith. Is it out of misinformation that every modern society has embraced this view and rejected the alternative? Societies differ greatly in their attitude toward the income people may have, the relations among their various races, and the distribution of political power. But they differ scarcely at all over the distinctions between heterosexual and homosexual couples. The former are overwhelmingly preferred over the latter. The reason, I believe, is that these distinctions involve the nature of marriage and thus the very meaning—even more, the very possibility—of society.

## The Civil Rights Argument

The final argument over homosexual marriage is the liberal one, based on civil rights.

As we have seen, the Hawaiian supreme court ruled that any state-imposed sexual distinction would have to meet the test of strict scrutiny, a term used by the U.S. Supreme Court only for racial and similar classifications. In doing this, the Hawaiian court distanced itself from every other state court decision—there are several—in this area so far. A variant of the suspect-class argument, though, has been suggested by some scholars who contend that denying access to a marriage license by two people of the same sex is no different from denying access to two people of different sexes but also different races. The Hawaiian Supreme Court embraced this argument as well, explicitly comparing its decision to that of the U.S. Supreme Court when it overturned state laws banning marriages involving miscegenation.

But the comparison with black-white marriages is itself suspect. Beginning around 1964, and no doubt powerfully affected by the passage of the Civil Rights Act of that year, public attitudes toward race began to change dramatically. Even allowing for exaggerated statements to pollsters, there is little doubt that people in fact acquired a new view of blacks. Not so with homosexuals. Though the campaign to aid them has been going on vigorously for about a quarter of a century, it has produced few, if any, gains in public acceptance, and the greatest resistance, I think, has been with respect to homosexual marriages.

> *"Marriage is a different issue from the issue of social integration."*

Consider the difference. What has been at issue in race relations is not marriage among blacks (for over a century, that right has been universally granted) or even miscegenation (long before the civil-rights movement, many Southern states had repealed such laws). Rather, it has been the routine contact between the races in schools, jobs, and neighborhoods. Our own history, in other words, has long made it clear that marriage is a different issue from the issue of social integration.

There is another way, too, in which the comparison with race is less than helpful, as Sullivan himself points out. Thanks to the changes in public attitudes I mentioned a moment ago, gradually race was held to be not central to decisions about hiring, firing, promoting, and schooling, and blacks began to make extraordinary advances in society. But then, in an effort to enforce this new view, liberals came to embrace affirmative action, a policy that said that race *was* central to just such issues, in order to ensure that *real* mixing occurred. This move created a crisis, for liberalism had always been based on the proposition that a liberal political system should encourage, as John Stuart Mill put it, "experiments in living" free of religious or political direction. To contemporary liberals, however, being neutral about race was tantamount to being neutral about a set of human preferences that in such matters as neighborhood and schooling left groups largely (but not entirely) separate.

Sullivan, who wisely sees that hardly anybody is really prepared to ignore a political opportunity to change lives, is not disposed to have much of this either in the area of race or in that of sex. And he points out with great clarity that popular attitudes toward sexuality are anyway quite different from those about race, as is evident from the fact that wherever sexual orientation is subject to local regulations, such regulations are rarely invoked. Why? Because homosexuals can "pass" or not, as they wish; they can and do accumulate education and wealth; they exercise political power. The two things a homosexual cannot do are join the military as an avowed homosexual or marry another homosexual.

The result, Sullivan asserts, is a wrenching paradox. On the one hand, society has historically tolerated the brutalization inflicted on people because of the color of their skin, but freely allowed them to marry; on the other hand, it has given equal opportunity to homosexuals, while denying them the right to marry. This, indeed, is where Sullivan draws the line. A black or Hispanic child, if heterosexual, has many friends, he writes, but a gay child "generally has no one." And that is why the social stigma attached to homosexuality is different from that attached to race or ethnicity—"because it attacks the very heart of what makes a human being human: the ability to love and be loved." Here is the essence of Sullivan's case. It is a powerful one, even if (as I suspect) his pro-marriage sentiments are not shared by all homosexuals. . . .

## Homosexual Promiscuity

Of course, homosexual "families," with or without children, might be rather few in number. Just how few, it is hard to say. Perhaps Sullivan himself would marry, but, given the great tendency of homosexual males to be promiscuous, many more like him would not, or if they did, would not marry with as much seriousness.

That is problematic in itself. At one point, Sullivan suggests that most homosexuals would enter a marriage "with as much (if not more) commitment as heterosexuals." Toward the end of his book, however, he seems to withdraw from so optimistic a view. He admits that the label "virtually" in the title of his book is deliberately ambiguous, because homosexuals as a group are *not* "normal." At another point, he writes that the "openness of the contract" between two homosexual males means that such a union will in fact be more durable than a heterosexual marriage because the contract contains an "*understanding of the need for extramarital outlets*" (emphasis added). But no such "understanding" exists in heterosexual marriage; to suggest that it might in homosexual ones is tantamount to saying that we are now referring to two different kinds of arrangements. To justify this difference, perhaps, Sullivan adds that the very "lack of children" will

> *"Given the great tendency of homosexual males to be promiscuous, many . . . would not marry."*

give "gay couples greater freedom." Freedom for what? Freedom, I think, to do more of those things that heterosexual couples do less of because they might hurt the children.

## A Fundamental Error

The courts in Hawaii and in the nation's capital must struggle with all these issues under the added encumbrance of a contemporary outlook that makes law the search for rights, and responsibility the recognition of rights. Indeed, thinking of laws about marriage as documents that confer or withhold rights is itself an error of fundamental importance—one that the highest court in Hawaii has already committed. "Marriage," it wrote, "is a state-conferred legal-partnership status, the existence of which gives rise to a multiplicity of rights and benefits. . . ." A state-conferred legal partnership? To lawyers, perhaps; to mankind, I think not. The Hawaiian court has thus set itself on the same course of action as the misguided Supreme Court in 1973 when it thought that laws about abortion were merely an assertion of the rights of a living mother and an unborn fetus.

I have few favorable things to say about the political systems of other modern nations, but on these fundamental matters—abortion, marriage, military service—they often do better by allowing legislatures to operate than we do by deferring to courts. Our challenge is to find a way of formulating a policy with respect to homosexual unions that is not the result of a reflexive act of judicial rights-conferring, but is instead a considered expression of the moral convictions of a people.

# Gays and Lesbians Should Not Seek State-Sanctioned Marriage

**by Alisa Solomon**

**About the author:** *Alisa Solomon is a staff writer for the* Village Voice.

I'm definitely the marrying kind—a nester, monogamous, and corny as Kansas. My partner and I had a commitment ceremony a few years ago to celebrate our relationship and declare it publicly. The rings we exchanged are engraved with the Hebrew words *ahuvot l'olam*—beloveds forever. (I *said* I was corny.)

But if Hawaii legalizes gay and lesbian marriages, we won't be hurrying to Honolulu. The way we see it, if the state has no business in our bedrooms, what business does it have in our bonding? Of course equality is a bottom-line principle. As long as the state awards benefits to heterosexuals who marry, those benefits ought to be available to lesbian and gay couples, too. That's the simple logic of fairness; any disputing of lesbians' or gay men's "fitness" for such privileges is bigotry plain and simple. Nonetheless, the debate over same-sex marriage offers an opportunity to examine the institution of matrimony, the values it serves, and the state's interest in them. Indeed, this debate can challenge the lesbian and gay movement to imagine new models for achieving a just society for all.

## Male Control

State-sanctioned marriage is not a neutral structure we can slip into and reshape to our liking. Gayle Rubin said it best in her influential essay, "The Traffic in Women: Notes on the Political Economy of Sex": "Kinship and marriage are always parts of total social systems, and are always tied into economic and political arrangements." The historical purpose of legal matrimony has been the promotion of patriarchal control over property—understood to include land, wealth, women, and children.

Alisa Solomon, "Get Married? Yes, but Not by State," *Village Voice*, January 9, 1996. Reprinted by permission.

Changes in marriage law over the last few decades have certainly reflected women's increased economic independence (sometimes detrimentally, as when alimony is denied a divorcing woman who has been tending home and kids for years). But in the eyes of the law—and in the rhetoric of Promise Keepers, the Million Man March, and all the other scary folks promoting "family values"— the family is a man's fiefdom. He may be disenfranchised and disempowered by unemployment or government indifference, but in the precincts of legal matrimony, the state pronounces him king.

Certainly we can inhabit this structure and resist its strictures, as do heterosexuals committed to egalitarianism. But we can't puncture the paradigm. The institution of marriage serves the state as an instrument for regulating its version of morality: It codifies sexual behavior and promotes a particular arrangement of child rearing. In doing so, the state aims to preserve social stability. And indeed, this is precisely why it rewards married couples with the privileges lesbians and gays, in the name of fairness, seek.

The state confers tax benefits, inheritance rights, and other incentives on hetero mates, and the commercial world follows suit—workplaces offer health benefits to employees' spouses and insurance companies grant lower rates to married folks. As the argument for queer marriage goes, why can't we get the same?

> *"If the state has no business in our bedrooms, what business does it have in our bonding?"*

Yet what is all this but special rights for the coupled? Shouldn't anyone caring for an infirm individual be able to claim a tax deduction, whether or not the state recognizes a "familial" relationship? Shouldn't we *all* be able to designate who can visit us in the hospital, inherit our property, or serve as powers of attorney? Does someone have to vow lifelong fidelity in order to get decent health coverage? Universal health care was a demand of the lesbian and gay movement not too long ago (at least it was included on the list for the 1993 March on Washington), but it's been drowned out lately by the demand to be lawfully wed. Yet such health coverage—along with other rational and inclusive policies—would obviate the need for legalizing gay unions. Except insofar as that need is more symbolic than substantive. What's really at the heart of the push for queer marriage is social sanction: By allowing us to marry, the state literally licenses our love.

## Marriage Will Not Help Gays

That's a heady prospect in these days when our very existence is under perpetual attack. As reactionaries seek to preempt our civil rights all across the country, it's tempting to seek state support for what the courts have called a "most basic right": to marry whom one chooses. Like the ban on gays in the military, the exclusion of gays from matrimony reveals that we aren't fully recognized as citizens.

Yet when we seek to lift these bans, we can't turn away from exposing the power relations these institutions serve. We might like to think that marrying with the state's blessing will help diminish homophobia, but to countenance monogamy and the nuclear family unit, and affirm their value for social cohesion, is to hang the promiscuous, the nonmonogamous, even the woefully single, out to dry.

> *"The question isn't whether the state should marry gays, but whether it should marry anyone."*

The Supreme Court's 1967 declaration that antimiscegenation laws were unconstitutional has had little impact on racism in this country. Indeed, racism is still served by the demonization of black sexuality that isn't maritally contained. There's no bigger villain for American conservatism these days than black women who have babies out of wedlock—which is to say, sex outside of marriage. Except, perhaps, for queers. The images of gyrating Gay Pride revelers, drag queens, and dykes on bikes that are the stuff of right-wing propaganda films will be no less potent when the state has heard some of us say "I do." Gay marriage would achieve approval of gay marriage, nothing more. It could grant queer couples some privileges, but it won't advance the community.

The language of constitutional law makes that clear enough. Never mind arguments based on privacy: In *Bowers* v. *Hardwick*, the case upholding Georgia's sodomy laws, the Supreme Court ruled that homosexual claims to a constitutional right of privacy for sexual relations are "at best, facetious." We might be more successful arguing for equal protection, but that requires demonstrating that people who are alike must be treated alike. Thus we must argue that we are, in every way that counts, just like straight couples. Which is fine, I suppose, for those who feel they are. But what about the rest of us?

Queer relationships are forged outside the assumptions that are attached to gender. Banished from the privileges of marriage, we've been spared its imperatives; coupling without the presumption of procreation, we exalt our love in and for itself. So can straight couples, of course; but *all* queer lovers, for better and for worse, must constantly invent the terms of their relationships. If anything, such creativity should be encouraged—and extended to straights. At the very least, we have to consider what damage we do to our movement by creating law that denies our difference.

Besides, if we win the right to marry, we might cut off those couples who choose not to do so. Lesbians, for instance, who escaped a bad marriage to a man and found eternal bliss with a dyke might nonetheless choose not to reenter an institution they experienced as oppressive. Will they (like straight couples who don't marry) be excluded from spousal benefits? Marriage could also work to *restrict* benefits. For example, a gay man with AIDS who relies on social security and medicare would lose those resources if he were deemed to have a spouse. Yet if they've declined to marry, his lover might not be granted "next of kin" status at the hospital.

As gay organizations lead the charge to the altar, there's been little opportunity to admit impediments. The press quotes lesbian and gay activists who hold that legalizing queer matrimony is the movement's central concern, and no one raises doubts. So one has to ask how well they've prepared for the backlash that's sure to come. Utah, for instance, has already passed legislation saying it will not recognize same-sex marriages knotted elsewhere.

If Hawaii rules in favor of queer marriage, how many states will seek similar statutes? What if the right pushes a constitutional amendment enshrining the ban on gay marriage—how many members of Congress could resist voting yes? And in turn, how many of our activist hours and resources will be drained as we attempt to defeat them? What issues will be neglected as a result?

Right-wing opponents of gay marriage froth about how sanctioning our unions would threaten "the building block of civilization," as Robert Knight of the Family Research Council has put it. On the contrary. It says we don't want to topple the edifice, just add some lavender bricks.

Instead, this debate should be an opportunity to reveal the narrow way in which a particular model of family puts those who adhere to it inside the loop, and leaves more and more Americans outside. It should provide the opening to ask why access to basic benefits, which are granted to *individuals* in the rest of the developed world, requires certified membership in a nuclear family. And it should lay bare how the state steers heterosexuals into particular lifestyles by rewarding certain "choices."

How much better to marry just for love. Party on the beach, proclaim vows before the goddess, holler from the mountaintops, huddle under a *chuppa*—whatever. But leave the government out of it. The question isn't whether the state should marry gays, but whether it should marry anyone.

# Homosexual Parents Are Not in a Child's Best Interests

**by Robert H. Knight**

**About the author:** *Robert H. Knight is the director of cultural studies at the Family Research Council and author of the monograph* Sexual Disorientation: Faulty Research in the Homosexual Debate.

In deciding who should raise children, society's primary concern must be what is in the best interest of the child. Parents' rights should be protected and the state should intrude only when a child is in a high-risk situation. An openly homosexual household constitutes such a risk.

This issue is climaxing in child custody litigation, with mixed rulings. In June 1994, a Virginia appeals court overruled a decision to award custody of a 2-year-old boy to his grandmother because his mother, Sharon Lynne Bottoms, has a live-in lesbian lover. The appeals court ruled that the mother's sexual preference is irrelevant. In April 1994, a Washington judge denied custody of a 2-year-old girl to two gay men, citing a District of Columbia law forbidding an unmarried couple—homosexual or heterosexual—from adopting the same child. Homosexual "marriage" is not legal in Washington or anywhere else in the United States.

## What Children Need

Regardless of what courts rule, children need a same-sex and an opposite-sex parent to have the best chance to develop healthy sexual identities. Those in single-parent households already are disadvantaged because one of the sexes is missing. Some single parents understand this "gender deficit" and work mightily to ensure that their children receive guidance from grandparents or other role models who represent the sexes evenly. In a homosexual household, the problem is compounded by the embrace of same-sex sexuality within the home itself. Children, who in an androgynous culture are having an increasingly hard time trying to establish basic, confident gender identities, cannot possibly be helped by seeing "mom" kiss "mom" or "dad" kiss "dad."

Proponents of homosexual parenting often defend their view as an issue of freedom and individual rights. But adopting children is not a right. Children are not commodities to be parceled out. Nor are they guinea pigs to be used in experiments in "alternative" sexuality. They are individuals with psychological, emotional, social and developmental needs. And societies the world over, for thousands of years, have found that children thrive best in families with mothers and fathers.

The driving force behind gay parenting seems to be legitimation of the homosexual lifestyle more than what is best for children. In *The Lesbian and Gay Parenting Handbook*, author April Martin reveals why she and her lesbian lover decided to switch sperm donors for "their" second child: The donor "might become a great deal more psychologically important in our lives than we intended. The children would be biologically related to each other through the sperm donor, deriving from the donor a link that we could never give them. It felt more comfortable, then, to have different donors."

So the children's genetic history, in effect, is being engineered to comfortably facilitate a lesbian relationship. Never mind that the children are missing out on life with father.

## Family Makeup Is Important

Homosexual activists often say that family makeup is irrelevant because homosexuals are "born that way," just like heterosexuals. But the weight of studies—even those by homosexual researchers—shows that children in homosexual households are four times as likely to identify with homosexuality. Furthermore, no credible evidence exists that homosexuality has a genetic link. Seventy years of studies and therapeutic experience clearly indicate that homosexuality is a gender-identity problem stemming from environmental factors in early childhood. Masters and Johnson reported in 1984 a 71 percent success rate in therapy for homosexuals wanting to change their orientation, and thousands of homosexuals have been freed with help from gender-identity therapy and ex-gay ministries.

Homosexual-parenting activists also assert that if a parent loves the child, the parent's sexuality or sexual preferences make no difference. The

> *"Children need a same-sex and an opposite-sex parent to have the best chance to develop healthy sexual identities."*

good intentions of all would-be homosexual parents are not being challenged here. But the character, behavior and biological sexuality of parents are extremely important to a child's development. In a homosexual household, children miss out on seeing important relationships between mothers and fathers, men and women, and husbands and wives, plus the personal relationships that parents of both sexes have with children.

In terms of sexual development, boys need fathers so they can develop their own sexual identity; they need mothers so they can learn how to interact with the opposite sex. Girls have similar needs.

Activists often use hypothetical situations to make a homosexual household seem like a haven. They ask: If a loving homosexual couple wants to adopt a child who is now living with an abusive father, wouldn't the child

> *"Societies the world over, for thousands of years, have found that children thrive best in families with mothers and fathers."*

be better off with the gay couple? But such scenarios do not validate homosexual households. Purely for debate, one could imagine thousands of situations: A child is in a burning house; wouldn't he be better off over in the gay household which is not burning? The question should be: What is best for children's development? The research and common sense tell us that children do best in mom-and-dad households. Given that as many as 1 million heterosexual couples are waiting to adopt, there is no excuse for validating homosexual adoption when there are healthier alternatives.

According to the most reliable surveys, homosexuals comprise less than 2 percent of the population—not the inflated 10 percent from the discredited Kinsey studies—and homosexual couples comprise a microscopic portion of that subset. But numbers alone would not dictate whether homosexuality was a healthy development. If 90 percent of people in a community were smoking two packs of cigarettes a day, they would not be healthy. Just because many people exhibit certain behaviors does not mean that they should gain social acceptance based on that behavior; acceptance and civil rights must be based on other characteristics shared by all, including homosexuals.

## Biased Research

Studies on the effects of homosexual parenting on children are scant, highly politicized and conducted largely by lesbian researchers in tightly limited samples. The research often is biased and by design screens out any "problem" households. Most scientists have deduced that placing a child in a homosexual household is an unwarranted risk, and they would not do so willingly for the sake of scientific experimentation. Those who have reservations about such an arrangement would be unable to develop a rapport with homosexual parents and thus gain the data necessary for a study. So the field is left to homosexual activists, who already support the notion of homosexual parenting.

In any case, just as we don't need studies to tell us that it is unwise to let children play unprotected near highways, we don't need research to tell us that it is unwise to have children raised by homosexuals. Only two states—Florida and

New Hampshire—have laws prohibiting homosexual adoption, and they enacted them in 1989. But the absence of such laws is not an endorsement of homosexual adoption. It's a reflection of the societal wisdom that the practice is so obviously inappropriate that laws barring it were not even needed.

Researcher Frederick W. Bozett acknowledges in *Homosexuality and the Family* that: "Most studies of gay fathers are based on nonrandom, small-sample sizes, with subjects who are Caucasian, middle- to upper-class, well-educated with occupations commensurate with their education, who come mostly from urban centers and who are relatively accepting of their homosexuality. There is severely limited knowledge of gay fathers who vary from these demographics. Moreover, the validity and reliability of the instruments used in the studies reported are not always addressed." Other shortcomings of homosexual parenting studies, according to Brigham Young University psychologist J. Craig Peery, include: "unsuitable philosophical approaches, logical inconsistencies, inappropriate theoretical models, limitations on sample size, sample selection, control groups, data collection and analysis and lack of a longitudinal perspective."

## Risks to Children

Nonetheless, even within these biased studies, greater risks to children raised in homosexual households are evident. Most of the studies compare children in homosexual households to those in single-parent households instead of mom-and-dad households. Research shows that children in single-parent households are at higher risk for susceptibility to peer pressure, early sexual activity, drug abuse, delinquency and other problems. Again, not all children raised in single-parent households suffer from such maladies, but they are statistically at a higher risk. So comparing homosexual households with single-parent households is a way to avoid the obvious, documentable desirability of the mom-and-dad household.

In addition, the studies reveal some examples of elevated risks for children raised in homosexual households. Dr. Jerry Binger, himself a homosexual parent and a coinvestigator with Bozett, writes: "12 percent [of children raised in homosexual households] tend to develop a homosexual orientation." His finding appears to match that of a 1989 survey of women once married to men who practice homosexuality, in which nearly 12 percent report homosexual behavior in their children. Considering that homosexuals make up less than 2 percent of the general population, these numbers show a dramatically elevated risk of gender-identity confusion.

> *"The driving force behind gay parenting seems to be legitimation of the homosexual lifestyle more than what is best for children."*

Children raised in homosexual households also experience emotional problems associated with their parents' homosexuality. The 1989 study of women once married to men who practice homosexuality also showed that one in three mothers with older children report that their children have "problems in relationships with members of the opposite sex." Another study featured in *Homosexuality and the Family* showed that five of nine daughters of divorced lesbians had "felt

> *"Children in homosexual households are four times as likely to identify with homosexuality."*

negatively about their mothers' lesbianism." Psychologist Paul Cameron also found that "58.8 percent of the children of lesbians and 21.1 percent of the children of homosexual fathers experience relationship problems with other people because of their knowledge of their parents' homosexuality."

Other studies by researchers who do not openly promote homosexual parenting find even greater risks to children in homosexual households. In one of the few random studies on homosexual parenting, Cameron found that children in these households are at far greater risk in a number of areas, including greater risk of sexual involvement with a parent, of becoming homosexual and of having social or psychological problems such as sexual adventurism. Psychological counselor Jaki Edwards says of her upbringing in a lesbian household: "I had to 'prove' my femininity, and I did that by becoming promiscuous with men." She observes that this is a common reaction among children raised in lesbian households.

Children, for better or worse, grow up to be much like their parents. Children in Roman Catholic families tend to become Roman Catholics; children in Republican families tend to vote Republican; children in households where alcohol is abused are more likely to become alcoholics themselves. It is reasonable to assume that children raised in homosexual households would be more likely either to become homosexual themselves or to become sexually promiscuous, and the little research available bears this out.

## The Natural Environment

The mom-and-dad family is the natural environment for child rearing and is the foundation of civilization. Homosexuals want to appropriate marital and family status, but insemination with donated sperm, surrogate birthing and other technological monstrosities cannot contribute to cross-generation kinship. It still takes two opposite-sex people to biologically create children and to provide the full dimension of family life.

Elizabeth Moberly, a research psychologist who specializes in gender-identity research, says homosexual behavior is an unconscious effort on the part of homosexuals to recover their natural sexual identity. In her groundbreaking 1979 book *Psychogenesis*, Moberly describes how homosexuality is "an unmet need for love from the parent of the same sex," rather than a rejection of the opposite sex: "The homosexual's love for men is but the boy's thwarted love for his father . . . [that] is in no way analogous to the love of the female for the male, since this latter kind of love does not aim at fulfilling an incomplete gender identity, but rather presupposes the completion of the identificatory process."

Since homosexual love is quite different from the love a wife gives to her husband, a wife cannot simply be replaced by a male partner without a monumental change in the entire psychology of the household. Nor can a husband and father be replaced by a female roommate. Only if one thinks that sexual differences are trivial would one assume that the sexuality of the partners makes no difference. Children in a homosexual household will not see, hear and experience what they would in a mom-and-dad family.

It also may be argued that the typical homosexual lifestyle is inconsistent with the proper raising of children. David McWhirter and Andrew Mattison, authors of *The Male Couple*, have documented that gay relationships characteristically are unstable. It follows that they are less likely to provide children with the security they need. The average male homosexual has 50 sex partners each year. One study found that 43 percent of white, male homosexuals estimated that they had sex with 500 or more partners and 28 percent had sex with 1,000 or more. Only 2 percent of homosexuals could be considered monogamous.

> *"In a homosexual household, children miss out on seeing important relationships between mothers and fathers, men and women, and husbands and wives."*

While there are some homosexuals who have stable, monogamous relationships and live what appear to be conventional lives, most do not.

Apart from the heightened possibility of the child in a homosexual household being exposed to his or her parents' outside partners, gay male sex practices are inherently unhealthy and lesbian culture is rife with anti-male sentiment—as evidenced by hostility toward men in lesbian publications and public references. Even if lesbian parents of a male child work hard to conceal their own bitterness toward men, their social milieu consists of people who largely are hostile to the very people that a boy needs to observe to develop a secure gender identity. Likewise, a gay male household is missing a proper appreciation of the feminine.

Children need and deserve the best environment possible in which to learn and grow. The traditional mom-and-dad family provides this, while homosexual relationships do not. Homosexual relationships, however well-meant, are not the equivalent of marriage and family. Children deserve better.

# Chapter 3

# Should Gays and Lesbians Be Allowed in the Military?

# The "Don't Ask, Don't Tell" Ban: An Overview

## by Craig Donegan

**About the author:** *Craig Donegan is a staff writer for* CQ Researcher.

Since the 1970s, the number of African-Americans and women in the armed forces has skyrocketed. There are more black officers than ever; women now hold scores of military jobs once reserved for men; and President Bill Clinton's "Don't Ask, Don't Tell" policy has given homosexuals official sanction to serve in the military. The changes have subjected the military to what have been called the most significant cultural shocks since President Harry Truman desegregated the military in 1948. The role changes have been accompanied by reports of extremist activity on military bases, a surge in sexual harassment cases and a fierce battle over the right of homosexuals to serve. Some observers are asking whether the military is dealing fairly with minorities, women and gays. . . .

## A Nightmare Policy

Sexual harassment . . . is a nightmare for homosexuals, says Michelle M. Benecke, co-director of the Servicemembers Legal Defense Network (SLDN). This is particularly true, she says, because of how the services enforce the Clinton administration's policy toward homosexuals in the military. Put into effect in 1994, "Don't Ask, Don't Tell" allows homosexuals to serve if they keep their sexual orientation private. But Benecke says the military routinely undermines the policy. According to SLDN, the three services investigated and discharged 21 percent more homosexuals in 1995 than in 1994, many of whom were women.

"The DOD's [Department of Defense's] own figures show that 21 percent of those discharged under the gay policy are women although they make up only 13 percent of the active forces," says SLDN Co-Director C. Dixon Osburn. "Lesbian baiting is used as a tool to harass women and to root them out of the service," Benecke adds.

"I would say that's intolerable if that's the case," says John Luddy, an aide to Sen. James M. Inhofe, R-Okla., who serves on the Armed Services Committee

From Craig Donegan, "New Military Culture," *CQ Researcher*, April 26, 1996. Reprinted by permission of Congressional Quarterly, Inc.

staff. "Still, we should not force an unnatural situation by putting 18- and 19-year-old women or openly gay soldiers together with heterosexual men in forward, austere environments."

Some observers say, however, that the military could better use the time and money it spends dogging homosexuals to ferret out extremists. "The military has overreacted to the one while not reacting strongly enough to the other," says Lawrence Korb, a senior fellow at the Brookings Institution and former assistant secretary of Defense in the Reagan administration. "We've spent $20 million investigating gays, even calling up mothers and fathers to ask about their children's sexuality. We should be more worried about the signs of fascism, of soldiers with swastikas in their barracks.". . .

## "Don't Ask, Don't Tell"

Launched in 1994, "Don't Ask, Don't Tell" was a compromise between President Clinton and military and political leaders who opposed his promise to lift the ban on homosexuals in the military. The policy promises not to ask soldiers about their sexual orientation, not to investigate them for homosexuality without credible cause and to let gays and lesbians serve unless they openly reveal their homosexuality.

Opponents of homosexuals serving in the military say they disrupt discipline, lower morale and unit cohesion and threaten combat readiness. Supporters say they have served honorably in the military over the years

> *"'Don't Ask, Don't Tell' allows homosexuals to serve if they keep their sexual orientation private."*

and that the opposition is rooted in bigotry. Moreover, they argue, the military should reflect the civilian population, which includes gays.

"'Don't Ask, Don't Tell' is the worst of all possible worlds," says Brookings' Korb. "It says we're making the ban on gay soldiers less stringent when we have not. Under the current policy, they're just as hard on homosexuals as they were under the old.". . .

As far as Cornell University's Mary Katzenstein, an associate professor of government and women's studies, is concerned, "It would be best for the military to drop the ban altogether." Adjusting to the change would require some effort, she says, because young men are typically very nervous about their sexuality. To deal with that, the military should establish and enforce strict rules governing sexual conduct, as it has tried to do with heterosexual relations."

"If the military can't tell its uniformed servicemen how to behave, then the military has a problem," Katzenstein adds.

The real problem, says Luddy, a former Marine rifle platoon leader, is that "Don't Ask, Don't Tell" undermines the military's credibility on the issue of sexuality. "To have a policy that says 'Don't Ask, Don't Tell,' is saying that homosexuality is incompatible with military service, but we're going to officially, passively, accept it," he says. "That contributes to the corruption of a certain morality—the integrity of the service."

"There are very sound reasons for not allowing homosexuality in the military," he adds, "and we ought to just say that." Most important among them, Luddy says, is that "distractions in combat—sexual or otherwise—get people killed."

SLDN's Osburn agrees that "Don't Ask, Don't Tell" sends mixed signals, and says he would like to see the ban abolished. It "has made things as bad or worse than prior policy," he says. "Many of our clients say they feel trapped. They feel they were lied to."

Nevertheless, says Osburn, axing the policy would be a mistake because the only alternative available today is a return to exclusion. "Congress will not change anytime soon," he says, "so this issue will have to wend its way through the federal courts and be settled on constitutional grounds.". . .

## An Issue of Sexuality or Human Rights?

In a study of the "Don't Ask, Don't Tell" policy released in February 1996, the SLDN reported that the military had discharged 722 service members for homosexuality in fiscal 1995—an increase of 21 percent over 1994. During that period, SLDN says the policy was violated at least 363 times.

Each service is different in how it enforces the policy, says SLDN's Osburn, but all of them have destroyed the soldiers' "zone of privacy" that the policy promised to protect.

Under the policy, declared homosexuals are excluded from military service based on the assumption that once they announce their sexual orientation, homosexual behavior may follow. And that behavior, critics say, destroys the morale and fighting ability of troops who must trust one another absolutely to be effective. If, for example, an officer plays favorites because of sexual attraction toward certain soldiers, then trust breaks down and endangers the unit, says Luddy.

"The clearest and strongest reason for the [policy]," Luddy writes, "is to remove the influence of sexuality—not heterosexuality, not homosexuality, just sexuality, period—from an environment where the stakes are literally life and death."

Some argue, however, that the issue is not sexuality but human rights. To them, there is no difference between African-American soldiers who began winning equal treatment nearly 50 years ago and homosexual soldiers today.

> *"Some argue . . . that the issue is not sexuality but human rights."*

Supporters of the policy, however, say that Gen. Colin Powell has laid that argument to rest. Powell, who initially opposed "Don't Ask, Don't Tell," argues that skin color and sexual orientation are completely different. "Skin color is a benign, non-behavioral characteristic," he writes. "Sexual orientation is perhaps the most profound of human behavioral characteristics. Comparison of the two is a convenient but invalid argument."

"Racial integration increased military efficiency," adds military sociologist Charles Moskos of Northwestern University. "The acceptance of declared homosexuals will likely have the opposite effect, at least for a time."

Still, SLDN's Benecke argues that banning or restricting homosexuals is unreasonable. There are 18 people serving openly as homosexuals in the military today, she says. And many have received superior performance evaluations. "If logic prevailed, we wouldn't have two classes of soldier," she says. "But logic and the facts have never been the basis for these policies."

# Homosexuality Is Incompatible with Military Service

## by James A. Donovan

**About the author:** *James A. Donovan is a retired colonel of the U.S. Marine Corps.*

Ranking military officials and other spokesmen defending the policy denying official recognition and acceptance of homosexuals in the armed services are not articulating their case adequately. Much more must be explained to a confused public and to ill-informed and inexperienced journalists and media commentators.

First, it should be reiterated that current laws, regulations, and the Uniform Code of Military Justice prescribe punishments, including court martial and/or dismissal from the service, for homosexual activities in the military services. These laws cannot be abrogated by simple executive order or policy but would have to be changed by Congress, preceded by lengthy and emotional hearings and debates.

Second, there is much more to the issue than the individual rights and desires of a homosexual minority. Much more important are the standards, values, and beliefs of the U.S. military.

The policy banning gays from U.S. military service has evolved since World War II. The flat ban on homosexuals that went into effect in 1982 prohibits homosexuals from joining the armed forces and prohibits those in uniform from performing sex acts with partners of the same sex. The punishment is dishonorable discharge except in cases of forced acts (rape) or certain other narrowly defined circumstances. Violated individuals can press charges resulting in court martial, discharge, and imprisonment.

The Uniform Code of Military Justice also forbids oral and anal sex among both homosexuals and heterosexuals. This law, however, has been to a large degree impractical to enforce.

James A. Donovan, "Preserving Esprit de Corps." This article appeared in the April 1993 issue and is reprinted with permission from the *World & I*, a publication of The Washington Times Corporation, ©1993.

Department of Defense policy requires known homosexuals to be immediately discharged. Homosexual acts do not need to be proved. The policy presumes that one who admits to being homosexual will engage in the conduct that defines the class.

## Special Interests Do Not Fit

Within the military, good order and discipline must prevail. Sexual orientation, gender, race, and religious differences are subordinate to the common good and to the effective performance of the military mission. Special interests and minority demands have no place in the armed services.

The military imposes many special standards for acceptance to serve, including weights, height, health, vision, strength, and education. A crippled illiterate cannot be accepted. Neither can an avowed homosexual.

The current debate has been missing one crucial point: The vast majority of men and women in the armed forces do not want to be in close association with homosexuals. The propaganda of homosexual lobbyists has convinced many naive journalists that the ban should be lifted, but most of these young media people have never served in uniform, have never been in a war, and simply do not know what they are talking about.

Polls say a narrow majority of American people support lifting the gay ban, but these polls have little meaning or value, because they do not ask the people directly concerned. A more meaningful poll of active duty personnel, reservists, retirees, and veterans would reveal that a vast and indignant majority do not want the ban on homosexuals lifted.

> *"Homosexuals openly recognized in the ranks will not foster pride, trust, or mutual respect typical of warriors."*

Gays do not fit the "self-image" of the military, where men (who are still a majority in the services) desire to be manly, tough, courageous, and rugged. Military leaders describe their troops as "warriors," trained and ready for any demanding mission. Gays wearing earrings and holding hands simply do not fit this image. Even the suggestion of perverted sex makes most healthy, straight men uncomfortable. Such problems would not foster the male bonding of "comrades in arms," unit pride, and esprit de corps so carefully developed in military organizations.

Each of the services recognizes the advantages gained in martial spirit from loyalty and pride engendered in such esprit, and this sets the armed forces apart from other large organizations. Professional military men and women belong to a cohesive team with its own standards of discipline and self-regulation, with traditions that are jealously guarded from weakness, distortion, or contamination from the civilian world.

The inculcation of ideals and loyalties is a vital aspect of military training.

Military ideology, codes, and creeds of conduct and belief are almost unique to the armed services in a society that has little discipline and few ideals beyond self-interest, self-expression, and personal comfort. Self-centered, hedonistic behavior is contrary to military ideals. The impact of military ideals, firm beliefs in the unit's purpose, and pride in belonging to a special group of courageous men and women prepared to risk their lives in service to the country bind young servicemen together. The public image of gays does not fit this pattern.

In recent conflicts, American professional service members have been motivated mainly by professional pride in their military skills, loyalty to their units, and trust and confidence in their comrades. Homosexuals openly recognized in the ranks will not foster pride, trust, or mutual respect typical of warriors.

## Little Privacy

Homosexuals have a recognized right to follow their lifestyles in private. But there is little privacy in most military barracks and combat units. As head of the Joint Chiefs of Staff Gen. Colin Powell said in congressional testimony: "It is difficult in a military setting where there is no privacy, where you don't get choice of association, where you don't get choice of where you live, to introduce a group of individuals who are proud, brave, loyal, good Americans, but who favor a homosexual life-style, and put them in with heterosexuals who would prefer not to have somebody of the same sex find them sexually attractive. . . . I think that is a very difficult problem to give the military."

Young battalion, squadron, ship, and company officers are already overwhelmed with demands for social indoctrination regarding servicewomen, sexual harassment, affirmative action, racial management, and drug control. They should be devoting their time to military training, readiness planning, and property management.

## A Can of Worms

The armed forces are institutions that were never intended to be a means for social change. The military has one purpose: to fight and win wars. Official approval of homosexuals in the ranks will lead to further demands by the gay/lesbian activists. They will want special clubs, special social activities, special permission for dress and conduct, and even acceptance of gay couples and their housing needs. This is a can of worms the armed forces do not need at a time of reorganiza-

> *"Official approval of homosexuals in the ranks will lead to further demands by the gay/lesbian activists."*

tion, reduced funds, downsizing, and new missions. As General Powell testified, "Am I then forced to face the problem of different accommodations for homosexuals and heterosexuals, and then by sex within the homosexual community?"

Sen. Sam Nunn (D-Georgia) supports General Powell's position and backs it with a list of searching questions that he proposes to explore in future hearings. For example, Nunn asked, "What restrictions, if any, should be placed on conduct between members of the same sex? Should such restrictions apply in circumstances in which such conduct would not be prohibited if engaged in between members of the opposite sex"—for example, "displays of affection that are otherwise permissible while in uniform, such as dancing at a formal event?"

Other questions Nunn put forward include:

"Should homosexual couples receive the same benefits as legally married couples," such as "housing, medical care, exchange and commissary privileges, and similar benefits?" Would military gay couples "benefit from policies that accommodate marriages, such as joint assignment programs? . . . Will there be a need for extensive sensitivity training for members of the armed forces? What accommodation, if any, should be made to a heterosexual who objects to rooming or sharing bathroom facilities with a homosexual?" Finally, "What will be the effect on the tens of thousands of past cases, particularly in terms of claims for back pay, reinstatement, promotions, and similar forms of relief?"

> *"Very few homosexuals desire to serve in the military. Their goal is to destroy a bastion of traditional manliness and heterosexual morality."*

Homosexuals are not bad people, but through various physical and/or personality aberrations, they seek abnormal sexual relations. Unlike other minority groups seeking rights or privileges, gays have no common ethnic, religious, political, or intellectual focus. Gay and lesbian associations are unique in that they are oriented toward sexual relationships and activities.

## Conservative Values

Most men and women who serve in our fine volunteer armed forces have conservative, middle-class, family values. They want to be loyal to their service, to their country, and their leaders. They are disciplined conformists who willingly follow sensible orders for meaningful missions. They want and accept a military society very different from civilian society because they understand that it allows them to function with good order, discipline, and pride. They do not want homosexuals with questionable values, morals, and habits forced upon them and their orderly military life.

The effort to remove the ban on homosexuals actually affects only a small special-interest minority. Very few homosexuals desire to serve in the military. Their goal is to destroy a bastion of traditional manliness and heterosexual morality.

A new president [Bill Clinton] who avoided service in our last big war [Vietnam], who has no idea what goes on in a barracks, a berthing compartment, or a foxhole, who attempts to solve a complex social matter with an executive order, will seriously detract from the loyalty and respect he should normally get from his troops.

The friendships experienced in military service are usually the most unreserved and lasting ever found. The relationships of comrades or buddies is peculiar to military life. Men in business or industry rarely have the bonds of trust and unselfishness that fighting men of the armed forces do. It is not a sexual or physical relationship, but one of shared confidence, shared hardship, and shared danger. It results in relationships wherein men have died for their comrades. Right or wrong, homosexuals do not appear to fit this profile.

## Not in the Nation's Interest

A homosexual minority should not be allowed to determine military policy contrary to the beliefs and wishes of millions of active, reserve, and retired military people. President Clinton's primary duty is to assure the most efficient and effective military establishment that the taxpayers can afford. Yet he has bowed to the pressures of people who know little or nothing about military duty, military codes and standards, or the basic principles of national defense. Forcing major value changes upon professional military service members to placate a minority of noisy homosexuals is not in the national interest. This is a distortion of the purpose of civil rights and ignores the mission of the armed forces.

# Allowing Gays and Lesbians in the Military Will Adversely Affect Morale

**by Mark E. Cantrell**

**About the author:** *Mark E. Cantrell is a major in the U.S. Marine Corps.*

Judging from newspaper accounts, Marine leadership training will soon need to incorporate the following scenarios into its curriculum:

## Scenario #1

*You are the officer in charge of a disbursing office at Camp Lejeune. One Monday morning, you are surprised to learn that Johnson, a promising young private first class, has failed to report for duty. Then, just before lunch, you receive a phone call from Johnson's enraged father. With considerable effort, you calm the father. He then explains that his son unexpectedly showed up at home over the weekend. Eventually, the father got the son to reveal the reason for his unauthorized absence. On Friday night, after drinking at the club, Johnson went to sleep in his bachelor enlisted quarters (BEQ) room. Hours later, he awoke to find LCpl Clarke, his roommate, performing oral sex on him. Due to a combination of shock, alcohol, and his own arousal, Johnson hesitated for a moment. Then, fully awake, he leaped out of the rack and started screaming at the lance corporal. Unable to calm his victim, LCpl Clarke left the room. Confused, angry, scared, and feeling guilty, Johnson packed his bag and left for the bus station.*

*That Friday, just before lunch, your admin chief enters your office and shuts the door. Obviously very concerned, he shows you an anonymous note left on his desk. Although you have made every effort to keep the investigation quiet, the Naval Investigative Service interviews and the commotion in the BEQ ap-*

*parently tipped off the Marines. The anonymous writer claims that several friends of Johnson are conspiring to kill LCpl Clarke at the beach over the weekend. An hour earlier you remember overhearing Clarke and several Marines planning a beach trip.*

What now lieutenant?

## Scenario #2

*You are a rifle platoon commander. Your platoon has established a patrol base while on a drug interdiction mission in South America. Late at night, your platoon sergeant notifies you that your two-man listening post is no longer answering the sound-powered phone. As is customary in the battalion, you will be the one to crawl out along the telephone wire, through the claymore mines, to investigate. The mines don't bother you. But the Marines are a little edgy after days of sniping and ambushes. You are concerned that one of them may shoot you if startled.*

*As you crawl quietly up to the listening post, you hear what sounds like a wounded man. You ready your pistol and crawl closer. Then, expecting to find a man dying of machete wounds you instead find your listening post engaged in illicit sex.*

What now lieutenant?

## Scenario #3

*You are ordered to take over a rifle platoon between skirmishes. The platoon has a bad reputation. During the last firefight, the platoon was overrun by little more than an enemy squad. As a result, the platoon sergeant was killed and the former platoon commander badly wounded. Anxious to determine their weaknesses, you immediately schedule some patrolling and immediate action drills. Although the Marines seem to be technically proficient, they repeatedly bicker during the drills. Two squad leaders even come to blows during a critique.*

*You meet with the squad leaders and acting platoon sergeant to discuss morale and discipline. But none of them offer any explanation for the friction in the platoon. Finally, your radio operator confides in you after the two of you are left alone. He explains that the dead platoon sergeant was romantically involved with the second squad leader. As the romance surfaced, the other squads began to complain that second squad no longer got its share of the dirty work, to include the dangerous assignments. During the firefight, a fragmentation grenade, possibly American, finished off the platoon sergeant, but not the internal conflicts. The second squad leader accused the third squad leader of throwing the grenade.*

> **"It would be no more reasonable to force heterosexuals to room with homosexuals than it would be to force women Marines to room with male Marines."**

101

*The first squad leader mistrusted both of the other squad leaders. Most of the junior Marines took sides with one of the three squad leaders but not necessarily their own. No one is willing to talk about the problems for fear of implicating himself, the platoon sergeant, or whoever threw the grenade.*

What now lieutenant?

## Concrete Arguments

Marine leaders may have to deal with situations such as these because of the influence of two groups of people—first, well-meaning people who are themselves tolerant of homosexuals but do not fully realize their potential impact on military effectiveness and, second, gay rights proponents who either won't believe that homosexuals will harm military effectiveness or who consider the impact to be an acceptable price to pay. Members of the latter group have made up their minds, and we cannot hope to sway them. However, the first group may still listen to reason and may still have enough influence to affect the outcome. It is in hope of reaching this group, through you, that I now write. . . .

Most military professionals instinctively support the ban on homosexuals in the military. But too few are prepared to offer concrete arguments

*"Homosexuals will present unsolvable problems that are certain to hurt morale, retention, and unit cohesiveness."*

in the policy debate we now face. Should you be lucky enough to be asked for an opinion, consider the issues that follow.

## Privacy

Military service necessarily takes a heavy toll on personal freedoms and privacy. At best, a junior unmarried or unaccompanied Marine can expect to live in a small single BEQ room with at least one other Marine. Three- or four-man rooms are still fairly common and squad bays are often used by deployed units or in training commands. Communal heads and showers are typical, regardless of room type. Privacy is even more restricted on shipboard or in the field; there is no such thing as personal space in a two-man fighting hole or tent.

Under these circumstances, homosexuals would thoroughly demoralize servicemembers who seldom get to choose their roommates. It would be no more reasonable to force heterosexuals to room with homosexuals than it would be to force women Marines to room with male Marines. It is irrelevant whether the homosexual is actually attracted to the heterosexual. The point is that the heterosexual would be completely uncomfortable undressing, showering, or sleeping under those conditions. Most Marines would also be terrified of the rumors and assumptions that would inevitably start among their peers. Gay rights activists will no doubt argue that the heterosexual's discomfort is his problem, the result of Neanderthal attitudes. But few parents would be ready to let the military train or regulate modesty out of their sons and daughters, even if it could be done.

Commanders will have no workable solutions for dealing with this privacy problem. The cost of private rooms would be staggering. Privacy on ships or in the field is simply unachievable at any price. Homosexuals cannot be given private rooms without infuriating heterosexuals. Billeting homosexuals together would complicate billeting assignments and draw protests from heterosexuals who are not allowed to room with their girlfriends or boyfriends. If we authorize quarters allowance for homosexuals to live off-base, we will, once again, draw protests from heterosexuals who are forced to live on base. In short, homosexuals will present unsolvable problems that are certain to hurt morale, retention, and unit cohesiveness.

## Marriages

Some states recognize marriages between homosexuals. How will we respond to requests for basic allowance for quarters from homosexual "newlyweds?" Will we be obligated to transfer them to the same duty station if both are servicemembers? Will they qualify for married family housing? If the military is forced to accept homosexuals, it may be difficult to convince the courts that they should be denied such benefits. Yet many taxpayers will be reluctant to pay the rent for homosexuals who choose to play house. Married servicemembers, many with children, will likewise balk at waiting in line behind homosexual "couples" for family housing.

## Conduct Unbecoming

We think nothing of seeing uniformed servicemembers kissing their spouses goodbye in an airport. What will it do to morale and public opinion of the military to have servicemen kissing their boyfriends goodbye on CNN? What will happen to esprit de corps when males in dress blues start dancing cheek to cheek at the Marine Corps Birthday Ball? Before answering these questions, consider the fact that society is by no means unanimous in tolerating homosexual behavior. More important, the majority of servicemembers are conservative and traditional in their views. We take pride in our uniform and most of us are infuriated at the sight of a Marine with his hands in his pockets. Openly homosexual behavior by uniformed servicemembers would be completely intolerable. Yet how can we prohibit public displays of affection among homosexuals while permitting them among heterosexuals? Gay

> *"What will it do to morale and public opinion of the military to have servicemen kissing their boyfriends goodbye on CNN?"*

rights activists apparently hope the military will lead society into acceptance of homosexuality. Instead, openly homosexual behavior will destroy morale and esprit de corps like no enemy ever could.

## Sexual Assault

The sexual assault described in this article's opening is actually based on direct knowledge of two very real incidents. The first involved a sergeant in charge of a platoon of students at one of the Schools of Infantry. At the end of one of the daily briefings he dismissed all but one of the student squad leaders. He then proceeded to lock the office door, unbutton the student's fly, and pin him against the wall and perform oral sex on him. The sergeant was convicted by a general court-martial of forced sodomy. But the student, until then a model Marine, was so emotionally disturbed by the experience that he deserted and eventually had to be discharged.

The second assault occurred exactly as described in Scenario 1. This victim too was emotionally devastated by the incident. The homosexual had to be removed from the unit, for his own safety, while awaiting a discharge in lieu of trial.

Gay rights supporters are quick to claim that homosexuals are no more likely to commit sexual assault than heterosexuals. But, in contrast to the two incidents just described, I have yet to serve with a heterosexual guilty of sexual assault. This is in spite of the fact that the average junior serviceman is about 19 years old and composed almost entirely of hormones. Then again, we don't make female Marines room with male Marines. Nor do we permit male Marines to put on a duty

> *"Openly homosexual behavior will destroy morale and esprit de corps like no enemy ever could."*

belt and stalk communal women's showers. How can we expect homosexuals to exercise greater restraint than we would expect of heterosexuals in the face of similar temptations?

## Counseling in Private

For most young servicemembers, their initial enlistment is also their first prolonged period away from home and family. Many become deeply troubled by personal and professional problems. It takes skilled counseling from trusted leaders to deal with such problems. Often, it takes one-on-one counseling from someone of the same sex, particularly when the problem is personal.

Now, consider the problem of counseling in a military that includes homosexuals. How many officers and noncommissioned officers are prepared to advise a serviceman who has just been dumped or abused by his homosexual lover? Once sexual allegations against same-sex counselors become credible, who will be willing to risk closed door, one-on-one counseling sessions? These questions are doubly important in view of the extra emotional baggage that homosexuals will bring with them to the Service. According to a 1984 American Psychological Association study (quoted in the *Boston Herald*), the average homosexual has in excess of 50 sex partners a year. Also, homosexuals, numbering between

2 and 10 percent of the population, account for 80 percent of America's most serious sexually transmitted diseases, and two-thirds of all AIDS cases are directly attributable to homosexual conduct. On top of all this, add the less than enthusiastic reception that homosexuals will receive from their peers. It doesn't take a psychologist to foresee a greatly increased need for professional counseling. Because the military will have difficulty providing that counseling, we can reasonably expect discipline problems and the suicide rate, already high among homosexuals, to increase.

## Crisis of Confidence

Consider how this debate opened. Shortly after his election, word leaks out that President Bill Clinton would, within days of inauguration in 1993, sign an executive order overturning a long-standing military policy. This decision was apparently made completely absent any advice from military professionals. Then, a number of highly respected policy experts—military, civilian, Republican, and Democratic—strongly advised against the move. The American Legion, Veterans of Foreign Wars, Retired Officers Association, and other veteran's groups joined in criticizing the plan. Shortly after taking office, the President agreed to consult with military leaders on how to implement the change, but made clear that the change itself was not negotiable. These events were disturbing to almost everyone who wears a uniform and believes that the advice of military professionals is essential to sound decisionmaking. In a world where regional conflicts are increasingly common, this action raises questions that are vitally important to everyone. Furthermore, it raises doubts about the competency and judgment of civilian leadership and how future military operations will be conducted.

## Morale and Esprit de Corps

It has become increasingly popular since the end of the draft to look upon military service as just another job. But the military demands far more from servicemembers than any civilian employer. We are asked to endure long separations from family, frequent moves to places we do not choose, and long hours without overtime. Many have missed the birth of a child; others have had children set back in school or upset at the loss of friends due to midyear moves. We have given up many of what most people consider God-given rights. Most important, we are required to entrust our lives to our

> *"We cannot expect a soldier to concentrate on a military mission when his lover, male or female, is in danger in the next fighting hole."*

appointed leaders. Servicemembers make these sacrifices and continue to serve for a variety of reasons. Pay, which we are told lags well behind pay for "comparable" civilian jobs, is certainly not the most important motivator. Morale and esprit de corps, on the other hand, are a large part of the volunteer military's success. But thousands of servicemembers, who had no part or representation in the decisionmaking, will now find their living and working conditions radically altered. They will be forced to choose between continued service under conditions they find intolerable, or resignation after faithfully investing years of their lives in a military career. Widespread resentment and anger are inevitable. In a corporation, such a leadership blunder could cause lost productivity and high employee turnover. In the military, the costs could be measured in lost lives and failed missions.

## Fighting Hole Romances

Intraoffice romances can be disruptive in any organization. Employees spend time courting when they should be working. Those who fail to win a maiden's affection become jealous of those who do. Employees who cannot take "no" for an answer pester other employees for dates. Junior employees grumble about romances, real and imagined, between their peers and supervisors. In short, tension and bickering can take the place of teamwork and productivity. While such

> *"No amount of sensitivity training will allow openly homosexual people to serve harmoniously in the military."*

problems might be tolerable in the normal office where people have the opportunity to live a normal life, they would take on disastrous proportions in combat or in deployed, isolated military units. For example, we cannot expect a soldier to concentrate on a military mission when his lover, male or female, is in danger in the next fighting hole. Nor can we expect soldiers to trust a platoon leader who may put his affection for one of the squad leaders ahead of his objectivity when deciding who will walk point. Most important, we cannot expect a platoon riddled with jealousy and mistrust to function as a team under fire. No amount of training and no body of regulations can prevent romantic entanglements if homosexuals are permitted in combat units. And the threat of court-martial cannot take the place of camaraderie and trust as a motivator once these romantic entanglements come between the Marines of those units.

Some have suggested assignment restrictions as an answer to the special demands of combat units. But no person concerned with morale would consider filling noncombat billets with male homosexuals while forcing only heterosexual males to face direct combat. Few males take issue with the exclusion of women from direct combat. But many would object to rewarding, with safe jobs, what they consider to be aberrant behavior.

## The Military's Role in the Debate

The American military is traditionally, and rightfully, reluctant to become involved in politics. It is customary to voice our concerns in private, and then do our best to execute our orders, whether we agree with them or not. But the press and gay right proponents have portrayed this as a case of a few stodgy old generals and admirals standing in the way of social progress. Those who acknowledge that there will be considerable resistance in the ranks are inclined to blame it on homophobia. Few have taken the time to interview more than a handful of junior officers and enlisted servicemen. In fact, the papers seem to contain more interviews with discharged homosexuals than with ordinary servicemen.

> *"Fighting hole romances can gut combat effectiveness."*

Under the circumstances, we cannot afford to be spectators in the debate. We have a right as citizens, and a responsibility as officers and noncommissioned officers, to reinforce the warnings of our senior military leaders. Specifically, anyone concerned with the outcome of this debate should make known their concerns to their elected representatives, their family, their friends, and to editors of hometown newspapers and favorite magazines. Additionally, while it would be inappropriate to coerce or lobby your subordinates, there is nothing wrong with encouraging them to participate in the democratic process by writing as well, whatever their views.

Those in favor of lifting the ban obviously expect that the most visceral of objections can be magically swept away with a simple executive order. Presumably, we in the military will keep our mouths shut, follow orders, and thereby prove to ourselves and society that homosexuals and heterosexuals can work side by side. But no amount of sensitivity training will allow openly homosexual people to serve harmoniously in the military. Moreover, the problems will not disappear until it becomes as socially acceptable for men to prefer men as it is for men to prefer brunettes or blondes. Even in such an enlightened age, we would find that fighting hole romances can gut combat effectiveness.

# Homosexuals in the Military Present a Medical Risk

**by Ronald D. Ray**

**About the author:** *Ronald D. Ray is a retired Marine colonel and the author of* Military Necessity and Homosexuality.

The military ban against homosexuals rests historically and legally upon government deference, particularly by Congress and the U.S. Supreme Court, to the judgment of military leaders on the basis of "military necessity." The military's singular mission is, as stated by the Secretary of Defense, on March 26, 1992, "*to fight and win our wars*," to defend America from enemies foreign and domestic. Anything or anyone who interferes with or inhibits the military's ability to accomplish that high calling with the fewest casualties threatens America's national security.

## Different Rules and Standards

The military is entirely separate and apart from the civilian society it defends and is necessarily governed by different rules and standards. Soldiers are recruited and selected from classified groups. These classifications, based upon military selection criteria, have been developed over time and proven on the battlefield.

First and foremost, the battlefield demands that young recruits between the ages of 18–26 be able-bodied. The military for the good of the services selects certain classifications of people and excludes classifications with characteristics shown to be unfit for military service such as convicted felons; non–high school graduates; drug users, physically disabled, etc. This is especially true when the military is reducing forces and ample numbers of able-bodied men are available for combat service. The extraordinary physical demands of combat on land, sea and air are unchanging and are still critically important in war. Military leaders

Ronald D. Ray, "A Question of Health," *American Legion Magazine*, June 1993. Reprinted by permission of the *American Legion Magazine*, ©1993.

declare that the battlefield has not become less demanding because of today's advanced technology, but rather more lethal.

In its effort to adhere to this standard and keep combat readiness at peak effi-ciency, service chiefs have consis-tently determined that there are no military reasons for allowing open homosexuals to serve in the Armed Forces. Among the many significant military reasons cited for maintaining the ban are sagging morale and cohe-

> *"Homosexual men are extraordinarily promiscuous, which only aggravates their medical risk to the military."*

sion, lack of privacy, fraternization, favoritism, sexual harassment and unneces-sary disorder. While these are important considerations, any decision to allow homosexuals to serve is fundamentally flawed for one primary reason: Homo-sexuals as a group are simply not able-bodied.

## Defining Homosexual Behavior

*"It is very difficult for me to make love, even safely, when the very act is now so inextricably bound up with death."*—Larry Kramer

*"In the first place, these people are involved in what I consider to be a filthy, disease-ridden practice. . . ."*—Admiral Thomas H. Moorer, USN (Ret.), for-mer Chairman of the Joint Chiefs of Staff

Without some understanding of what homosexuals actually do, a valid ap-praisal of the serious dangers homosexuals present to themselves, to others and to America is not possible.

Many homosexuals engage in sexual practices that are virtually unknown among heterosexuals. Almost all homosexuals engage in sexual practices in-volving degradation or humiliation that are rarely practiced by heterosexuals. Furthermore, study after study indicates that homosexual men are extraordinar-ily promiscuous, which only aggravates their medical risk to the military.

A 1981 study found that only 2 percent of homosexuals could be considered monogamous or semi-monogamous (having 10 or fewer lifetime partners). Larry Kramer, a homosexual and AIDS activist, put it this way: Those with AIDS may be described sexually as the "genuinely promiscuous and the nearly monogamous."

A 1983 study that required homosexuals to keep a diary of their sexual expe-riences found that the average male homosexual, in one year, 1) fellated 106 different men and swallowed seminal fluid 50 times, 2) experienced 72 penile penetrations of the anus, and 3) ingested the fecal matter of 23 different men.

Despite the onset of AIDS, many male homosexuals, particularly younger men of military age, are still very promiscuous and have merely cut back on the number of partners: in one study, from 70 different partners per year to 50; in another study, from 76 different partners per year to 47. This is in contrast to a study published in 1990 which reported that for the U.S. population as a whole, the estimated number of sex partners since age 18 is seven to nine.

## Homosexuals Practice Unsafe Sex

In addition, most homosexuals still engage in unsafe sex. A study of 823 homosexual and bisexual males in 1989 found that 64 percent had engaged in at least one unsafe sexual practice during the previous two months. Only 9 percent claimed to consistently practice safe sex. Almost one quarter reported having unprotected anal intercourse during the previous two months.

A compilation of recent health studies shows that homosexuals account for 80 percent of America's most serious sexually transmitted diseases, and that they account for less than 2 percent of the total American population.

Youths engaging in homosexual behavior are 23 times more likely to contract a sexually transmitted disease than strictly heterosexual youths. Lesbians are 19 times more likely than heterosexual women to have had syphilis, twice as likely to suffer from genital warts, and four times as likely to have scabies.

Male homosexuals are 14 times more likely to have had syphilis than male heterosexuals. They are also thousands of times more likely to contract AIDS. According to the Centers for Disease Control, at least two-thirds of all AIDS cases in the United States are directly attributable to homosexual conduct.

> *"Homosexuals account for 80 percent of America's most serious sexually transmitted diseases."*

Even more ominous than this blasé attitude towards promiscuity and sexually transmitted diseases, leaders of the homosexual/"gay rights" movement have consistently been willing to suppress data concerning the direct link between promiscuous homosexual behavior and AIDS in an effort to preserve public acceptance and empathy, or at least public neutrality and apathy.

The "cultural elites," including the media, have presented the matter entirely as a "civil rights" issue and have succeeded in concealing from the public their deadly activities while putting the nation at risk. An informed public would be outraged at the truth and would undo all the gains that homosexuals have made in the name of "gay rights."

## The Medical Facts of AIDS

Among the most obvious dangers homosexuals pose for the military is the threat of AIDS, which would undoubtedly increase for all military members if homosexuals were openly admitted to the services.

Once relieved of the necessity to restrain their sexual behavior in order to suppress or hide their homosexual tendencies, homosexual and bisexual service members themselves would be more likely to contract and spread the AIDS virus while in the service.

Heterosexual service members would also be more likely to contract the AIDS virus through peacetime training injuries or from the blood supply during wartime, when there may not be the opportunity to test blood before battlefield transfusions. Recent studies have shown these blood tests to be ineffective where infection has recently occurred and significant symptoms have not manifested themselves.

At present, AIDS in the military remains almost exclusively a homosexual phenomenon. As noted earlier, according to an Army survey, 80 percent of soldiers who tested positive for the HIV virus admitted to contracting the virus through homosexual contact.

We may assume that many of the remainder contracted the virus in the same way, though they would not want to admit it for personal reasons. Some claim that virtually all AIDS cases in the military are the result of homosexual behavior. All the same, AIDS is a product of promiscuous sexual behavior, behavior which the military has a demonstrated and compelling interest in proscribing.

With an increase in AIDS cases among homosexual members, the military can expect a dramatic increase in personnel costs related to medical care and personnel turnover. At present, HIV-positive service members are deemed "non-deployable."

Sodomy is still a crime under the Uniform Code of Military Justice, and scarce military resources should be better utilized. At present, each AIDS patient costs the military a total of about $250,000 in medical care alone. By the year 2003 at the present rate of infection, the military will have spent about $3 billion in AIDS treatment—enough money to buy three Aegis cruisers.

In the absence of the ban on homosexuals, there are solid reasons to fear—and anticipate—that the military's generous medical benefits would provide an incentive to increase the number of homosexuals entering the military.

Homosexual apologists, in fact, argue that the military is the best place to get AIDS on account of their efficient diagnostic procedures, treatment programs and facilities, and comprehensive medical coverage. Homosexuals would be expected to seek admittance into the military on this basis alone, thereby straining an already burdened healthcare delivery system.

> *"The threat of AIDS . . . would undoubtedly increase for all military members if homosexuals were openly admitted to the services."*

Homosexual behavior, however reckless or restrained, has shown itself to be a greater threat than even drug addiction. Homosexual behavior presents the greatest risk for passing or contracting the AIDS virus.

One report describes AIDS as follows:

"AIDS is a breakdown of the natural immune mechanism of the body. In patients with AIDS, the immune system breaks down and the body can no longer effectively fight infection. Organisms normally resisted by healthy persons invade the body and cause serious diseases (opportunistic infections).

"In the early stages the condition is characterized by weight loss, fever, thrush (especially of the throat), diarrhea and swollen lymph glands. Unusual forms of herpes, cytomegalovirus, TB and toxoplasmosis may develop. Invasion of the brain by organisms usually never found there can occur. A previously rare form of cancer (Kaposi's sarcoma) may develop; eventually most patients will contract Pneumocystis carnii pneumonia.

> *"By the year 2003 at the present rate of infection, the military will have spent about $3 billion in AIDS treatment— enough money to buy three Aegis cruisers."*

"For many of the infections afflicting AIDS victims there is no treatment. Where drug treatment can be used, it proves less effective and more toxic. The fatality rate appears to be 100 percent. No one has ever recovered."

Furthermore, *Time* magazine stated in 1985:

"They [homosexual men suffering from AIDS] had other infections as well: Candida albicans, a fungus that cakes the mouth and throat, making it difficult and painful to speak or eat; herpes, not the garden variety of sores, but ulcerating infections of the mouth, genitals or anus that raged for months. The patients fell prey to exotic bugs seen more often in animals than humans, like Toxoplasma gondii, and Cryptosporidium, which causes diarrhea."

## Other Medical Problems

AIDS aside, homosexuals present a substantial medical risk to themselves, to others and to the military, owing to their promiscuous and generally reckless lifestyle. An Army study of male soldiers found dramatically higher rates of morbidity among soldiers infected with the AIDS virus in the years prior to their diagnosis. These soldiers were:

- 41 times more apt to have contracted syphilis;
- 32 times more apt to have had enlarged lymph nodes;
- 10 times more likely to have had hepatitis B;
- 5 times more likely to have contracted other sexually transmitted diseases and hepatitis A;
- 4 times more likely to have had disorders of the anal/rectal region;
- twice as apt to have had acute pharyngitis and mononucleosis;
- 6 times more apt to have had urethral scarring and acute bronchitis;
- and 8 times more likely to have had herpes zoster.

Though morbidity rates for these soldiers declined as they became aware of the AIDS threat, they continued to suffer "lifestyle-related" infections and disorders nearly four times more often than male soldiers without the AIDS virus.

There is more, as reported by Patrick J. Buchanan and J. Gordon Muir in their article "Gay Times and Diseases" in the *American Spectator*, August 1984.

"The 'Gay Bowel Syndrome,' [is] a group of rare bowel diseases, previously considered 'tropical,' now epidemic in urban gay communities. . . .

"The main conditions normally considered under the GBS are amebiasis (a disease of the colon caused by parasites that results in dysentery and sometimes liver abscesses), giardiasis (a parasitic bowel disease causing diarrhea), shigellosis (a bacterial bowel disease that can cause severe dysentery), and hepatitis A (a viral liver disease [less serious than B or non-A, non-B] spread by fecal contamination: e.g., food, water, and close person-to-person contact). From a public health viewpoint there are several alarming features in these diseases: the rapidly expanding pool of infection in the homosexual community; the ease of spread to the wider public; the tendency for persons to be infected with two or more organisms at once; the difficulty of laboratory diagnosis; the difficulty of clinical diagnosis (they all have common symptoms); the likelihood of active homosexuals repeatedly reinfecting themselves; and the fact that nearly all the GBS groups of diseases have symptomless carrier states. . . .

"Hepatitis A is also common in homosexuals. Among gay men attending a venereal disease clinic in Seattle there was evidence of previous hepatitis A infection in 30 percent. The yearly attack rate was about 22 percent. . . .

> *"The military's generous medical benefits would provide an incentive to increase the number of homosexuals entering the military."*

"Finally, gonorrhea is also rampant in the homosexual community. In one large survey of U.S. gays, 40 percent reported known infection with gonorrhea.

"Common homosexual varieties of this disease (oral and rectal) are also more difficult to detect and treat. Antibiotic-resistant gonocci are now making an appearance; the pharmaceutical industry is only about one drug ahead of these strains, and there is no guarantee it will remain so.

"Syphilis, an old disease that was in decline, is also making a comeback. In the same gay survey, 13.5 percent reported a previous infection with syphilis. Among gays attending saunas in Amsterdam there was evidence of old or recent syphilis in 34 percent; only half the men were aware of their infection . . ."

In summary, and as one gay writer told the *Washington Post* (emphasis added): *"You can take away AIDS and you're still looking at a community that happens to be a diseased community.* I'm sorry. The bulk of your venereal diseases now reside within the gay community. The bulk of enteric (intestinal) diseases is now within the gay community."

## Homosexuals Are a Health Risk

In weighing the incompatibility of homosexuality with military service, the military must therefore consider:

1) the added cost of medical care incurred by homosexuals for infectious

venereal diseases and serious injuries;

2) the added burden on strained military and VA hospitals;

3) risk of injury, illness and infection of other military personnel caused by the incubation of rare diseases in homosexual carriers;

4) the personnel cost of aggravated attrition and "workarounds" caused by temporary medical disability; and

5) the loss of unit effectiveness caused by the absence of key personnel due to injury or medical disability.

The evidence shows plainly that homosexuals are a terrible and unnecessary medical risk especially for a military reducing its forces. If America's elected officials permit homosexuals to openly serve in the military with America's sons and daughters, knowing full well that homosexuals carry, in overwhelming numbers, a disease more deadly than war's killing fields, they will answer to America's families.

In view of the fact that homosexuals, as a classification of people, are not able-bodied, there is no military necessity to place American servicemen and women at risk by lifting the ban against homosexuals openly serving in the Armed Forces.

# Gays and Lesbians Should Be Allowed to Serve in the Military

## by Barry M. Goldwater

**About the author:** *Barry M. Goldwater is a former senator from Arizona and was the Republican nominee for president in 1964.*

After more than 50 years in the military and politics, I am still amazed to see how upset people can get over nothing. Lifting the ban on gays in the military isn't exactly nothing, but it's pretty damned close.

Everyone knows that gays have served honorably in the military since at least the time of Julius Caesar. They'll still be serving long after we're all dead and buried. That should not surprise anyone.

But most Americans should be shocked to know that while the country's economy is going down the tubes, the military has wasted a half-billion dollars over the past decade chasing down gays and running them out of the armed services.

### No Valid Reason

It's no great secret that military studies have proven again and again that there's no valid reason for keeping the ban on gays. Some thought gays were crazy, but then found that wasn't true. Then they decided gays were a security risk, but again the Department of Defense decided that wasn't so—in fact, one study by the Navy in 1956 that has never been made public found gays to be good security risks. Even Larry Korb, President Ronald Reagan's man in charge of implementing the Pentagon ban on gays, now admits it was a dumb idea. No wonder my friend Dick Cheney, secretary of Defense under President Bush, called it "a bit of an old chestnut."

When the facts lead to one conclusion, I say it's time to act, not to hide. The country and the military know that eventually the ban will be lifted. The only remaining questions are how much muck we will all be dragged through, and

Barry M. Goldwater, "The Gay Ban: Just Plain Un-American," *Washington Post National Weekly Edition*, June 21–27, 1993; ©1993 The Washington Post.

how many brave Americans like Tom Paniccia and Col. Margarethe Cammer-meyer will have their lives and careers destroyed in a senseless attempt to stall the inevitable.

Some in Congress think I'm wrong. They say we absolutely must continue to discriminate, or all hell will break loose. Who knows, they say, perhaps our soldiers may even take up arms against each other.

Well, that's just stupid.

Years ago I was a lieutenant in charge of an all-black unit. Military leaders at the time believed that blacks lacked leadership potential—period. That seems ridiculous now, as it should. Now, each and every man and woman who serves this nation takes orders from a black man—our own Gen. Colin Powell.

Nobody thought blacks or women could ever be integrated into the military. Many thought an all-volunteer force could never protect our national interest. Well, it has—and despite those who feared the worst, I among them, we are still the best and will continue to be.

The point is that decisions are always a lot easier to make in hindsight, but we seldom have that luxury. That's why the future of our country depends on leadership, and that's what we need now.

I served in the armed forces. I have flown more than 150 of the best fighter planes and bombers this country manufactured. I founded the Arizona National Guard. I chaired the Senate Armed Services Committee. And I think it's high time to pull the curtains on this charade of policy.

We have the strongest military in the world because our service people respect the chain of command and know how to follow orders. The military didn't want blacks in integrated units, or women, and now it doesn't want gays. Well, a soldier may not like every order, or every member of his or her unit, but a good soldier will always follow orders—and, in time, respect those who get the job done.

> *"Gays have served honorably in the military since at least the time of Julius Caesar."*

What would undermine our readiness would be a compromise policy like "Don't ask, don't tell." That compromise doesn't deal with the issue—it tries to hide it.

We have wasted enough precious time, money and talent trying to persecute and pretend. It's time to stop burying our heads in the sand and denying reality for the sake of politics. It's time to deal with this straight on and be done with it. It's time to get on with more important business.

## Discrimination Against Gays

The conservative movement, to which I subscribe, has as one of its basic tenets the belief that government should stay out of people's private lives. Government governs best when it governs least—and stays out of the impossible task of legislating morality. But legislating someone's version of morality is exactly what we do by perpetuating discrimination against gays.

We can take polls. We can visit submarines to get opinions on who are the best citizens. But that is not the role of a democratic government in a free society. Under our Constitution, everyone is guaranteed the right to do as he pleases as long as it does not harm someone else. You don't need to be "straight" to fight and die for your country. You just need to shoot straight.

> *"Military studies have proven again and again that there's no valid reason for keeping the ban on gays."*

With all the good this country has accomplished and stood for, I know that we can rise to the challenge, do the right thing and lift the ban on gays in the military. Countries with far less leadership and discipline have traveled this way, and successfully.

When you get down to it, no American able to serve should be allowed, much less given an excuse, not to serve his or her country. We need all our talent.

If I were in the Senate today [1993], I would rise on the Senate floor in support of our commander in chief [Bill Clinton]. He may be a Democrat, but he happens to be right on this question.

When the government sets policy, it has a responsibility to acknowledge facts, tell the truth and lead the country forward, not backward. Congress would best serve our national interest by finding the courage to rally the troops in support of ending this un-American discrimination.

# Homosexuals Can Enhance Military Effectiveness

## by Richard H. Kohn

**About the author:** *Richard H. Kohn chairs the Curriculum in Peace, War, and Defense at the University of North Carolina at Chapel Hill. He is the editor of* The United States Military Under the Constitution of the United States, 1789– 1989 *and a former president of the Society for Military History.*

Bill Clinton's promise to end the ban on homosexuals serving openly in the military, and the continuing furor over women in combat, threaten an ongoing civil-military battle that could damage military professionalism, alienate an otherwise friendly incoming Administration, and, ultimately, ruin the military effectiveness of the American armed forces for the foreseeable future. Military leaders who oppose these changes ought to consider some facts and principles that might change their minds.

## Reasons to Change

First, history. Women have fought successfully, sometimes integrated with men, as in the World War II Allied underground, where they proved just as adept at slitting throats, leading men in battle, suffering torture, and dying, as men; sometimes segregated, as in Soviet air force units, which produced many female aces fighting the Germans. Homosexuals have for centuries served honorably and effectively, in the United States and abroad. Arguments against open service assume that proper policies and effective leadership will fail, even though the services succeeded in integrating African-Americans and women, switching to a draft military in 1940 and then back to an all-volunteer force after 1973, and adjusting to other very divisive social changes over the last half century.

Second, there is fairness. In times of emergency, service is a fundamental obligation no citizen should escape unless disqualified physically or excused on reli-

Richard H. Kohn, "Women in Combat, Homosexuals in Uniform: The Challenge of Military Leadership," *Parameters*, Spring 1993. Reprinted by permission.

gious or moral grounds, or because their skills need to be used in some other capacity. But also, participation in combat—dying for one's country—has historically enabled minorities to claim the full privileges of equal participation in society, something basic to our form of government. That is why African-Americans for generations "fought for the right to fight" and why combat and military service are so important to women and homosexuals. Combat and service promote equal protection of the laws and undermine prejudice and discrimination.

Third, the very real practical problems can be overcome. Without question, change will be complicated and costly and take time, and military efficiency will suffer in the short term. Unless carefully explained to the American people, these changes could harm recruiting, precisely in those areas and among those groups which have been traditionally supportive of military service. To accommodate women on combat ships and in flying units (few advocate women in ground combat units), facilities and perhaps weapon systems will need modification. There will be ticklish, perhaps intractable, problems of privacy and personal discomfort (there already *are* in the military). The services will be distracted from their primary peacetime duties of readiness, preparation, and modernization.

Leadership at all levels will be challenged to maintain morale and effectiveness in circumstances where, historically, macho behavior and explicit sexual banter helped forge the personal bonds that enabled units to train and fight effectively.

> *"In the long run, the services should find that their effectiveness . . . will be enhanced rather than diminished."*

Cohesion, the key to military success, will be more difficult without traditional methods of male bonding. The strict authority, harsh discipline, and instant obedience required for victory in battle have always been subject to abuse, and adding more women and ending discrimination against gay men and lesbians will increase the problem. To deal with it, military leaders will have to redouble their efforts to define appropriate conduct and to punish or expel those in the ranks who cannot or will not control their language and their behavior. The problem, as Tailhook so clearly reveals, already exists; the fundamental issue in the short run will not be attitude, but behavior, and the military can be extremely effective in controlling behavior. The services will have to review policies on acceptable conduct, on and off duty. Research on maintaining cohesion without scapegoating homosexuals and treating women as sex objects will have to be undertaken. The challenge to our military leadership, at all levels, will be enormous, and it will last as long as sexism and homophobia afflict significant portions of our population.

## The Military Can Adjust

And yet, our military can adjust—once again. It is natural to resist because change poses a diversion from the primary purposes of preparing for and deterring war, and engaging in combat. That is why as outstanding a public servant as General George C. Marshall during World War II opposed racial integration, believing it divisive and concerned that the Army could not afford to act as a "social laboratory" during a national emergency. But civilian control means that our military will be organized and will operate according to the nation's needs and desires. Historically our national security and our social, legal, and constitutional practices have had to be balanced. The services know that military efficiency and combat effectiveness do not always determine our military policies, and less so in times of peace and lessened threat.

> *"The armed forces will be stronger the more they reflect the values and ideals of the society they serve."*

If President Clinton follows through on the promise to let gay men and lesbians serve openly, and if, for reasons of fairness and justice, he permits women to fight in combat units at sea and in the air, then the American military must comply, and without resistance. To resist would only make the adjustment more time-consuming and disruptive, and would itself undermine military effectiveness.

In the long run, the services should find that their effectiveness, as in the experience of racial and gender integration, will be enhanced rather than diminished. The strength of our military depends ultimately upon its bonds to the people; the armed forces will be stronger the more they reflect the values and ideals of the society they serve.

# Homosexuals in the Military Are Not a Threat to National Security

**by Franklin D. Jones and Ronald J. Koshes**

**About the authors:** *Franklin D. Jones and Ronald J. Koshes are psychiatrists in the Washington, D.C., area.*

During World War II some 5,500 persons were admitted to hospitals with a diagnosis of "pathologic sexuality," primarily homosexuality. It has been estimated that the number of homosexual service members serving in World War II may have been 5–10 times this number. Such discovered homosexual service members were court martialed (for offenses) or given "blue" discharges (without honor). A War Department directive issued in January 1944 allowed the issuing of blue discharges in lieu of courts martial to offenders not deemed "reclaimable" and encouraged psychiatric rehabilitation of other service members. Among this latter category of service members were individuals acting out of intoxication or curiosity or acting "under undue influence," such as one who was seduced by a person of superior rank. The number who were "reclaimed" is unknown, but it is probably less than 1,000, or fewer than one-fifth of those hospitalized. No figures on homosexuality among the Women's Army Corps are available; however, the rate was lower than for men in spite of initial fears that a Women's Army Corps would attract overtly homosexual women.

During World War II attempts by the Army Surgeon General's Office to separate honorably homosexual service members who had not engaged in sexual misconduct in the Army were thwarted by other War Department agencies, who feared this would create an "evacuation syndrome," i.e., attempts by soldiers to evade duty by false claims of a medical or mental disorder. Finally, by late October 1945 the Army Surgeon General's Office secured acceptance by the Adjutant General's Office of a policy of administratively separating nonoffending homosexuals under honorable conditions similar to those for other persons un-

Excerpted from Franklin D. Jones and Ronald J. Koshes, "Homosexuality and the Military," *American Journal of Psychiatry*, January 1995; ©1995 American Psychiatric Association. Reprinted by permission.

able to adapt because of personality aberrations or immaturities. Officers were allowed to resign for the good of the service.

## Homosexuality as a Mental Illness

Considering homosexuality a mental illness has long been used as a defense of the exclusionary and separation policy. This reason was specifically used in the opinion in *Crawford v. Davis*, in 1966. A homosexual soldier sought a preliminary injunction to restrain his impending dismissal. In denying the motion, Judge Higginbotham stated, "I think it would be clearly inappropriate to hobble the Army by forcing it to retain even one soldier for an indefinite period of time when there are serious questions concerning his emotional health."

This attitude may have been a carryover from the hereditary degeneration theory of mental illness. Authors such as E. Kraepelin and R. Krafft-Ebing viewed mental illness as a progressive spectrum of behaviors ranging from masturbation through sexual deviance to severe mental illness. After this "degeneration" theory was successfully debunked, Freudian psychoanalytic theory replaced it but retained the idea that homosexuality, as well as neurotic and other mental illnesses, represented a fixation at an immature level of psychosexual development. While Sigmund Freud clearly did not consider this an illness or a serious disorder, many who followed him did. This view seems to have been reinforced by the fact that those with homosexual orientations who seek psychiatric help, like others seeking such help, tend to have more psychopathology than those not seeking help.

> *"Position statements by . . . the American Medical Association have reversed the claim that homosexual individuals are mentally ill."*

The finding of homosexuality in a patient presents particular difficulties for the military psychiatrist since current regulations not only do not permit privileged medical communication but actually enjoin the physician to report such cases. Ordinarily, the psychiatrist is called on to render a medical evaluation after homosexual acts have been established. This is important for two reasons: 1) the psychiatrist may find such acts to have been a manifestation of mental illness, for instance, schizophrenia, in which case psychiatric treatment and medical disposition are indicated; and 2) the psychiatrist can render an opinion as to whether a person who has committed a homosexual act should be retained in the service, without reference to the homosexual act. The regulation indicates only that a mental status evaluation must be obtained when a service member is to be processed for separation. Recent Army practice has been not to retain such persons, although during times of war homosexual service members have been retained on active duty status and later separated during peacetime. The Navy has retained some identified homosexual sailors on active duty during peacetime. . . .

Since the formation of George Washington's army, countless homosexual individuals have been excluded from military service. An Army regulation (July 15, 1966) titled "Personnel Separations—Homosexuality" described military policy regarding homosexual soldiers:

> Personnel who voluntarily engage in homosexual acts, irrespective of sex, will not be permitted to serve in the Army in any capacity, and their prompt separation is mandatory. Homosexuality is a manifestation of a severe personality defect which appreciably limits the ability of such individuals to function effectively in a military environment. Members who engage in homosexual acts, even though they are not homosexuals within the meaning of this regulation, are considered unfit for military service because their presence impairs the morale and discipline of the Army.

Thus, this policy statement implies two of the three main arguments of military personnel officers for excluding and separating homosexual individuals from military duty:

1. Homosexuality denotes a severe underlying mental disorder, making such a person inherently unstable.

2. Homosexual service members would cause poor morale among other service members.

3. Homosexual service members would be poor security risks because of blackmail or easy seduction in a military environment that increasingly requires security classification.

## Mental Disorder

The first argument is of questionable validity, and in fact, a study of homosexual individuals who effectively concealed their homosexuality indicated acceptable functioning. A survey of 183 former college students who were known from detailed pre–World War II studies to be homosexual in orientation revealed that 51 were rejected at induction, but only 29 for neuropsychiatric reasons. Only 14 were prematurely discharged from the service, for various reasons. Thus, 118 of these 183 men served with credible records for 1 to 5 years, and 58% served as officers.

*"Since most of the arguments about homosexual seduction and blackmail could be made about heterosexual seduction and blackmail, this argument has lost much of its force."*

It was probably not because of such studies that the military dropped alleged mental illness as a justification for excluding and separating homosexual individuals. Rather, the change was probably due to a series of civilian court challenges and APA's [American Psychiatric Association's] elimination of homosexuality from DSM-II [Diagnostic and Statistical Manual of Mental Disorders, second edition]. The text originally listed homosexuality as a mental disorder, as it had in the previous edition. A series of proposals, discussions, and votes by the many relevant components of APA and then a vote by APA's Board of Trustees in 1973 resulted in the replacement of "homosexuality" by "sexual orientation disorder" in DSM-II. The new term applied not to homosexuality per se but to conflict over sexual orientation, homosexual or heterosexual. A subsequent referendum in APA to try to overturn this change failed. The American Psychological Association promptly concurred that homosexuality per se is not a mental disorder, and APA subsequently dropped even "sexual orientation disorder" from DSM-III. Position statements by APA and the American Medical Association have reversed the claim that homosexual individuals are mentally ill and affirm the civil rights of these people. A 1991 position statement of APA opposed the exclusion and dismissal from the armed services of individuals with homosexual orientation.

> *"Arguments for exclusion and separation on the basis of sexual orientation alone have no validity."*

## Poor Morale

The second of the arguments may currently be the most compelling, since many recruits, who may be insecure in their own sexual orientation, may react with various forms of discomfort to the presence of an identified homosexual person. That such discomfort has in the past reportedly contributed to violence may be associated with both individual and group psychological factors, both probably modifiable by different official military rules and expectations. Many psychiatrists who have been stationed at basic training facilities can cite such cases.

We believe that the major current argument for exclusion and separation would be a threat to military order and morale, especially in the case of an identified homosexual service member in basic training or a small unit. Whether this phenomenon results from homophobia or "homo-ignorance" (lack of knowledge and experience regarding individuals who are homosexual) is not clear. The important topic of homophobia in the military has been well described by other authors and deserves further psychiatric study.

Nevertheless, a number of morale issues are raised by the presence of a subculture in the military, whether it is based on religious, ethnic, racial, drug use, or other grounds.

1. What effects do homosexual or antihomosexual cliques have on discipline? Subcultures in a military organization can disrupt functioning of the unit by encouraging favoritism, through *sub rosa* communication channels, which are threats to leadership and command. Since the military copes with many subcultures, it remains for the military to make a convincing case that this subculture is substantially and essentially so much more damaging than, for instance, racial and religious subcultures that it justifies the costs of current policy.

2. In the many military settings in which soldiers do not have ready access to

heterosexual partners, what are the effects of the presence of a known homosexual person? What role do fears and labels of homosexuals play in military training? An example is a drill instructor's calling Marine recruits "faggots." How much of the military concern about homosexuality is actually related to the aggressive characteristics of the pseudo-homosexual dominance-submission theme?

Generally, we believe these answers to be socially and culturally based and outdated. As acceptance of homosexuality in American society at large increases, we expect that acceptance of homosexuals in the military will increase, negating the need for a walled-off subculture and resulting in more respect for the homosexual soldier. Regulations concerning fraternization and sexual harassment can be legitimately enforced, upholding a general standard of conduct. These regulations ban such practices irrespective of sex or sexual orientation.

## Security Risk

The argument that homosexual service members are security risks, since they would be subject to blackmail or seduction, does not take into account the fact that heterosexual blackmail is also possible and heterosexual seduction has been a favored spy method since before Mata Hari. This reason has not fared well in the courts. In commenting on the case of Dennis Beller, a 15-year Navy veteran, Judge Harris stated, "The Navy does itself and the public little good by removing an experienced and able serviceman such as Beller from its ranks. . . . It would seem more reasonable to believe that if, as the Navy posits, the great majority of its members are heterosexual, then there is a graver danger of blackmail from illicit heterosexual than homosexual liaisons."

In a number of cases involving homosexual civilian workers for the military who required security clearances, the use of homosexuality as a criterion for automatic denial of such clearances was found to be illegal. The argument that evolved has been called the "nexus" issue, the need to show a nexus, or connection, between the presence of homosexuality in an individual and the way in which this would interfere with his or her performance of duty. . . .

The courts now take the position that the government must show how homosexuality makes the person a security risk. Since most of the arguments about homosexual seduction and blackmail could be made about heterosexual seduction and blackmail, this argument has lost much of its force, particularly if the person acknowledges his or her homosexuality. . . .

In summary, the strongest argument for excluding and separating homosexual persons from military service is not mental illness or security risks but the presence of social strictures and adverse attitudes. How malleable these attitudes will be remains to be seen. We believe that arguments for exclusion and separation on the basis of sexual orientation alone have no validity and that homosexual acts and antihomosexual harassment can be dealt with appropriately by personnel regulations informed by courteous respect for all military persons.

# The Military Ban on Gays and Lesbians Is Based on Prejudice

by Alasdair Palmer

**About the author:** *Alasdair Palmer is a writer for the* Spectator, *a weekly British magazine.*

In June 1995, British Lord Justice Simon Brown ruled against three men and one woman who had been dismissed from the Armed Forces for being homosexual. They were appealing against their dismissal on the grounds that the policy which led to it is 'unreasonable'. The judge accepted the arguments of the Ministry of Defence (MoD) that it is not. Roger Freeman, the Minister for Defence Procurement, put the Ministry's case in Parliament in May 1995. 'The Ministry of Defence has long taken the view that homosexuality is not compatible with securing the aims of the Armed Forces because it undermines the good order and discipline necessary for military effectiveness. This is not a moral judgment but a practical assessment, by those best placed to make it, of the implications of homosexual orientation on military life.'

## Cool Reason or Hot Prejudice

The Ministry of Defence is adamant that the policy of dismissing homosexuals is the result of cool reason rather than hot prejudice. The considered pronouncements of those best placed to make the decision—the senior officers in the Armed Forces—do not, however, always support that claim as clearly as one might hope. Consider, for example, Air Chief Marshal Michael Armitage, former Chief of Defence Intelligence, responding to a request from the BBC programme *Taking Liberties* to explain his views on homosexuality: 'Dear Sir,' he wrote. 'Many thanks for your letter about fairies in the Armed Forces.' In an interview, he went on to say that 'the genital activities of these people make . . . almost all normal people very queasy indeed. . . . Almost all normal people

Alasdair Palmer, "Prejudices on Parade," *Spectator*, June 10, 1995. Reprinted by permission of the *Spectator*.

would be repelled.' Or consider this statement from a senior officer about a man under his command whom he considered might be homosexual. His evidence was that the man 'showed an unmanly interest in soft furnishings . . . and a lack of interest during a female striptease'. Or the remarks of Admiral Sandy Woodward, the hero of the Falklands, who in 1994 opposed a plan to make it illegal to imprison homosexual servicemen on the grounds that 'it is precisely because Britain remains one of the few countries where homosexuality is an offence in the

> *"Most officers . . . do not have direct experience of unit cohesion and discipline being disrupted by homosexuals."*

Armed Forces that our forces still command such respect around the world'. Or the letter written by Surgeon Commander Richard Jolly OBE, Principal Medical Officer at Britannia Naval College, in reply to a heterosexual officer who had complained of his description of homosexuality as 'biologically unsound'. Commander Jolly replied, 'If such a simple (but entirely accurate) labelling caused you to be "deeply offended", then stand by to become *really* upset. Here are some of the common terms I could have used: arse grabber, shirt lifter, bowel troweller, botty bandit, turd burglar. . . . You'll never be able to convince me of the merits of a way of life in which the main sewer gets regular usage as a playground.'

Britain's senior servicemen evidently feel extremely strongly about maintaining the ban on homosexuals. Where does that feeling come from? Generals, admirals and air-marshals stress that it is born of experience: homosexuals are disruptive of unit cohesion and discipline. Homosexuals are liable to fall in love with men in their unit, thereby undermining the trust in the absolute impartiality and fairness of command, a development which is fatal to the smooth functioning of any military organisation involved in combat.

That claim has been made many times. The evidence for it is difficult to pinpoint. Most officers, even those who reach senior rank, do not have direct experience of unit cohesion and discipline being disrupted by homosexuals. In fact, as far as I can discover, no one in living memory has had direct experience of it, for the simple reason that the policy of discharging homosexuals has been rigidly and effectively enforced: whenever their presence has been identified, they have been discharged. The Armed Forces have two organisations—the Special Investigations Bureau (SIB) for the Army and Navy, the Provost & Security Service for the RAF [Royal Air Force]—whose job it is to identify homosexuals and ensure they are dismissed. They do their job very thoroughly. They have set up cameras outside a gay club in Portsmouth, and will secretly follow servicemen when they consider it necessary. They can tap into a network of informants: doctors and priests are not bound by the usual requirements of confidentiality, and are required to report anyone who admits, in the intimacy of the confessional or consulting-room, to being homosexual.

Between 1991 and 1995, the activities of SIB have ensured that over 250 people have been dismissed from the services for being homosexual or admitting to homosexual leanings. Ian Waterhouse, who used to be a corporal in the RAF, was dismissed in 1994 after he was reported to have been seen on a Gay Pride march in London. His room was searched, his diaries, letters and address book confiscated, along with videos of *Another Country* and *The Torch Song Trilogy*. He was questioned in detail about the names that appeared in his private correspondence and papers: whom he had had sex with, when and how it had been done. He was also pressured to reveal any other RAF men who might be homosexual. Graeme Grady, also of the RAF, was dismissed in May 1994 after he was reported to have been seen at a self-help group for married homosexuals.

## No Evidence

Neither Waterhouse nor Grady had had any sexual relations with anyone in the forces. They had never disrupted anything. On the contrary, they both had exemplary records. To quote the report on the investigation into Waterhouse: 'There is no evidence to suggest that Corporal Waterhouse is, or has been, involved in homosexual relationships with any member of HM [Her Majesty's] Forces, or that criminal offences have been committed in the course of those relationships. Waterhouse has confessed that he is a homosexual, although there is no evidence to suggest misconduct, corruption, blatant or promiscuous activities or unnatural behaviour on Service establishments.'

> *"Any argument for allowing women [in the military] is also an argument for allowing homosexuals."*

The effectiveness of the way homosexuality is policed ensures the absence of concrete examples of homosexuals causing the kind of disruption that the generals fear. The MoD is convinced that nevertheless there is 'overwhelming evidence' that homosexuals are disruptive. Where does that evidence come from? The answer is that the best evidence that homosexuals are potentially disruptive of unit discipline does not come from homosexuals at all. It comes from heterosexuals. The Armed Forces' decision to employ women in frontline positions has involved—as lifting the ban on homosexuals would—placing people who may find each other sexually attractive in very close proximity. That policy has certainly, on occasion, been disruptive of discipline. In one famous case in 1992, Chief Petty Officer Ian Luff and Petty Officer Sylvia Panter, who both had spouses waiting for them back in England, stole over £11,000 from HMS *Invincible*, the aircraft-carrier on which they were serving. When the *Invincible* docked at Corfu, Greece, they proceeded to jump ship together, disappearing for two weeks—and spending most of the money—before finally giving themselves up in Barcelona, Spain.

There have been numerous similar cases where the bond of love has proved stronger than the chain of command. All of them, so far, have been heterosexual. Surprisingly, the Ministry of Defence has no plans whatever to abandon the use of women in the Army, Navy and Air Force. On the contrary, the plan is to recruit more women and to give them more responsibility. The official view is that the policy of introducing women has not been 'disruptive of discipline'. Ministry of Defence spokesmen insist that it has been a great success.

The MoD's admirably dogged defence of the policy of introducing women into the Armed Forces—in the face of undeniable evidence of its disruptive effects—makes it difficult to maintain, as the Ministry and its military advisers do, that the ban on homosexuals 'is not a moral judgment but a practical assessment'. If the concern is simply to avoid whatever might disrupt smooth and efficient discipline, what are women doing on board ships and in army units? The MoD cannot have it both ways: either the presence of individuals in a unit which other members may find sexually attractive poses an unacceptable risk to military discipline, or it does not. If it does pose an unacceptable risk, women pose exactly the same threat as homosexuals. If it does not, then any argument for allowing women is also an argument for allowing homosexuals.

The suspicion that the roots of the ban on homosexuals lie more in prejudice than practical experience is reinforced by the way the Armed Forces treat those they suspect are homosexual. John Beckett, one of the plaintiffs in the case Judge Brown decided, became aware that he was homosexual after having joined the Royal Navy at the age of 19. He told the Navy padre, who advised him to report it to his commanding officer. Beckett did so. He was referred to Commander Churcher-Brown, a naval psychiatrist. Beckett claims that Commander Churcher-Brown offered to 'treat' Beckett's homosexual leanings by electric shock therapy. (Commander Churcher-Brown says he may have discussed electric shock therapy with Beckett; he does not recall offering it as treatment.)

All those who have been interrogated on the suspicion that they may be homosexual have experienced extremely hostile questioning, even when they have begun the interview with a frank admission that they are homosexual. Duncan Lustig-Prean, a former naval lieutenant-commander with an outstanding record, went to his commanding officer in May 1994 and confessed to being homosexual after a man attempted to blackmail him. Nevertheless, when interviewed by the SIB, he was asked to supply precise details of exactly what sexual acts he had performed. The point of the degrading and prurient questioning is obscure. The MoD alleges that the services need 'proof' that a man (or woman) is homosexual, as opposed to

> *"The roots of the ban on homosexuals lie more in prejudice than practical experience."*

merely pretending to be in order to ensure immediate discharge. Grant the intriguing idea that servicemen will try to fake homosexuality in order to be instantly sacked, can anyone seriously maintain that the way to distinguish the false from the true homosexual is to demand anatomical details of his sexual practices?

Our generals tend to be contemptuous of other armies which have relaxed the ban on homosexuals serving, which includes all other NATO countries except Turkey and Luxembourg. But there is no evidence that the morale, efficiency and discipline of those nations' armies have collapsed as a consequence. Israel—to take another example—has one of the toughest and most successful armies in the world, with a record worthy of respect. . . . The Israeli army has lifted the ban. It has replaced it with a rigid code of conduct, which includes a ban on sexual activity of any kind between ranks and on military bases. Allowing homosexuals has had no noticeable effect. British soldiers are even serving in Bosnia as part of the UN peace-keeping force alongside soldiers from the French, Dutch and Irish armies—all of which allow homosexuals to serve.

> *"Homosexuality has . . . a distinguished history in warfare."*

Britain's firmness in ejecting homosexuals has led to the strange situation in which servicemen from other countries who take up posts here can find themselves instantly dismissed. Sergeant Mark Livingston of the Australian Air Force came over to Britain for a fixed posting with the RAF. He was sacked here when he admitted to being homosexual, but was immediately reinstated on his arrival in Australia, where the ban has been lifted. The Australian General Peter Gration, who had opposed allowing homosexuals, admitted after the policy had been changed that it had had 'no effect on morale or efficiency'.

A prejudice, if widely enough held, may have to be accommodated, on the grounds that failing to do so would be disruptive: the men would take their own revenge on the 'outsiders' they would not accept as part of the group. That was the main reason for excluding blacks and Jews from certain regiments in the past. It would be a brave minister who stood up in the House of Commons to defend the exclusion of homosexuals from the Armed Forces on that basis, although it may actually be the reason why there is so much resistance to lifting the ban.

## A Waste of Tax Money

The four ex-servicemen who lost their bid for reinstatement are not going to give up. They plan to appeal as far as the House of Lords, and, if that fails, they will move to the European Court of Human Rights—where they will almost certainly win. Lord Justice Simon Brown stressed that point in his judgment. The leaders of Britain's Armed Forces will then be forced to pay large sums in compensation, and to reinstate, against their better judgment, men and women they have dismissed for being homosexual. In financial terms, the costs will be enormous. But the ban is already costing the forces several million pounds a year. Robert Nunn, for instance, was an instructor for pilots of nuclear submarines. When he was dismissed for homosexuality, the Navy was waving goodbye to several million pounds' worth of investment and training. There are six pilots waiting to appeal against their dismissal. Together, their departure represents about £25 million. It is a lot of taxpayers' money to waste.

Politicians are reluctant to overrule their generals, despite the fact that the generals are nominally their juniors. Tories are naturally deferential to the virility of military men. Tony Blair's New Model Labour seems to have adopted the same inferiority complex. When Labour's defence spokesman said his party would lift the ban, Tony Blair [the Labour Party chair] moved swiftly to explain that Labour only proposed a commission to look at the issue, not an immediate overthrow of the present policy.

It will be unfortunate if the services are forced, as the result of decisions given in the courts, to change their policy. That will be bad for discipline, morale and efficiency—as bad as it has been in the case of the women officers to whom the service chiefs have been forced to pay enormous sums in compensation. But the generals ought to change the policy of their own accord. There are already many homosexual servicemen. The rate in the Armed Forces is probably more or less the same as it is in the general population, which means there are plenty more in the services than are being expelled from them, despite the sterling efforts of the SIB.

All the evidence is that the consequences of not dismissing homosexuals will be no more—and probably considerably less—disruptive than allowing women. Homosexuality has, after all, a distinguished history in warfare. From Achilles onwards, many of the greatest fighters and commanders have been experienced homosexuals: Alexander the Great, Julius Caesar, Richard the Lionheart and, in more recent times, Lord Kitchener [who helped win the Boer War in South Africa], Lawrence of Arabia and Lord Mountbatten [who supervised the end of British rule in India]. Air-Marshal Armitage stressed that his main objection to homosexuals was that he 'wouldn't care to sleep between two of them in the barrack room'. The truth is that he probably has already done so, many times. The experience obviously didn't do him any harm.

The Army, Navy and Air Force have survived homosexual servicemen unscathed. Recognising that fact voluntarily, rather than being forced to do it, is the best way that the MoD can maintain the British Armed Forces' reputation for efficiency.

# Chapter 4

# Do Gays and Lesbians Need Antidiscrimination Laws?

CURRENT CONTROVERSIES

# Antidiscrimination Laws for Gays and Lesbians: An Overview

by Richard L. Worsnop

**About the author:** *Richard L. Worsnop is an associate editor for the* CQ Researcher, *a weekly report on public policy issues.*

Homosexuals, once hesitant about declaring their sexual orientation and fighting discrimination, are now demanding equal treatment. . . . They seek passage of a federal civil rights law giving them the same sort of protection enjoyed by racial and ethnic minorities. Homosexuality deserves such protection, they say, because it is biologically determined and immutable. Conservatives, on the other hand, insist that homosexuality is a freely chosen behavior that can be modified. Thus, they say, gays and lesbians are demanding "special rights." The special-rights argument helped win approval of an anti-gay-rights law in Colorado in 1992. . . .

## Is Homosexuality Innate or Acquired?

Much of the conflict between homosexual activists and their foes springs from disagreement over the nature of homosexuality. Most gays and lesbians contend their sexual leaning is either an inborn trait or an immutable and healthy psychological condition developed in the early years of life. In contrast, conservative opponents of gay rights insist homosexuality is a consciously acquired mode of behavior that can be changed or discarded at will. It is basically the old "nature vs. nurture" debate in a politically charged context.

Homosexuals themselves once lent support to the conservative thesis. For years many gays and lesbians used the term "sexual preference," which implied that homosexuality was an adopted lifestyle. Today, "sexual orientation" is their term of choice.

The debate is of far more than academic interest to both sides. If conserva-

Excerpted from Richard L. Worsnop, "Gay Rights," *CQ Researcher*, March 5, 1993. Reprinted with permission of Congressional Quarterly, Inc.

tives persuade a substantial majority of Americans that homosexuals could change their sexual behavior if they tried, the movement for gay and lesbian civil rights might grind to a halt. No other population group covered by existing civil rights laws, conservatives note, is defined by a common denominator as malleable as behavior.

On the other hand, if homosexuals convince the nation that their condition is inborn and immutable, their case for broader civil-rights protections would seem stronger. For example, they might win recognition as a "suspect class" in legal actions alleging violation of constitutional rights. To qualify as a suspect class, a group must be the subject of historical discrimination, the discrimination must be unfair and the group must lack political power. Courts apply a "strict scrutiny standard" in such cases, imposing a greater burden of proof on defendants than they do in cases not involving members of a suspect class.

> *"Much of the conflict between homosexual activists and their foes springs from disagreement over the nature of homosexuality."*

As they try to sway popular opinion on this crucial point, homosexuals and conservatives look to psychiatrists, psychologists and neuroscientists for ammunition. Both sides can cite clinical studies and expert opinion to support their views—at least in part. But since the evidence often is inconclusive, the question remains open. . . .

## "Special" Rights Versus Equal Rights

The debate on whether homosexuality is innate or acquired is closely tied to another question—whether gay and lesbian pressure for legal protection amounts to a demand for "special" rights.

Robert Knight, director of the Cultural Studies Project of the Family Research Council, a conservative think tank that seeks to preserve traditional family values, believes the answer is yes. "Homosexuals are trying to carve out an entirely new area of civil rights law," he says, "by basing protections for minorities on behavior rather than religion or immutable characteristics, such as skin color, ethnicity, national origin—things you can't change. In doing this, they would open up a Pandora's box of behavioral claims of minority status. Alcoholics could claim minority status, for instance, saying, 'Gee, I've been this way ever since I can remember, and I can't help it. Therefore, I should get special treatment and I shouldn't be discriminated against based on my behavior.'"

Knight also argues that "homosexuals already have all the civil rights everyone else has. But they want to be able to claim that whatever happens to them is as a result of their being gay. So if you have a homosexual employee who performs badly or is insubordinate, you would have a lawsuit on your hands if you fired that person for those reasons, because he would claim it's because he's gay."

Robert Bray of the National Gay and Lesbian Task Force disagrees. "What we are talking about is the same rules of conduct for both straights and gays—nothing more, nothing less; nothing special, just the same." And he predicts that "When people realize this, we will garner moral support."

Franklin E. Kameny, president of The Mattachine Society of Washington, one of the country's oldest gay-rights organizations, makes a similar point. "We are the victims of special abuses, and we are trying to eliminate those to even off the playing field," he says. "We don't say that civil rights laws designed to protect blacks, Jews and other classic victims of discrimination are special rights. The laws simply even the playing field for them. And that's exactly what we want, too."

Bray felt sure the "special rights" question would surface during the Senate hearings on the military's gay ban in 1993. If he is right, 1992's campaign in Colorado over Amendment 2, a ballot initiative to bar any legal claims of discrimination by homosexuals, could serve as a refresher course in what to expect. Many who followed the campaign closely credit the special-rights argument with persuading a majority of Coloradans to vote in favor of the proposal. [Colorado's Amendment 2 was struck down by the U.S. Supreme Court in 1996.]

Vincent Carroll, editorial page editor of the *Rocky Mountain News*, shares that view. The debate on Amendment 2, he noted in an op-ed page column printed in the *Wall Street Journal*, "centered on an unexpected topic: not on the morality of gay behavior, although that discussion of course occurred, but on the very nature of civil rights enforcement. It is safe to say that public resentment over affirmative action policies was indispensable to the amendment's success."

To gain a more accurate reading of public opinion on the issue, Carroll separated 100 letters to the *News* on Amendment 2 into three broad categories. About one-third of the writers "offered moral reasons" for backing the proposal; about one-fourth "cited idiosyncratic reasons . . . or simply weren't fully coherent"; and the remainder "staked their case on an opposition to 'special rights' for any group of Americans." One letter quoted by Carroll declared that homosexuals "already have equal rights. They want preferential rights."

Executive Director Tim McFeeley of the Human Rights Campaign Fund, a Washington-based homosexual advocacy group, took issue with Carroll's analysis in a letter to the *Journal*. Rejecting the notion that homosexuals seek "special" treatment,

> *"The debate on whether homosexuality is innate or acquired is closely tied to another question—whether . . . legal protection amounts to a demand for 'special' rights."*

McFeeley wrote that "there is nothing special about wanting to live as an equal member of society, protected from irrational discrimination." Regardless of what motivated Coloradans to support Amendment 2, he added, the result was to "sanction discrimination and promote bigotry."

# Gays and Lesbians Are Entitled to Protection Against Discrimination

**by Michael Nava and Robert Dawidoff**

**About the authors:** *Michael Nava, a lawyer, and Robert Dawidoff, a historian, are the authors of* Created Equal: Why Gay Rights Matter to America.

Gay men and lesbians . . . do not want to continue through life abused, bashed, and discriminated against in their own country. They do not want to labor under the vicious stereotypes that incite violence and justify denial of their civil rights. They do not want to have to struggle so hard to live their lives. Life is trouble enough without the distracting burden of defending yourself from fear and prejudice at every turn.

## What Gays and Lesbians Want

So what do gays and lesbians want? What do we want? We want more than the absence of abuse. We want our rights as citizens; we want the chance to live our lives happily and morally; we want the chance to make our ways individually and as members of a loosely associated community without being taxed or pressed into service to support institutions and laws that oppress us. We also want things that go beyond the cessation of pain. Marriage is crucially important to many gays and lesbians, as is support for their parenting of children. We want the material benefits society gives to preserve families; the right to serve openly in the military, in public life, in entertainment; the right to be open about being gay; the right to genuine privacy, not the secrecy that passes for privacy for far too many of us.

Some of these matters can be legislated or decided by the judiciary, and some cannot, but this is no reason not to effect the changes that are possible. Martin Luther King, Jr., was right when he said you can't legislate the hearts of men, but so was Thurgood Marshall when he added that you can legislate their conduct. We have already witnessed the beginning of the public struggle to end discrimination against lesbians and gay men in the military. The protection of civilians who are lesbian and gay is, if anything, more urgent; it will require amending federal civil rights laws to include sexual orientation as a protected class. Sodomy laws must either be repealed or be overturned by the courts. Initiatives, constitutional amendments, or statutes that, like Colorado's, legalize discrimination against gays and lesbians must be ruled unconstitutional violations of the right to equal protection.

> *"The protection of civilians who are lesbian and gay . . . will require amending federal civil rights laws to include sexual orientation as a protected class."*

Gays and lesbians must be given the statutory right to marry, to obtain custody of their children if they are fit parents, to adopt, to leave their property to one another at death, to do all the other things that people in heterosexual unions are permitted to do. The accomplishments of homosexual Americans and respect for their lives and their privacy must be taught as part of the social studies curriculum in every public school in America. The epidemic of AIDS must be fought with every resource this country has committed to every other epidemic that has assailed it. These are the things that need to be done to protect gay Americans and integrate them into the society. We are under no illusion that these things will be done in the next ten years or even the next fifty, but they must be done.

## A Nation of Equals

The debate about any changes in the power arrangements of the society is always framed in terms of what women, African-Americans, gays, or whatever social minority group want. The fantasies of the Lou Sheldons [minister and chair of the Traditional Values Coalition] and William Dannemeyers [former U.S. representative from California] of the world are consumed with that question. George Bush, Sam Nunn, Bill Clinton, and just about everybody else who isn't gay assumes that what gays and lesbians want is the legitimization and approval of their "lifestyles." This is not entirely correct. Gay Americans have individually and collectively created customs and institutions and families that help give us the solidity and clarity that in our own eyes legitimate our lives. We do not expect American society to give us some seal of approval. It is not within the scope of government to do that. We have our own approval. What we do want is equal protection of the laws and *all* that implies, and we want our fellow citizens to acknowledge that our constitutionally protected choices about what is, after all, our own business should not disqualify us from equal membership in the multitude of American communities.

There will always be lesbians and gay men who prefer a gay-oriented way of living, who live in urban gay communities and pursue the attractions and diversions those communities offer. Other gays and lesbians live lives undistinguished by sexual orientation except in their private lives. Most, of course, will mix the two. We ask and deserve that our fellow citizens recognize our existence and accept us into the common life. This is neither begging for acceptance nor looking for approval. It is the corollary of the Bill of Rights that creates a nation of equals, equally free. The constitutional protections we are entitled to must go along with the effort to educate nongay Americans out of their hostile conditioning. Again, this is not to win approval, but to change perceptions enough to prevent majority prejudices from being acted out against us.

It is incumbent on minority groups to acquaint their fellow citizens with the facts of their lives and to remind their fellow citizens of the elements common to everybody's life. In the end, acceptance does matter—acceptance not of the way other people live their lives, but of their right to live them. This kind of acceptance of our membership in the American family is not, as bigots fear, conversion of heterosexuals to homosexuality, but democratic acceptance, which means that our differences do not disqualify us from the exercise of our rights as citizens. What we seek agreement on, acceptance of, is the proposition that all of us have the right to our own lives without someone battering down the door, calling us names, beating us up, denying us work or shelter or medical care, or refusing to honor our intimate unions.

## The Anti-Gay Faction's Beliefs

The zealous opponents of gay rights understand that what we want is to be equal as citizens and to establish the principle of equality between gay and straight lives. What they refuse to understand is what we are really like, because they refuse to understand—or perhaps accept—what people are really like. Pluralism and individualism terrify them, because both present opportunities to which they are afraid to expose themselves or their families, so they believe the answer is to wipe out these things. The fact that this is impossible only redoubles their efforts. They want to keep us the creatures of their own fears and prejudices, the scarecrows of their own furious campaigns against individual liberty and individual freedom of choice about the most important and private matters.

Just as it was once assumed that African-American men lusted after white women and suffragists wanted to be men, the anti-gay lobby seems to think that gays and lesbians want to seduce adult and child alike, recruit new queers, and destroy the family. They think the heterosexual

> *"In the end, acceptance does matter—acceptance not of the way other people live their lives, but of their right to live them."*

two-parent family cannot coexist with alternative families (Adam and Eve, who were not married and had a troubled family life are preferable to Adam and Steve). And what do the opponents of our rights think we want *then*? To conquer the world? Redecorate their houses?

The opposition's version of what we want tells you more about what they fear and desire than it does about us. Likely as not, what they fear is their own sexual impulses, but their focus is on seduction and corruption by others. This is interesting psychologically but not of much account otherwise. Gay people are not recruited. Heterosexuals recruit and attempt to convert homosexuals, not the reverse. If the opponents of gay rights are truly concerned about predatory sexual behavior, they ought to educate their heterosexual sons, who are the most likely to grow up to be sex offenders, to respect the physical integrity of women and children.

> *"Our differences do not disqualify us from the exercise of our rights as citizens."*

What gays and lesbians want is for our rights as citizens to be recognized as readily as our responsibilities as taxpayers; we want an end to the systematic discrimination against us on the basis of prejudice whether grounded in religious or other opinion. Our opponents believe we are not fully human and deserve to remain disenfranchised and subject to intimidation and violence. They do not believe the Constitution protects anything that goes against their own selective views of what their religions tell them.

## No Special Rights

Stated generally, what gays and lesbians want is not very different from what most Americans want: to live as little disturbed by government as possible but secure in the knowledge that social institutions will serve them equally and that laws affecting them will be enforced fairly. We are not asking for "special rights" or special treatment. We are not a special interest. On the contrary, we are the victims of special-interest pleading by our opponents attempting to foist their minority religious views on the rest of us. We are demanding our basic rights, rights that Americans are not supposed to be deprived of without due process of law and that are nevertheless denied to us, without due process, as a matter of routine.

It would be nice if our families, friends, neighbors, leaders, and other fellow citizens could just get over their prejudices about us. It is really difficult sometimes to see what in the lives we lead should be a source of such interest to so many people. It would be possible to make a list of things we all might like, but there is little consensus among gays and lesbians beyond the basics of equal protection and individual freedom. One thing we agree on is that we want to be left alone, to be free from the constant pressures and prejudices that assail us whether we are out of the closet or not.

At the very least, public institutions should treat gay and lesbian Americans and their lives with the same respect they give heterosexual Americans. The culture has no business promoting heterosexuality at the expense of homosexuality, and if this sounds radical, then ask yourself if you agree that the interests of white Americans or male Americans should not be promoted at the expense of black or female Americans. The same principle of equality is at work in all three cases. People's inclinations, orientation, preference, nature, and private lives should be respected, unless it can be shown that some harm to the public interest would result. This is the principle of equal protection under the law. Although we would like to see reasonable representations of gays and lesbians in the world around us, to have our numbers acknowledged, our needs addressed, our feelings respected, and our accomplishments noted and rewarded, most of us would be happy to gain equal protection and make do without the special attentions society lavishes on heterosexuals. But equal protection is our minimal demand, because the absence of rights is not the same as being let alone. Rights are required to protect individuals from undue interference with their lives by government or majority prejudice. Gay rights activist David Mixner said it well in an interview with NBC: "We are going to be free."

## Individual Liberty

*Freedom.* Gay Americans want freedom.

The right to be left alone to live your life was supposed to be the point of this constitutional regime. Many Americans share the feeling that our society has forgotten how to mind its own business. Our lives as individuals seem less important than they should be. No class in America is more familiar with the obstacles to individual thriving than lesbians and gay men. When all Americans think about sexual orientation, they should not think about the sex they do not want to have, but whether the sex they do want to have is anyone's business but their own.

For those who believe that meaningful individuality has lost its force in the complex, harried world, gay issues may not resonate. For those who believe that the appropriate response to the modern world is precisely to bolster and reinforce the capacities of the individual, gay rights must resonate powerfully. Heterosexuals who value their own self-knowledge are no more inclined than homosexuals to give in to the moral bullies who would rather yell than reason and who seem to know how everyone ought to live. The point of education, progress, freedom is to liberate internal truths so that our lives may prove more responsive to them.

> *"We are not asking for 'special rights' or special treatment."*

That was the point of the Declaration of Independence: to stick the principle of individual liberty into the craw of any potential tyranny, whether British, racial, or moral. Gays and lesbians have to struggle very hard to earn our inner freedom. Having done this in significant numbers over the past quarter century, we are determined to secure our civil freedom so that our lives can be as good and safe and decent as anybody else's.

Why should heterosexual Americans care about gay rights? Beyond fairness and decency, what concern is it of theirs? In one of those odd twists of fate that makes history something more or less than a science, the majority of Americans face issues in their lives that gays and lesbians have pioneered. The identification and understanding of the self, apart from family and social and conventional expectations, is what is required for gay people to survive. Such self-understanding is what the reexamination of gender roles, the predominance of serial monogamy or single-parent families, the recasting of families in a more extended and complicated fashion have brought about for people who are not gay. The traditional family is no longer normative. Only one family in five, according to a survey by the Population Reference Bureau, fits the image of a wage-earner father, a wife at home, and two children.

> *"We are determined to secure our civil freedom so that our lives can be as good and safe and decent as anybody else's."*

## The New Model Family

Whether or not one deplores the change in normative family structure, the fact is that more and more Americans have to make personal decisions on the basis of economic, psychological, and sexual realities that force them to re-imagine family rather than to pursue the ideal of family they learned as children. They can no longer depend—nor do many want to depend—on the old, and inherently troubled, ideal of one marriage, one career, one house and two kids equals one family. The inclusion of gays and lesbians in the model of family, and the model of gay families, are important in a society full of people trying to make their way through life, and to lead good lives, in what have been considered unconventional settings. The great majority of Americans live unconventional lives, if judged by the "traditional" family—which, of course, is not traditional at all but an aberration of the post–World War II era. What gays and lesbians have to teach other Americans is that morality is how you live and how you conduct yourself, not what you happen to be; that family values, like cooperation and respect for the rights of others, have to do with the values inside a family, not whether that family conforms to someone else's idea of what a family should be. What gays and lesbians have to teach other Americans is that an authentic life can be difficult but also satisfying, moving, and rich, and that the kind of openness it can create permits precisely the tolerance for others that must exist in a democratic society.

Individuality requires self-consciousness above all. Making choices for ourselves in public and private life is the challenge of a free democratic society. The pitfalls of this are many; most of the world still falters and reverts to regimes under which people are told what to believe, what to think, and how to act. The totalitarianism of communism is being replaced by the totalitarianism of religion and nationalism throughout the world. The United States has a tradition of freedom to hold on to, but, as always, the challenge freedom presents is uncomfortable for many.

As a people, we are learning about the differences of race, religion, gender, ethnicity that will either divide or unite us. But it is as individuals, which we all have the right and capacity to be, that we make the choices about our personal lives based on inner necessity and principled concern for what is good and what will make us happy. That is, of course, what the "pursuit of happiness" is all about. Those choices are about more than recreation, possessions, and pleasure; they are about identity and private life. Freedom makes one gamble on the private decisions other free citizens make about their lives and the common life. These decisions and choices are the core of freedom, and their protection is the paramount issue of our times.

## The Case for Gay Rights

To acquiesce in the denial to gay and lesbian Americans of equal protection of the law because the idea of their equality worries you or because you don't want to think about homosexuality is bad citizenship. To refuse to recognize yourself in our struggles shows shortsighted self-interest. The forces that seek to oppose our equality are the forces that aim to restrict everyone's right to a truly private life. The more Americans live private lives they have chosen or have hewed out of unexpected circumstance—and that appears to be

> *"Morality is how you live and how you conduct yourself, not what you happen to be."*

most of us—the more compelling for everyone is the case for gay rights. We want what you want. We have a right to what you have a right to. The enemies of our right to live freely as individuals are the enemies of your right to live freely as individuals. We all come from your families, and your families cannot survive if we are persecuted. The individualism foreseen by Emerson, the challenge to people to live their lives from the inside out and to make custom and convention respond to the indwelling human truth, has at last become a majority cause; gay rights is the most telling instance of it in our times.

# Antidiscrimination Laws Protect Equal Rights for Gays and Lesbians

by American Civil Liberties Union

**About the author:** *The American Civil Liberties Union is a national organization that works to defend civil rights guaranteed by the U.S. Constitution.*

The struggle of lesbians and gay men for equal rights has moved to the center of the American stage. At no time in our nation's history have gay people been more visible: Lesbians and gay men are battling for their civil rights in Congress, in courtrooms and in the streets; well-known figures are discussing their sexual orientation in public; gay characters are featured in movies and on prime time television shows. More Americans today than ever before are aware of the concerns and needs of lesbians and gay men.

Historically, our legal system has sought to enforce presumed cultural and moral norms through laws that dictate what combinations of individuals may have sex with one another and how. Adultery, for example, is still a crime in nearly half of the states, and a few states still criminalize premarital sex. Not until 1967 did the U.S. Supreme Court strike down "anti-miscegenation laws," criminalizing interracial marriages, as unconstitutional. This type of government regulation has been particularly punitive for lesbians and gay men. Sodomy laws, which invade the intimate realm of sexual expression, have provided the legal basis for justifying a wide range of discrimination against lesbians and gay men in areas from housing and employment to parenting.

## History of the Gay Rights Movement

The modern movement to end discrimination against lesbians and gay men began dramatically in June 1969, when the patrons of the Stonewall Inn, a tavern frequented by gay people in New York City's Greenwich Village fought back against police violence during a raid on the bar. Using the same strategies

From "Lesbian and Gay Rights," American Civil Liberties Union Briefing Paper No. 18, June 1996. Reprinted with permission.

of grass-roots activism and litigation used by other 20th century movements for social change, the nationwide movement spawned by the Stonewall rebellion has achieved significant progress. After two decades of struggle:

• Sodomy laws that previously existed in all 50 states now exist in only 21 states;

• eight states, the District of Columbia, and over 100 municipalities ban discrimination based on sexual orientation in areas such as employment, housing and public accommodations, and

• dozens of municipalities and many more private institutions, including some of the country's largest corporations and universities, have "domestic partnership" programs that recognize and accord various benefits, such as health insurance coverage, to gay and lesbian partners.

But as lesbians and gay men have become empowered, and issues concerning them have gained national attention, anti-gay hostility has become more open and virulent.

• Sexual orientation, although unrelated to an individual's ability, is still the basis for employment decisions in both the public and private sectors.

• State and local laws aimed at blocking equal rights for gay people are proliferating nationwide.

• A homophobic backlash has sparked a dramatic rise in "hate crimes" against gay people or those perceived to be gay, including murder—for example, a 127 percent rise in five major cities that keep anti-gay violence records between 1988 and 1993.

• Millions of Americans are still denied equality, including custody of their children, and access to housing and public accommodations, because they are openly lesbian or gay or are so perceived.

• Gay organizations on college campuses are denied official recognition, access to funding and campus services.

• The federal government continues its tradition of sanctioning anti-gay bigotry, which led, in the late 1940s and 1950s McCarthy era, to the firing of at least 1,700 federal workers who were suspected of being lesbian or gay and were branded "perverts" and "subversives." Today, the government maintains discriminatory policies in, among other areas, the military and in access to security clearances.

> *"Millions of Americans are still denied equality ... because they are openly lesbian or gay."*

In 1986, after more than two decades of support for lesbian and gay struggles, the American Civil Liberties Union (ACLU) established a national Lesbian and Gay Rights Project to coordinate the nation's most extensive program advocating equal rights for lesbians and gay men. The ACLU's work is cut out: Well-organized and well-funded radical right-wingers and religious fundamentalists have pledged that "gay rights will be the 'abortion' issue of the 1990s"—meaning that the gay community's every advance toward equality will be challenged.

Here are the ACLU's answers to some questions frequently asked by the public about the rights of lesbians and gay men.

## What Is the Constitutional Basis for Supporting Lesbian and Gay Rights?

The struggle for legal equality for lesbians and gay men rests on several fundamental constitutional principles.

*Equal protection of the law* is guaranteed by the Fifth and Fourteenth Amendments and reinforced by hundreds of local, state and federal civil rights laws. Although the Fourteenth Amendment, ratified at the end of the Civil War, was originally intended to ensure full legal equality for African Americans, courts have interpreted the Equal Protection Clause to prohibit discrimination on other bases as well, such as gender, religion and disability.

*The right to privacy*, or "the right to be left alone," is guaranteed by the Fourth, Fifth, Ninth and Fourteenth Amendments and further secured by a series of Supreme Court rulings: In 1965, the landmark *Griswold v. Connecticut* struck down a state law that prohibited even married couples from obtaining contraceptives, citing "zones of privacy" into which the government cannot intrude; in 1967, *Loving v. Virginia* decriminalized interracial marriage; in 1972, *Eisenstadt v. Baird* recognized unmarried persons' right to use contraceptives, and in 1973 *Roe v. Wade* recognized women's right to terminate pregnancy.

> *"The struggle for legal equality for lesbians and gay men rests on several fundamental constitutional principles."*

*Freedom of speech and association* are protected under the First Amendment and include the rights to form social and political organizations, to socialize in bars and restaurants, to march or protest peacefully, to produce works of art or popular culture with homosexual themes, and to speak out publicly about lesbian and gay issues.

## What Exactly Do Sodomy Statutes Prohibit?

Sodomy statutes generally prohibit oral and anal sex, even between consenting adults in the privacy of their homes. "Sodomy" is variously referred to as "deviate sexual intercourse," "a crime against nature" or "unnatural or perverted sexual practice." The language of some statutes is extremely vague and subjective. Michigan, for example, outlaws "gross lewdness" and "gross indecency." Penalties for violating sodomy laws range from a $200 fine to 20 years imprisonment. In most of the 21 states that still retain consensual sodomy statutes, these laws apply to both homosexual and heterosexual sex. However, six states limit the laws' application to same-sex couples. The primary effect of sodomy laws is to sanction the suppression of lesbian and gay male sex.

## What Has the Supreme Court Said About Sodomy Laws?

Sodomy laws invade one of the sexual "zones of privacy" defined by the Supreme Court in 1965. But unfortunately, the Court ignored its own standard in 1986 by upholding the constitutionality of Georgia's sodomy law. *Bowers v. Hardwick* involved an Atlanta resident who was arrested when a police officer entered his home and found him in bed with another man. Stating that a majority of Georgians regarded homosexuality as immoral, the Court ruled that the constitutional right to privacy did not prevent states from criminalizing sodomy.

> *"By criminalizing lesbian and gay sex, sodomy laws institutionalize the concept that ... mistreatment [of gays and lesbians] by government and society is ... justified."*

Justice Harry A. Blackmun, representing four Justices, dissented sharply and forcefully. "[W]hat the Court really has refused to recognize," he wrote, "is the fundamental interest all individuals have in controlling the nature of their intimate associations with others." Four years later, Justice Lewis F. Powell, who had provided the decision's swing vote, stated publicly that he regretted having voted to uphold sodomy statutes.

## Why Is It Necessary to Seek Repeal of Sodomy Laws When They Are So Rarely Enforced?

Though infrequently enforced, consensual sodomy laws can be used against gay people for as long as they remain on the books, as illustrated by the *Hardwick* case. Thus, even their occasional use is a good reason to seek repeal. Moreover, such statutes are the cornerstone of the oppression of lesbians and gay men: By criminalizing lesbian and gay sex, sodomy laws institutionalize the concept that gay people are by nature outlaws, and that their mistreatment by government and society is, therefore, justified.

The Supreme Court decision in *Hardwick* was a disappointing setback, but the effort to achieve equality for lesbians and gay men has since continued on the state level. Indeed, that effort has met with some success. Courts in Kentucky, Michigan and Texas have declared sodomy laws unconstitutional under their state constitutions' guarantees of privacy and equal protection. In *Kentucky v. Wasson*, the Kentucky Supreme Court explained:

> ... [W]e hold the guarantees of individual liberty provided in our 1891 Kentucky Constitution offer greater protection of the right of privacy than provided by the Federal Constitution as interpreted by the United States Supreme

Court, and that the statute in question [prohibiting 'deviate sexual inter-course'] is a violation of such rights. . . .

The fight to repeal sodomy laws will continue, in both legislatures and the courts, until such laws have been consigned to history in every state.

### Are Gay Men and Lesbians Protected from Discrimination Anywhere in the Country?

Yes. Eight states (California, Connecticut, Hawaii, Massachusetts, Minnesota, New Jersey, Vermont and Wisconsin), the District of Columbia and more than 100 municipalities have enacted laws that protect gay people from employment discrimination. But in most locales in 42 states, such discrimination remains perfectly legal.

Every year, thousands of Americans are denied job opportunities and denied access to housing, restaurants, hotels and other public accommodations simply because they are gay or lesbian or are perceived to be so. Businesses openly fire lesbian and gay employees, many states maintain policies that exclude gay people from certain positions, and even the federal government maintains discriminatory employment policies.

The best way to redress pervasive discrimination against lesbians and gay men is to amend all existing federal civil rights laws to ban discrimination based on sexual orientation in employment, housing, public accommodations, public facilities and federally assisted programs. The ACLU, through its Lesbian and Gay Rights Project, is working to attain that goal.

### Aren't Lesbians and Gay Men Demanding Special Rights and Preferential Treatment?

Absolutely not. The gay community is demanding *equal* rights, not more or different rights than other Americans. Equal rights include the right to live free from persecution and violence based on sexual orientation.

The misleading term, "special rights," is used by those who hope to perpetuate discrimination against lesbians and gay men. For example, it was used successfully in November 1992 to convince a majority of Colorado voters that they should enact a state constitutional amendment—called Amendment 2—repealing all existing gay rights laws and barring any future enactment of such laws.

> *"The misleading term, 'special rights,' is used by those who hope to perpetuate discrimination against lesbians and gay men."*

What most Americans do not realize is that the many lesbians and gay men who face discrimination have *no* legal recourse: Federal law does *not* prohibit discrimination against gay people, and only a handful of states do. Therefore, laws prohibiting discrimination on the basis of sexual orientation are merely intended to provide *equal* rights—to level the playing field so that lesbians and gay men will be judged according to their abilities, not their sexual orientation.

## Do Any States Recognize Gay Marriage?

Not yet. But more than two dozen cities, including New York, Los Angeles, San Francisco, Seattle and Minneapolis, have "domestic partnership" programs that provide legal recognition for both heterosexual and homosexual unmarried cohabitants who register with the city. These programs, while not conferring all of the rights and responsibilities of marriage, generally grant registered partners some of the economic benefits accorded to married couples—typically, sick and bereavement leave and insurance and survivorship benefits for city employees.

## Why Does the ACLU Support Gay Marriage?

Lesbian and gay couples experience the law's hostility to their intimate relationships as a blatant enforcement of their status as second-class citizens.

To deny their relationships full legal recognition is to unfairly deprive lesbians and gay men of benefits that married heterosexuals take for granted. For example, married people automatically enjoy certain tax advantages; they can inherit property from one another without a will; one spouse can recover damages for the wrongful death of the other; they can adopt children more easily than singles can. Employers often extend health insurance, pension and other benefits on the basis of marital status. Thus, practically speaking, lesbians and gay men cannot achieve complete equality in American society until the government officially recognizes their relationships.

# Discrimination Against Gays and Lesbians Should Be Stopped

**by Richard Rorty**

**About the author:** *Richard Rorty is a professor of humanities at the University of Virginia. This viewpoint is from a speech Rorty delivered at Pomona College in Pomona, California, in February 1996.*

If one accepts the premise that the basic responsibility of the American left is to protect the poor against the rapacity of the rich, it's difficult to argue that the postwar years have been particularly successful ones. As Karl Marx pointed out, the history of the modern age is the history of class warfare, and in America today, it is a war in which the rich are winning, the poor are losing, and the left, for the most part, is standing by.

## "Rights" Rhetoric

Early American leftists, from William James to Walt Whitman to Eleanor Roosevelt, seeking to improve the standing of the country's poorest citizens, found their voice in a rhetoric of fraternity, arguing that Americans had a responsibility for the well-being of their fellow man. This argument has been replaced in current leftist discourse by a rhetoric of "rights." The shift has its roots in the fact that the left's one significant postwar triumph was the success of the civil-rights movement. The language of "rights" is the language of the documents that have sparked the most successful attempts to relieve human suffering in postwar America—the series of Supreme Court decisions that began with *Brown* v. *Board of Education* and continued through *Roe* v. *Wade*. The *Brown* decision launched the most successful appeal to the consciences of Americans since the Progressive Era.

Yet the trouble with rights talk, as the philosopher Mary Ann Glendon has suggested, is that it makes political morality not a result of political discourse—

From Richard Rorty, "The Intellectuals and the Poor," a speech delivered at Pomona College, Pomona, California, February 1996. Reprinted by permission of the author.

of reflection, compromise, and choice of the lesser evil—but rather an unconditional moral imperative: a matter of corresponding to something antecedently
given, in the way that the will of God or the law of nature is purportedly given.
Instead of saying, for example, that the absence of various legal protections
makes the lives of homosexuals unbearably difficult, that it creates unnecessary
human suffering for our fellow Americans, we have come to say that these protections must be instituted in order to protect homosexuals' rights.

The difference between an appeal to end suffering and an appeal to rights is
the difference between an appeal to fraternity, to fellow-feeling, to sympathetic
concern, and an appeal to something that exists quite independently from anybody's feelings about anything—something that issues unconditional commands. Debate about the existence of such commands, and discussion of which
rights exist and which do not, seems to me a philosophical blind alley, a pointless importation of legal discourse into politics, and a distraction from what is
really needed in this case: an attempt by the straights to put themselves in the
shoes of the gays.

Consider Colin Powell's indignant reaction to the suggestion that the exclusion of gays from the military is analogous to the pre–1950s exclusion of
African Americans from the military.
Powell angrily insists that there is no
analogy here—that gays simply do
not have the rights claimed by blacks.
As soon as the issue is phrased in
rights talk, those who agree with
Powell and oppose what they like to

> *"The absence of various legal protections makes the lives of homosexuals unbearably difficult."*

call "special rights for homosexuals" start citing the Supreme Court's decision
in *Bowers* v. *Hardwick*. The Court looked into the matter and solemnly found
that there is no constitutional protection for sodomy. So people arguing against
Powell have to contend that *Bowers* was wrongly decided. This leads to an ar-
gumentative impasse, one that suggests that rights talk is the wrong approach.

## Cruel Behavior

The *Brown* v. *Board of Education* decision was not a discovery of a hitherto
unnoticed constitutional right, or of the hitherto unnoticed intentions of the authors of constitutional amendments. Rather, it was the result of our society's
long-delayed willingness to admit that the behavior of white Americans toward
the descendants of black slaves was, and continued to be, incredibly cruel—that
it was intolerable that American citizens should be subjected to the humiliation
of segregation. If *Bowers* v. *Hardwick* is reversed, it will not be because a hitherto invisible right to sodomy has become manifest to the justices. It will be because the heterosexual majority has become more willing to concede that it has
been tormenting homosexuals for no better reason than to give itself the sadistic
pleasure of humiliating a group designated as inferior—designated as such for

no better reason than to give another group a sense of superiority.

I may seem to be stretching the term "sadistic," but I do not think I am. It seems reasonable to define "sadism" as the use of persons weaker than ourselves as outlets for our resentments and frustrations, and especially for the infliction of humiliation on such people in order to bolster our own sense of self-worth. All of us have been guilty, at some time in our lives, of this sort of casual, socially accepted sadism. But the most conspicuous instances of sadism, and the only ones relevant to politics, involve groups rather than individuals. Thus Cossacks and the Nazi storm troopers used Jews, and the white races have traditionally used the colored races, in order to bolster their group self-esteem. Men have traditionally humiliated women and beaten up gays in order to exalt their own sense of masculine privilege. The central dynamic behind this kind of sadism is the simple fact that it keeps up the spirits of a lot of desperate, beaten-down people to be able to say to themselves, "At least I'm not a nigger!" or "At least I'm not a faggot!"

> *"The heterosexual majority has . . . been tormenting homosexuals for no better reason than to give itself . . . sadistic pleasure."*

# Barring Antidiscrimination Laws for Gays and Lesbians Is Unconstitutional

**by Anthony Kennedy et al.**

**About the authors:** *Anthony Kennedy is a United States Supreme Court justice. He wrote the majority opinion in the case* Romer v. Evans, *which was joined by Justices John Paul Stevens, Sandra Day O'Connor, David Souter, Ruth Bader Ginsburg, and Steven Breyer.*

One century ago, the first Justice Harlan admonished this Court that the Constitution "neither knows nor tolerates classes among citizens." *Plessy v. Ferguson*, (1896) (dissenting opinion). Unheeded then, those words now are understood to state a commitment to the law's neutrality where the rights of persons are at stake. The Equal Protection Clause enforces this principle and today requires us to hold invalid a provision of Colorado's Constitution.

## Amendment 2

The enactment challenged in this case is an amendment to the Constitution of the State of Colorado, adopted in a 1992 statewide referendum. The parties and the state courts refer to it as "Amendment 2," its designation when submitted to the voters. The impetus for the amendment and the contentious campaign that preceded its adoption came in large part from ordinances that had been passed in various Colorado municipalities. For example, the cities of Aspen and Boulder and the City and County of Denver each had enacted ordinances which banned discrimination in many transactions and activities, including housing, employment, education, public accommodations, and health and welfare services. What gave rise to the statewide controversy was the protection the ordinances afforded to persons discriminated against by reason of their sexual orientation. Amendment 2 repeals these ordinances to the extent they prohibit discrimination on the basis of "homosexual, lesbian or bisexual orientation,

From *Roy Romer v. Richard G. Evans et al.*, 517 U.S. (May 20, 1996).

conduct, practices or relationships."

Yet Amendment 2, in explicit terms, does more than repeal or rescind these provisions. It prohibits all legislative, executive or judicial action at any level of state or local government designed to protect the named class, a class we shall refer to as homosexual persons or gays and lesbians. The amendment reads:

> No Protected Status Based on Homosexual, Lesbian, or Bisexual Orientation. Neither the State of Colorado, through any of its branches or departments, nor any of its agencies, political subdivisions, municipalities or school districts, shall enact, adopt or enforce any statute, regulation, ordinance or policy whereby homosexual, lesbian or bisexual orientation, conduct, practices or relationships shall constitute or otherwise be the basis of or entitle any person or class of persons to have or claim any minority status, quota preferences, protected status or claim of discrimination. This Section of the Constitution shall be in all respects self-executing.

Soon after Amendment 2 was adopted, this litigation to declare its invalidity and enjoin its enforcement was commenced in the District Court for the City and County of Denver. Among the plaintiffs (respondents here) were homosexual persons, some of them government employees. They alleged that enforcement of Amendment 2 would subject them to immediate and substantial risk of discrimination on the basis of their sexual orientation. Other plaintiffs (also respondents here) included the three municipalities whose ordinances we have cited and certain other governmental entities which had acted earlier to protect homosexuals from discrimination but would be prevented by Amendment 2 from continuing to do so. Although Governor Roy Romer had been on record opposing the adoption of Amendment 2, he was named in his official capacity as a defendant, together with the Colorado Attorney General and the State of Colorado.

The trial court granted a preliminary injunction to stay enforcement of Amendment 2, and an appeal was taken to the Supreme Court of Colorado. Sustaining the interim injunction and remanding the case for further proceedings, the State Supreme Court held in *Evans v. Romer* (*Evans I*) that Amendment 2 was subject to strict scrutiny under the Fourteenth Amendment because it infringed the fundamental right of gays and lesbians to participate in the political process. To reach this conclusion, the state court relied on our voting rights cases and on our precedents involving discriminatory restructuring of governmental decisionmaking. On remand, the State advanced various arguments in an effort to show that Amendment 2 was narrowly tailored to serve compelling interests, but the trial court found none sufficient. It enjoined enforcement of Amendment 2, and the Supreme Court of Colorado, in a

> *"The amendment withdraws from homosexuals, but no others, specific legal protection from the injuries caused by discrimination."*

second opinion, affirmed the ruling. We granted certiorari [review] and now affirm the judgment, but on a rationale different from that adopted by the State Supreme Court.

## An Invalid Argument

The State's principal argument in defense of Amendment 2 is that it puts gays and lesbians in the same position as all other persons. So, the State says, the measure does no more than deny homosexuals special rights. This reading of the amendment's language is implausible. We rely not upon our own interpretation of the amendment but upon the authoritative construction of Colorado's Supreme Court. The state court, deeming it unnecessary to determine the full extent of the amendment's reach, found it invalid even on a modest reading of its implications. The critical discussion of the amendment, set out in *Evans I*, is as follows:

> The immediate objective of Amendment 2 is, at a minimum, to repeal existing statutes, regulations, ordinances, and policies of state and local entities that barred discrimination based on sexual orientation.

> Metropolitan State College of Denver prohibits college-sponsored social clubs from discriminating in membership on the basis of sexual orientation and Colorado State University has an antidiscrimination policy which encompasses sexual orientation.

> The "ultimate effect" of Amendment 2 is to prohibit any governmental entity from adopting similar, or more protective statutes, regulations, ordinances, or policies in the future unless the state constitution is first amended to permit such measures.

Sweeping and comprehensive is the change in legal status effected by this law. So much is evident from the ordinances that the Colorado Supreme Court declared would be void by operation of Amendment 2. Homosexuals, by state decree, are put in a solitary class with respect to transactions and relations in both the private and governmental spheres. The amendment withdraws from homosexuals, but no others, specific legal protection from the injuries caused by discrimination, and it forbids reinstatement of these laws and policies.

The change that Amendment 2 works in the legal status of gays and lesbians in the private sphere is far-reaching, both on its own terms and when considered in light of the structure and operation of modern antidiscrimination laws. That structure is

*"Amendment 2 . . . nullifies specific legal protections for [homosexuals] in all transactions."*

well illustrated by contemporary statutes and ordinances prohibiting discrimination by providers of public accommodations. "At common law, innkeepers, smiths, and others who 'made profession of a public employment,' were prohibited from refusing, without good reason, to serve a customer." *Hurley v. Irish-American Gay, Lesbian and Bisexual Group of Boston, Inc.*, (1995). The duty was a general one and did not specify protection for particular groups. The common law rules, however, proved insufficient in many instances, and it was settled early that the Fourteenth Amendment did not give Congress a general power to prohibit discrimination in public accommodations. In consequence, most States have chosen to counter discrimination by enacting detailed statutory schemes.

## Listing Protected Groups

Colorado's state and municipal laws typify this emerging tradition of statutory protection and follow a consistent pattern. The laws first enumerate the persons or entities subject to a duty not to discriminate. The list goes well beyond the entities covered by the common law. The Boulder ordinance, for example, has a comprehensive definition of entities deemed places of "public accommodation." They include "any place of business engaged in any sales to the general public and any place that offers services, facilities, privileges, or advantages to the general public or that receives financial support through solicitation of the general public or through governmental subsidy of any kind." The Denver ordinance is of similar breadth, applying, for example, to hotels, restaurants, hospitals, dental clinics, theaters, banks, common carriers, travel and insurance agencies, and "shops and stores dealing with goods or services of any kind."

> *"The protections Amendment 2 withholds . . . are protections taken for granted by most people either because they already have them or do not need them."*

These statutes and ordinances also depart from the common law by enumerating the groups or persons within their ambit of protection. Enumeration is the essential device used to make the duty not to discriminate concrete and to provide guidance for those who must comply. In following this approach, Colorado's state and local governments have not limited antidiscrimination laws to groups that have so far been given the protection of heightened equal protection scrutiny under our cases. Rather, they set forth an extensive catalogue of traits which cannot be the basis for discrimination, including age, military status, marital status, pregnancy, parenthood, custody of a minor child, political affiliation, physical or mental disability of an individual or of his or her associates—and, in recent times, sexual orientation.

Amendment 2 bars homosexuals from securing protection against the injuries that these public-accommodations laws address. That in itself is a severe consequence, but there is more. Amendment 2, in addition, nullifies specific legal protections for this targeted class in all transactions in housing, sale of real estate, insurance, health and welfare services, private education, and employment.

Not confined to the private sphere, Amendment 2 also operates to repeal and forbid all laws or policies providing specific protection for gays or lesbians from discrimination by every level of Colorado government. The State Supreme Court cited two examples of protections in the governmental sphere that are now rescinded and may not be reintroduced. The first is Colorado Executive Order D0035 (1990), which forbids employment discrimination against "'all state employees, classified and exempt' on the basis of sexual orientation." Also repealed, and now forbidden, are "various provisions prohibiting discrimination based on sexual orientation at state colleges." The repeal of these measures and the prohibition against their future reenactment demonstrates that Amendment 2 has the same force and effect in Colorado's governmental sector as it does elsewhere and that it applies to policies as well as ordinary legislation.

Amendment 2's reach may not be limited to specific laws passed for the benefit of gays and lesbians. It is a fair, if not necessary, inference from the broad language of the amendment that it deprives gays and lesbians

> *"The resulting disqualification of a class of persons from the right to seek specific protection from the law is unprecedented."*

even of the protection of general laws and policies that prohibit arbitrary discrimination in governmental and private settings. At some point in the systematic administration of these laws, an official must determine whether homosexuality is an arbitrary and thus forbidden basis for decision. Yet a decision to that effect would itself amount to a policy prohibiting discrimination on the basis of homosexuality, and so would appear to be no more valid under Amendment 2 than the specific prohibitions against discrimination the state court held invalid.

If this consequence follows from Amendment 2, as its broad language suggests, it would compound the constitutional difficulties the law creates. The state court did not decide whether the amendment has this effect, however, and neither need we. In the course of rejecting the argument that Amendment 2 is intended to conserve resources to fight discrimination against suspect classes, the Colorado Supreme Court made the limited observation that the amendment is not intended to affect many antidiscrimination laws protecting nonsuspect classes. In our view that does not resolve the issue. In any event, even if, as we doubt, homosexuals could find some safe harbor in laws of general application, we cannot accept the view that Amendment 2's prohibition on specific legal protections does no more than deprive homosexuals of special rights. To the contrary, the amendment imposes a special disability upon those persons alone. Homosexuals are forbidden the safeguards that others enjoy or may seek without constraint. They can obtain specific protection against discrimination only by enlisting the citizenry of Colorado to amend the state constitution or perhaps, on the State's view, by trying to pass helpful laws of general applicability. This is so no matter how local or discrete the harm, no matter how public and widespread the injury. We find nothing special in the protections Amendment 2 withholds. These are protections taken for granted by most people either because they already have them or do not need them; these are protections against exclusion from an almost limitless number of transactions and endeavors that constitute ordinary civic life in a free society.

## Equal Protection of the Law

The Fourteenth Amendment's promise that no person shall be denied the equal protection of the laws must co-exist with the practical necessity that most legislation classifies for one purpose or another, with resulting disadvantage to various groups or persons. We have attempted to reconcile the principle with the reality by stating that, if a law neither burdens a fundamental right nor targets a suspect class, we will uphold the legislative classification so long as it bears a rational relation to some legitimate end.

Amendment 2 fails, indeed defies, even this conventional inquiry. First, the amendment has the peculiar property of imposing a broad and undifferentiated disability on a single named group, an exceptional and, as we shall explain, invalid form of legislation. Second, its sheer breadth is so discontinuous with the reasons offered for it that the amendment seems inexplicable by anything but animus toward the class that it affects; it lacks a rational relationship to legitimate state interests.

Taking the first point, even in the ordinary equal protection case calling for the most deferential of standards, we insist on knowing the relation between the classification adopted and the object to be attained. The search for the link between classification and objective gives substance to the Equal Protection Clause; it provides guidance and discipline for the legislature, which is entitled to know what sorts of laws it can pass; and it marks the limits of our own authority. In the ordinary case, a law will be sustained if it can be said to advance a legitimate government interest, even if the law seems unwise or works to the disadvantage of a particular group, or if the rationale for it seems tenuous. . . . By requiring that the classification bear a rational relationship to an independent and legitimate legislative end, we ensure that classifications are not drawn for the purpose of disadvantaging the group burdened by the law. "If the adverse impact on the disfavored class is an apparent aim of the legislature, its impartiality would be suspect." *United States Railroad Retirement Board v. Fritz*, (1980).

> *"The disadvantage imposed [by Amendment 2] is born of animosity toward [homosexuals]."*

Amendment 2 confounds this normal process of judicial review. It is at once too narrow and too broad. It identifies persons by a single trait and then denies them protection across the board. The resulting disqualification of a class of persons from the right to seek specific protection from the law is unprecedented in our jurisprudence. The absence of precedent for Amendment 2 is itself instructive; "[d]iscriminations of an unusual character especially suggest careful consideration to determine whether they are obnoxious to the constitutional provision." *Louisville Gas & Elec. Co. v. Coleman*, (1928).

It is not within our constitutional tradition to enact laws of this sort. Central both to the idea of the rule of law and to our own Constitution's guarantee of equal protection is the principle that government and each of its parts remain open on impartial terms to all who seek its assistance. "'Equal protection of the laws is not achieved through indiscriminate imposition of inequalities.'" *Sweatt v. Painter*, (1950) (quoting *Shelley v. Kraemer*, (1948)). Respect for this principle explains why laws singling out a certain class of citizens for disfavored legal status or general hardships are rare. A law declaring that in general it shall be more difficult for one group of citizens than for all others to seek aid from the government is itself a denial of equal protection of the laws in the most literal sense. "The guaranty of 'equal protection of the laws is a pledge of the protection of equal laws.'" *Skinner v. Oklahoma ex rel. Williamson*, (1942) (quoting *Yick Wo v. Hopkins*, (1886)).

*Davis v. Beason*, (1890), not cited by the parties but relied upon by the dissent,

> *"Amendment 2 classifies homosexuals not to further a proper legislative end but to make them unequal to everyone else."*

is not evidence that Amendment 2 is within our constitutional tradition, and any reliance upon it as authority for sustaining the amendment is misplaced. In *Davis*, the Court approved an Idaho territorial statute denying Mormons, polygamists, and advocates of polygamy the right to vote and to hold office because, as the Court construed the statute, it "simply excludes from the privilege of voting, or of holding any office of honor, trust or profit, those who have been convicted of certain offences, and those who advocate a practical resistance to the laws of the Territory and justify and approve the commission of crimes forbidden by it." To the extent *Davis* held that persons advocating a certain practice may be denied the right to vote, it is no longer good law. To the extent it held that the groups designated in the statute may be deprived of the right to vote because of their status, its ruling could not stand without surviving strict scrutiny, a most doubtful outcome. To the extent *Davis* held that a convicted felon may be denied the right to vote, its holding is not implicated by our decision and is unexceptionable.

## Disadvantage Is Born of Animosity

A second and related point is that laws of the kind now before us raise the inevitable inference that the disadvantage imposed is born of animosity toward the class of persons affected. "[I]f the constitutional conception of 'equal protection of the laws' means anything, it must at the very least mean that a bare . . . desire to harm a politically unpopular group cannot constitute a legitimate governmental interest." *Department of Agriculture v. Moreno*, (1973). Even laws enacted for broad and ambitious purposes often can be explained by reference to legitimate public policies which justify the incidental disadvantages they impose on certain persons. Amendment 2, however, in making a general announcement that gays and lesbians shall not have any particular protections from the law, inflicts on them immediate, continuing, and real injuries that outrun and belie any legitimate justifications that may be claimed for it. We conclude that, in addition to the far-reaching deficiencies of Amendment 2 that we have noted, the principles it offends, in another sense, are conventional and venerable; a law must bear a rational relationship to a legitimate governmental purpose, and Amendment 2 does not.

The primary rationale the State offers for Amendment 2 is respect for other citizens' freedom of association, and in particular the liberties of landlords or employers who have personal or religious objections to homosexuality. Colorado also cites its interest in conserving resources to fight discrimination against other groups. The breadth of the Amendment is so far removed from these particular justifications that we find it impossible to credit them. We cannot say that Amendment 2 is directed to any identifiable legitimate purpose or discrete objective. It is a status-based enactment divorced from any factual context from which we could discern a relationship to legitimate state interests; it is a classification of persons undertaken for its own sake, something the Equal Protection Clause does not permit. "[C]lass legislation . . . [is] obnoxious to the prohibitions of the Fourteenth Amendment. . . ." *Civil Rights Cases*, (1883).

> *"A State cannot so deem a class of persons a stranger to its laws."*

We must conclude that Amendment 2 classifies homosexuals not to further a proper legislative end but to make them unequal to everyone else. This Colorado cannot do. A State cannot so deem a class of persons a stranger to its laws. Amendment 2 violates the Equal Protection Clause, and the judgment of the Supreme Court of Colorado is affirmed.

# Homosexuals Should Not Be Granted Special Rights

**by Tony Marco**

**About the author:** *Tony Marco is the founder of Colorado for Family Values and is the author of Colorado's Amendment 2, which prohibited state and local governments from banning discrimination on the basis of sexual orientation. The amendment was struck down by the U.S. Supreme Court in May 1996.*

One of the most ambitious public image campaigns in American history is under way, with the mass media's generous help. Its message: Homosexuals are an oppressed, disadvantaged minority, much like African-Americans and Hispanics, and they deserve special legal status and privileges.

Two marketing experts outlined this campaign's goals in a homosexual magazine article, "The Overhauling of Straight America."

"Portray gays as victims, not as aggressive challengers. In any campaign to win over the public, gays must be cast as victims in need of protection so that straights will be inclined by reflex action to assume the role of protector. . . . Straight views must be able to identify with gays as victims. Mr. and Mrs. Public must be given no extra excuses to say 'they are not like us.'. . . Our campaign should not demand direct support for homosexual practices, but should instead take anti-discrimination as its theme."

## Homosexuals Claim Special Legal Privileges

Homosexuals claim they need special legal privileges that, among other things, would permit them to silence or punish their critics, coerce business to pay spousal benefits to their all-too-temporary partners, and express their sexuality whenever, wherever, and with whomever they choose.

Do homosexuals warrant the special legal status they seek? Historically, courts and civil rights authorities have employed three "touchstones" in awarding special protected status to disadvantaged minority classes.

*Criterion 1: A history of discrimination evidenced by lack of ability to obtain economic mean income, adequate education, or cultural opportunity.*

Tony Marco, "Oppressed Minority, or Counterfeits?" *St. Croix Review*, February 1993. Reprinted by permission.

Homosexuals claim they are economically, educationally, and culturally disadvantaged. Marketing studies refute those claims.

• Homosexuals have an average annual household income of $55,430, versus $32,144 for the general population and $12,166 for disadvantaged African-American households.

• More than three times as many homosexuals as average Americans are college graduates (59.6 percent v. 18 percent)—a percentage dwarfing that of truly disadvantaged African Americans and Hispanics.

> *"Homosexuals claim they are economically, educationally, and culturally disadvantaged. Marketing studies refute those claims."*

• More than three times as many homosexuals as average Americans hold professional or managerial positions (49 percent v. 15.9 percent)—again, making homosexuals embarrassingly more advantaged than true minorities in the job market.

• 65.8 percent of homosexuals are overseas travelers—more than four times the percentage (14 percent) of average Americans. More than 13 times as many homosexuals as average Americans (26.5 percent v. 1.9 percent) are frequent flyers.

"America's gay and lesbian community is emerging as one of the nation's most educated and affluent, and Madison Avenue is beginning to explore the potential for a market that may be worth hundreds of billions of dollars. . . . 'It's a market that screams opportunity,' said Eric Miller, editor of *Research Alert*, a consumer research newsletter based in New York."

Robert Bray, a spokesman for the National Gay and Lesbian Task Force, concurs as quoted in a recent article in the *Rocky Mountain News*: "Gay greenbacks are very powerful and the gay and lesbian community is a virtual motherlode of untapped sales."

*Editor and Publisher* estimates that there are more than 125 homosexual newspapers in the United States with a combined circulation of more than one million.

## Homosexual Behavior

*Criterion 2: Specially protected classes should exhibit obvious, immutable, or distinguishing characteristics, like race, color, gender or national origin, that define them as a discrete group.*

There is no credible scientific evidence to support homosexual claims that "gayness" is either genetically determined or immutable.

"The genetic theory of homosexuality has been generally discarded today. . . . Despite the interest in possible hormone mechanisms in the origin of homosexuality, no serious scientist today suggests that a simple cause-effect relationship applies," according to *Human Sexuality*, a 1984 textbook written by Masters, Johnson, and Kolodny.

It is unclear how sexual orientation evolves, but a study by the controversial Kinsey Institute found that 84 percent of homosexuals and 29 percent of heterosexuals shifted or changed their "sexual orientation" at least once; 32 percent of homosexuals and 4 percent of "straights" reported a second shift; and 13 percent of homosexuals and 1 percent of heterosexuals claimed at least five changes in sexual orientation.

Studies of prison inmate behavior, both male and female, clearly demonstrate that, behind bars, for a variety of reasons, homosexual behavior is practiced by inmates who have not previously engaged in homosexual behavior—and who do not practice "gay" behavior after their release from prison.

About lesbianism in women's prisons, one authority on inmate sociology remarked:

"Graphic excerpts from interviews seemed to suggest that (homosexual) social organization among the women prisoners had an institutional origin, since most of the participants had not been involved in homosexual liaisons prior to the prison experience and were evidently unlikely to continue homosexuality after leaving prison."

The same author discovered, about male homosexuality in prisons:

"For males (behind bars), homosexual activity seemed to focus primarily on physical gratification; in many instances it represented a commodity for economic exchange; and it was likely a transitory act."

A study by an avowed homosexual, publicized in a cover article in the Feb. 24, 1992, edition of *Newsweek*, purported to discover "homosexual brains." But on closer examination, the study doesn't hold up.

Simon LeVay's study of the brains of 19 homosexual male corpses (all died of AIDS complications) noted a difference in the size of a specific neuron group, INAH3, compared with that of a group comprised of 16 presumably heterosexual male and six female corpses.

One problem with LeVay's study is that the researcher presumed that the control group of 16 corpses had been heterosexual.

"It turns out that LeVay doesn't know anything about the sexual orientation of his control group, the 16 corpses 'presumed heterosexual.' A

> *"There is no credible scientific evidence to support homosexual claims that 'gayness' is either genetically determined or immutable."*

sloppy control like this is . . . enough by itself to invalidate the study," wrote homosexual reporter Michael Botkin in the *Bay Area Reporter.* "LeVay's defense? He knows his controls are heterosexual because their brains are different from the HIV corpses. Sorry, doctor; this is circular logic. You can use the sample to prove the theory or vice versa, but not at the same time."

The homosexual community cannot claim the study as proof of a genetic source for sexual orientation because the study was not designed to consider why the INAH3 neuron groups vary in size. (Based on the size of their INAH3s, a third of LeVay's subjects should have had the opposite sexual orientation than what he reported.) More study is required, but LeVay won't conduct it; he had left science to become a full-time gay activist.

## Homosexuals Do Not Lack Influence

*Criterion 3: "Protected classes" should clearly demonstrate political power-lessness.*

Far from being politically powerless, homosexual activists have in recent years demonstrated enormous political clout far beyond their numbers. Combining economical and educational advantage with high-pressure lobbying tactics, homosexual activists have ridden waves of tolerance emanating from the sexual revolution to a position of almost irresistible influence in today's America. They have:

• Won passage of legislation granting homosexuals protected class status in seven states and more than 90 cities across America.

• Secured political office both in the U.S. Congress and on numerous major U.S. city councils.

• Pressured the medical community to discard well-established public health measures and treat AIDS as history's first "politically protected" fatal plague.

• Received benefits for "domestic partners" identical to those of married couples, and other kinds of preferential treatment in several major U.S. corporations.

> *"Homosexual activists have . . . demonstrated enormous political clout far beyond their numbers."*

• Implemented homosexual-created curricula presenting homosexual sex as a valid, healthy alternative to heterosexuality, despite overwhelming evidence to the contrary.

• Gained ordination in mainline church denominations. Case in point: on April 1, 1992, a prominent Marin County, California, lesbian minister became a co-pastor of the Downtown United Presbyterian Church of Rochester, N.Y.

• Won National Endowment for the Arts (NEA) grants for "works of art" that graphically portray homosexual sex and savagely ridicule traditional religious and family values.

• Avoided prosecution for acts of violence and vandalism. Case in point: Homosexuals vandalized California State office buildings, burned state flags and California's governor in effigy after his veto in 1992 of a special-rights-for-gays bill, and pelted Gov. Pete Wilson himself with garbage at a speaking engagement following his veto. There were no arrests.

## Homosexual Protests

In 1989, "AIDS activists" invaded a Roman Catholic mass at New York City's St. Patrick's Cathedral, shouting obscenities and defiling Communion elements. A few participants in this blatant desecration incurred slight legal penalties.

No arrests were made and no charges were filed at San Francisco's 1990 and

1991 Gay and Lesbian Pride Parades. Videotapes from one such parade depict public nudity, both male and female; lewd and lascivious acts, including public fondling of genitalia and several acts of what appears to be public anal sex between homosexuals; and open promotion of pedophilia. In Madison, Wisconsin, on Sept. 8, 1991, homosexuals defaced the state Capitol and threatened the governor. *The Capital Times* gave this report:

> *"Once gayness was confirmed . . . , would protected class status and all accompanying entitlements then become retroactive to birth?"*

> About 100 ACT UP protesters charged the Capitol today, defacing the hallway leading to the governor's office with food and stickers and staging a "die-in" in the rotunda. They were protesting what they call "criminal" state policies against prison inmates with AIDS.

> The protesters were met by Capitol police and security officers, who closed the governor's office and blocked the group's entry. The protesters then tossed sandwiches and towels toward the door, and left numerous ACT UP stickers on the walls that portray (Wisconsin's Tommy) Thompson as a public health menace. . . . Other protesters used some type of black marker to write on the marble floor.

No arrests were reported in this incident.

## Too Many Questions

According to John N. Franklin, past chairman of the Colorado Civil Rights Commission, granting special privileges to homosexuals invites a number of questions.

How would class status be determined? Simply on the word of the applicant? After a homosexual performed homosexual acts before a panel of civil rights authorities? The first time someone engaged in sex with a member of the same gender—even accidentally, as in a drunken or drugged encounter? After someone became exclusively homosexual? For how long?

Once gayness was confirmed (whatever the confirmation process), would protected class status and all accompanying entitlements then become retroactive to birth?

In light of the extreme affluence of homosexuals relative to the general population, what would prevent opportunistic individuals from becoming closet heterosexuals status in order to secure benefits only available to legitimate minorities?

Under legislation granting special minority status to homosexuals, we can expect a plethora of nuisance suits and test cases to clog our legal system and bleed dry financially taxpayers and defendants.

Noted African-American civil rights leaders recognize the difference between their movement and the counterfeit of civil rights that homosexual activists have raised in their own interest:

"The equation of homosexuality with the noble history of civil rights in this country serves only to dilute, distort, and denigrate true civil rights," says Dr. Anthony Evans, executive director of The Urban Alternative, America's largest ministry to African Americans.

"'Gay rights' cannot be likened in any fashion to the black struggle for civil rights. 'Gay rights' is not, nor will it ever be, a civil rights issue, but rather a question of morality and individual values," says the Rev. Gill Ford, pastor of Salem Baptist Church in Denver, Colorado.

An African-American church pastor in Kansas City, Missouri, put it no less accurately, if a bit more colorfully: "The Freedom Bus that went to Selma was never intended to go on to Sodom."

If having "divergent" sex becomes all it takes to be considered "ethnic," with special protection and privileges, the concept of ethnicity will soon lose all traces of meaning or value, these civil rights leaders say.

---

### AMENDMENT 2
### TO COLORADO'S CONSTITUTION: FINAL DRAFT

PROPOSED INITIATIVE AMENDMENT TO THE CONSTITUTION OF THE STATE OF COLORADO:

Be it Enacted by the People of the State of Colorado:

Article _____, of the Colorado Constitution is amended by the addition of Section _____, which shall provide as follows:

NO PROTECTED STATUS BASED ON HOMOSEXUAL OR LESBIAN ORIENTATION.

Neither the State of Colorado, through any of its branches or departments, nor any of its agencies, political subdivisions, municipalities or school districts, shall enact, adopt or enforce any statute, regulation, ordinance or policy whereby homosexual, lesbian or bisexual orientation, conduct, practices or relationships shall constitute or otherwise be the basis of, or entitle any person or class of persons to have or claim any minority status, quota preferences, protected status, or claim of discrimination. This section of the Constitution shall be in all respects self-executing.

---

[Editor's note: Amendment 2 was struck down by the U.S. Supreme Court in May 1996.]

# Gay Rights Will Legitimize Homosexuality

**by Hadley Arkes**

**About the author:** *Hadley Arkes is the Ney Professor of Jurisprudence at Amherst College in Massachusetts and a contributing editor of the* National Review. *He was a consultant in the litigation over gay rights in Cincinnati.*

[*Editor's note: The U.S. Supreme Court struck down Amendment 2 in May 1996, subsequent to the original publication of this viewpoint.*]

The Supreme Court is moving to the threshold of a decision as portentous nearly as *Roe* v. *Wade*, and hardly anyone seems to be paying much attention. Only a handful of lawyers, in Colorado, Cincinnati, and Washington, D.C., share the agony now of waiting.

## *Romer* v. *Evans*

By any sober reckoning, there should have been nothing to strain the wit of judges in the so-called, miscalled case of "gay rights" in Colorado, *Romer* v. *Evans*. Miscalled, because the law in question creates no disabilities for gays, withdraws no protections, imparts no inequalities. But the jolt came on October 10, [1995], in the oral argument before the Supreme Court. Justices Anthony Kennedy and Sandra Day O'Connor opened with questions that not only were hostile to the conservative side but actually revealed two judges in a stupor of incomprehension. Even with the aid of the smartest clerks, these judges, holding pivotal votes, plainly had no firm hold on what this case was about.

On the other hand, the truth that dare not speak its name is that the judges know full well what *Romer* v. *Evans* is about, and Kennedy and O'Connor came into the oral arguments with their dispositions firmly fixed. [Since 1993,] a remarkable concert seems to have set in among judges, especially federal judges, on the matter of gay rights. There has been, among the jurists, an almost brazen willingness to strike down any law that implies an adverse judgment on homosexuality. The judges have moved here in rare harmony, as though they were being arranged by the same choreographer. [In November 1995] came an-

Abridged from Hadley Arkes, "Gay Marriage and the Courts: *Roe v. Wade* II?" *Weekly Standard*, November 20, 1995. Reprinted by permission.

other notable move: The highest court in New York removed the bar to adoption by unmarried couples, including couples of the same sex. Step by step, the judges have been dismantling any provisions in the law that refuse to regard homosexuality as something less than legitimate or desirable.

This new aggressiveness may have a political explanation: The judges have seen, in the advent of Ruth Bader Ginsburg, the fifth vote to overrule *Bowers* v. *Hardwick*. That was the case, in 1986, in which the court refused to overturn the statute on sodomy in Georgia. It refused, that is, to discover a constitutional right to engage in homosexuality. That

> *"What the gay activists were claiming here was not the equal right to participate in politics, but nothing less than the right to win."*

case was decided by one vote, and Ruth Ginsburg replaced Justice Byron White, who wrote the opinion in *Bowers*. There was every reason to expect that Justice Ginsburg would cast a decisive vote on the other side, and my own surmise is that some judges have been looking for a case—any case—that could be sent up on appeal and give the court the chance to revisit this question. To put it gently, the judges have been all too willing to give Providence a Helping Hand. In pursuing this mission, the judges have seemed willing to make use of any case, no matter how improbable; and in the case in Colorado, the judges embraced the most implausible argument in order to strike down the policy enacted in a referendum.

The voters had passed Amendment 2, an amendment to the state constitution, in November 1992. The aim of the amendment was to brake the tendency, spreading through the state, to treat "gays" as a class of victims on the same plane as groups suffering discrimination on the basis of race, religion, or gender. The amendment forbade governments at all levels to enact any statute that would treat homosexuals or bisexuals as a class entitled to "minority status, quota preferences, protected status or claim of discrimination."

## Restricting the Right to Make Moral Judgments

Plainly, the amendment did not license an active regimen of criminal enforcement, to seek out and prosecute homosexual acts. It did not represent a return to statutes on sodomy. It merely forestalled legislation that would work in a sweeping way to forbid or punish all acts of private discrimination against homosexuals. That kind of legislation could strike at domains of privacy and the free exercise of religion: It might deny people the right to discriminate in the sharing of their homes with people whose erotic interests they find objectionable on religious or moral grounds. To put it another way, the amendment merely preserved the right of people, in their private settings, to respect their own moral judgments on homosexuality.

And yet, one would hardly understand that version of the case from any account that has appeared on CNN or National Public Radio. After the success of Amendment 2 in Colorado, a similar measure was passed by the voters of Cincinnati as an amendment to the city charter. When that amendment was sustained [in 1995] by a federal court of appeals, the report in the *New York Times* was rather typical: As the *Times* construed it, the federal court had "upheld the right of Cincinnati voters to deny homosexuals specific legal protections." In that respect, the reports in the press have mirrored the line taken by gay activists as they have challenged these amendments in the courts. That line was as audacious as it was implausible, but the Supreme Court in Colorado and a federal judge in Cincinnati were willing to absorb that argument as their own and strike down these amendments as unconstitutional. As the judges declared, with straight faces, the amendments deprived gays and lesbians of an "equal" right to participate in the political process and advance their interests through the law.

What was so breathtakingly original in this construction was that the courts found this subtle denial of political rights without the aid of any of those measures that used to awaken our sensitivities in the past: The amendments disfranchised no one. They brought forth no literacy tests or contrivances to block voters from the rolls. They removed from no person the right to vote, to run for office, to contribute money or buy advertising to support any candidate or any proposition put before the voters in a referendum. Amendment 2 had passed by a vote of 813,966 to 710,151. The percentage of homosexuals in the state was estimated at

> *"What the [Colorado] amendment was really doing was removing from the legislature the power to legislate . . . on the matter of 'sexual orientation.'"*

about 4 percent, and yet this 4 percent managed to attract to its side the support of 46 percent of the voters. As Judge Jeffrey Bayless admitted, in the county court in Denver, "that is a demonstration of power, not powerlessness."

## The Amendment's Real Intent

Robert Bork put it bluntly in a commentary on the Colorado case: What the gay activists were claiming here was not the equal right to participate in politics, but nothing less than the right to win. And yet, when the oral arguments opened in the Supreme Court, Justice Kennedy remarked, "I've never seen a statute like that." He recalled another case, from California, in which the approval of the voters would be required for any project in public housing. The plan might have been fueled by an animus toward blacks, but it might have sprung quite as well from a concern about property values and the intrusion of cheaper housing. In that case, as Kennedy said, "we could measure the need, the importance, the objectives of the legislature to control low-cost housing against the classification that was adopted." But here, he argued, "the classification was just adopted for its own sake, with reference to all purposes of the law." In Kennedy's reading, the amendment seemed to be barring legislatures from legislating in favor of a whole class of people—namely, gays and lesbians—on any matter that touched the concerns of the law. But what the amendment was really doing was removing from the legislature the power to legislate on a certain class of cases—those involving private judgments, or private discriminations, on the matter of "sexual orientation."

Even some of the defenders of gay rights have conceded the inaptness of Kennedy's argument and that it is embarrassed, most notably, by the Thirteenth Amendment: In forbidding "involuntary servitude," that Amendment put beyond the power of legislatures all over the country the possibility of legislating to protect property in slaves. A whole class of people—owners of slaves—were now cut off from the possibility of securing legislation to advance their interests.

## No Dilution of Rights

When the filter of cliches is stripped away, it should become clear that gays are not faced here with the slightest dilution of their legal rights. If the law protects people, say, from assaults or racial discrimination, those protections of the law are still intact, and they cover homosexuals along with everyone else. So it was jarring, to say the least, to find Justice O'Connor utterly obtuse on this matter during the argument before the court. She raised the prospect of a public library refusing to allow homosexuals to borrow books, and it appeared to her that Amendment 2 would allow "no relief from that." In the same vein, Justice Stephen Breyer conjured up a city facing a rash of "gay-bashing." If the authorities put in a policy to forbid it, would the policy run afoul of Amendment 2? Justice Antonin Scalia quickly pointed out that the laws in Colorado already forbade the "bashing" of anyone, gay or non-gay. "So prohibiting the bashing of gays would not be a special protection, would it?" Or to put it more precisely, the law would not require any special provision to bar the bashing of gays. In the case of libraries and other public facilities, there may simply be a provision that bars discrimination on grounds that bear no connection to the service at hand. Gays may be protected from arbitrary discrimination in the provision of disaster relief, medical care, or library books—without the need to say anything about gays as a class apart, as a group deserving any special recognition or endorsement in the law.

> *"Gays are not faced here with the slightest dilution of their legal rights."*

When the slogans are cleared away, it becomes apparent that the rhetoric of gay rights has merely obscured to the judges the real class of victims here: The people who are threatened with the abridgment of their liberties or rights are the people who hold to the traditional Jewish and Christian teaching on homosexuality; the people who would have the temerity then to respect their own moral understanding in their own private settings. These people find themselves in the position of that wife of a shop owner in Boulder, Colorado, who gave literature on homosexuality to a gay employee. Her husband was then compelled,

> *"The people who are threatened with the abridgment of their liberties or rights are the people who hold to the traditional Jewish and Christian teaching on homosexuality."*

with the levers of the local law, to attend "sensitivity training." In this way has the new regime of "gay rights" made unmistakably clear just what moral understandings it means to punish and repress, even in their private expression.

My friend George Will is persuaded that when the justices settle down to the hard realities of judgment, they will concentrate their minds, read the briefs, and come down finally on the side of the state. Will, the most sober of men, has been strangely touched by the romance of "reason." Perhaps Kennedy and O'Connor will wake in time from their dogmatic slumber—or perhaps Will merely has an unbounded confidence in the power of "sleep-learning." But in any clear-eyed estimate, the side of "gay rights" seems to hold now a 6-3 majority. The same coalition that gave us the decision against term limits can add Justice O'Connor and easily put across this decision. There figures to be no political storm, no outrage in the land, because most people do not have even the faintest notion of what *Romer* v. *Evans* is about. Yet a loss in this case could bring about a vast remodeling of the laws on marriage and the family.

## Legitimizing Homosexuality

For the decision to strike down Amendment 2 would not be taken as a decision merely to guarantee "equal treatment" for gays. The decision would call into question any law that refuses to accord to homosexuality the same legitimacy or standing as that sexuality "imprinted in our natures." And with that decision, the court would also knock out the last prop that allows a state to hold back from accepting "same-sex marriage," the gift that is now being prepared for us by the courts in Hawaii. When a decision finally emerges from Hawaii, gay activists are counting on the "Full Faith and Credit" clause of the Constitution (Art. IV, Sec. 1) to spread the legalization of same-sex marriages to other states. That clause sustains the expectation that the driver's license granted in Illinois will be honored in California, or that the marriage legally performed in Kentucky will be honored in Massachusetts. The presumption would have to be set in favor of honoring these marriages from Hawaii—unless a state may still hold back, on moral grounds, from honoring certain kinds of union (such as the marriage of a man and his natural daughter). But with the case in Colorado, *the court is now likely to remove that ground of objection.* For if Amendment 2 were struck down, the point emerging from the case would be this: that a state may not incorporate, anywhere in its laws, an adverse judgment on homosexuality.

Some conservative writers have warned for over a year that the judges were heading in this direction, and they have suggested a simple move to head them off at the pass: a short constitutional amendment, of one sentence, that there is, in the Constitution, no right of homosexual marriage. (Prof. Charles Rice of the law school at Notre Dame has proposed a draft.) [The House passed a measure—the Defense of Marriage Act—in July 1996 that defines marriage as a union between one man and one woman only. The Senate was expected to pass the bill and Bill Clinton said he would sign it.] An amendment of that kind would not have to pass right away, or at all. The act of introducing or "moving" the amendment would itself send an important signal to the court: It would indicate that someone is watching; that the country is not going to remain passive while the judges add yet another revolution to *Roe* v. *Wade*. That might be enough to give some judges pause; it might encourage them finally to read the briefs, and concentrate their minds.

# Barring Antidiscrimination Laws for Gays and Lesbians Is Constitutional

**by Antonin Scalia, William H. Rehnquist, and Clarence Thomas**

**About the authors:** *Antonin Scalia has served as a U.S. Supreme Court justice since 1986 and is known for his conservative views on many issues. He is joined in his dissenting opinion by Chief Justice William H. Rehnquist and Justice Clarence Thomas.*

The U.S. Supreme Court has mistaken a Kulturkampf [culture struggle] for a fit of spite. The constitutional amendment before us here [Colorado's Amendment 2 in *Romer v. Evans*] is not the manifestation of a "bare . . . desire to harm" homosexuals, but is rather a modest attempt by seemingly tolerant Coloradans to preserve traditional sexual mores against the efforts of a politically powerful minority to revise those mores through use of the laws. That objective, and the means chosen to achieve it, are not only unimpeachable under any constitutional doctrine hitherto pronounced (hence the opinion's heavy reliance upon principles of righteousness rather than judicial holdings); they have been specifically approved by the Congress of the United States and by this Court.

In holding that homosexuality cannot be singled out for disfavorable treatment, the Court contradicts a decision, unchallenged here, pronounced only 10 years ago [*Bowers v. Hardwick*, (1986) upholding Georgia's laws against sodomy], and places the prestige of this institution behind the proposition that opposition to homosexuality is as reprehensible as racial or religious bias. Whether it is or not is precisely the cultural debate that gave rise to the Colorado constitutional amendment (and to the preferential laws against which the amendment was directed). Since the Constitution of the United States says nothing about this subject, it is left to be resolved by normal democratic means, including the democratic adoption of provisions in state constitutions. This Court has no business imposing upon all Americans the resolution favored by

From *Roy Romer v. Richard G. Evans et al.*, 517 U.S. (May 20, 1996).

the elite class from which the Members of this institution are selected, pronouncing that "animosity" toward homosexuality is evil. I vigorously dissent.

## The True Effect of Amendment 2

Let me first discuss Part II of the Court's opinion, its longest section, which is devoted to rejecting the State's arguments that Amendment 2 "puts gays and lesbians in the same position as all other persons," and "does no more than deny homosexuals special rights." The Court concludes that this reading of Amendment 2's language is "implausible" under the "authoritative construction" given Amendment 2 by the Supreme Court of Colorado.

In reaching this conclusion, the Court considers it unnecessary to decide the validity of the State's argument that Amendment 2 does not deprive homosexuals of the "protection [afforded by] general laws and policies that prohibit arbitrary discrimination in governmental and private settings." I agree that we need not resolve that dispute, because the Supreme Court of Colorado has resolved it for us. In *Evans v. Romer*, (1994), the Colorado court stated:

> [I]t is significant to note that Colorado law currently proscribes discrimination against persons who are not suspect classes, including discrimination based on age, marital or family status, veterans' status, and for any legal, off-duty conduct such as smoking tobacco. Of course Amendment 2 is not intended to have any effect on this legislation, but seeks only to prevent the adoption of antidiscrimination laws intended to protect gays, lesbians, and bisexuals.

The Court utterly fails to distinguish this portion of the Colorado court's opinion. Colorado Rev. Stat. 24-34-402.5 (Supp. 1995), which this passage authoritatively declares not to be affected by Amendment 2, was respondents' primary example of a generally applicable law whose protections would be unavailable to homosexuals under Amendment 2. The clear import of the Colorado court's conclusion that it is not affected is that "general laws and policies that prohibit arbitrary discrimination" would continue to prohibit discrimination on the basis of homosexual conduct as well. This analysis, which is fully in accord with (indeed, follows inescapably from) the text of the constitutional provision, lays to rest such horribles, raised in the course of oral argument, as the prospect that assaults upon homosexuals could not be prosecuted. The amendment prohibits special treatment of homosexuals, and nothing more. It would not affect, for example, a requirement of state law that pensions be paid to all retiring state employees with a certain length of service; homosexual employees, as well as others, would

> *"[Colorado's Amendment 2] is rather a modest attempt . . . to preserve traditional sexual mores."*

be entitled to that benefit. But it would prevent the State or any municipality from making death-benefit payments to the "life partner" of a homosexual when it does not make such payments to the long-time roommate of a nonhomosexual employee. Or again, it does not affect the requirement of the State's general insurance laws that customers be afforded coverage without discrimination unrelated to anticipated risk. Thus, homosexuals could not be denied coverage, or charged a greater premium, with respect to auto collision insurance; but neither the State nor any municipality could require that distinctive health insurance risks associated with homosexuality (if there are any) be ignored.

## Terminal Silliness

Despite all of its hand-wringing about the potential effect of Amendment 2 on general antidiscrimination laws, the Court's opinion ultimately does not dispute all this, but assumes it to be true. The only denial of equal treatment it contends homosexuals have suffered is this: They may not obtain preferential treatment without amending the state constitution. That is to say, the principle underlying the Court's opinion is that one who is accorded equal treatment under the laws, but cannot as readily as others obtain preferential treatment under the laws, has been denied equal protection of the laws. If merely stating this alleged "equal protection" violation does not suffice to refute it, our constitutional jurisprudence has achieved terminal silliness. . . .

> *"This Court has no business imposing upon all Americans the resolution . . . that 'animosity' toward homosexuality is evil."*

## A Legitimate, Rational Basis

I turn next to whether there was a legitimate rational basis for the substance of the constitutional amendment—for the prohibition of special protection for homosexuals. It is unsurprising that the Court avoids discussion of this question, since the answer is so obviously yes. The case most relevant to the issue is not even mentioned in the Court's opinion: In *Bowers v. Hardwick*, (1986), we held that the Constitution does not prohibit what virtually all States had done from the founding of the Republic until very recent years making homosexual conduct a crime. That holding is unassailable, except by those who think that the Constitution changes to suit current fashions. But in any event it is a given in the present case: Respondents' briefs did not urge overruling *Bowers*, and at oral argument respondents' counsel expressly disavowed any intent to seek such overruling. If it is constitutionally permissible for a State to make homosexual conduct criminal, surely it is constitutionally permissible for a State to enact other laws merely disfavoring homosexual conduct. (As the Court of Appeals for the District of Columbia Circuit has aptly put it: "If the Court [in *Bowers*] was unwilling to object to state laws that criminalize the behavior that defines the class, it is hardly open . . . to conclude that state sponsored discrimination against the class is invidious. After all, there can hardly be more palpable discrimination against a class than making the conduct that defines the class criminal." And a fortiori it is constitutionally permissible for a State to adopt a provision not even disfavoring homosexual conduct, but merely prohibiting all levels of state government from bestowing special protections upon homosexual conduct. Respondents (who, unlike the Court, cannot afford the luxury of ignoring inconvenient precedent) counter *Bowers* with the argument that a greater-includes-the-lesser rationale cannot justify Amendment 2's application to individuals who do not engage in homosexual acts, but are merely of homosexual "orientation." Some courts of appeals have concluded that, with respect to laws of this sort at least, that is a distinction without a difference. ("[F]or purposes of these proceedings, it is virtually impossible to distinguish or separate individuals of a particular orientation which predisposes them toward a particular sexual conduct from those who actually engage in that particular type of sexual conduct"); *Steffan v. Perry*, (1994). The Supreme Court of Colorado itself appears to be of this view: "Amendment 2 targets this class of persons based on four characteristics: sexual orientation; conduct; practices; and relationships. Each characteristic provides a potentially different way of identifying that class of persons who are gay, lesbian, or bisexual. These four characteristics are not truly severable from one another because each provides nothing more than a different way of identifying the same class of persons."

## No Violation of Equal Protection Laws

But assuming that, in Amendment 2, a person of homosexual "orientation" is someone who does not engage in homosexual conduct but merely has a tendency or desire to do so, *Bowers* still suffices to establish a rational basis for the provision. If it is rational to criminalize the conduct, surely it is rational to deny special favor and protection to those with a self-avowed tendency or desire to engage in the conduct. Indeed, where criminal sanctions are not involved, homosexual "orientation" is an acceptable stand-in for homosexual conduct. A State "does not violate the Equal Protection Clause merely because the classifications made by its laws are imperfect," *Dandridge v. Williams*, (1970). Just as a policy barring the hiring of methadone users as transit employees does not violate equal protection simply because some methadone users pose no threat to passenger safety, and just as a mandatory retirement age of 50 for police officers does not violate equal protection even though it prematurely ends the careers of many policemen over 50 who still have the capacity to do the job, Amendment 2 is not constitutionally invalid simply because it could have been drawn more precisely so as to withdraw special antidiscrimination protections only from those of homosexual "orientation" who actually engage in homosexual conduct. As Justice Anthony Kennedy wrote, when he was on the Court of Appeals, in a case in-

> *"The amendment prohibits special treatment of homosexuals, and nothing more."*

volving discharge of homosexuals from the Navy: "Nearly any statute which classifies people may be irrational as applied in particular cases. Discharge of the particular plaintiffs before us would be rational, under minimal scrutiny, not because their particular cases present the dangers which justify Navy policy, but instead because the general policy of discharging all homosexuals is rational.". . .

## No Constitutional Basis

The foregoing suffices to establish what the Court's failure to cite any case remotely in point would lead one to suspect: No principle set forth in the Constitution, nor even any imagined by this Court in the past 200 years, prohibits what Colorado has done here. But the case for Colorado is much stronger than that. What it has done is not only unprohibited, but eminently reasonable, with close, congressionally approved precedent in earlier constitutional practice.

First, as to its eminent reasonableness. The Court's opinion contains grim, disapproving hints that Coloradans have been guilty of "animus" or "animosity" toward homosexuality, as though that has been established as Unamerican. Of course it is our moral heritage that one should not hate any human being or class of human beings. But I had thought that one could consider certain conduct reprehensible—murder, for example, or polygamy, or cruelty to animals—and could exhibit even "animus" toward such conduct. Surely that is the only sort of "animus" at issue here: moral disapproval of homosexual conduct, the same sort of moral disapproval that produced the centuries-old criminal laws that we held constitutional in *Bowers*. The Colorado amendment does not, to speak entirely precisely, prohibit giving favored status to people who are homosexuals; they can be favored for many reasons—for example, because they are senior citizens or members of racial minorities. But it prohibits giving them favored status because of their homosexual conduct—that is, it prohibits favored status for homosexuality.

> *"If it is rational to criminalize the conduct, surely it is rational to deny special favor and protection to those . . . [who] desire to engage in the conduct."*

But though Coloradans are, as I say, entitled to be hostile toward homosexual conduct, the fact is that the degree of hostility reflected by Amendment 2 is the smallest conceivable. The Court's portrayal of Coloradans as a society fallen victim to pointless, hate-filled "gay-bashing" is so false as to be comical. Colorado not only is one of the 25 States that have repealed their antisodomy laws, but was among the first to do so. But the society that eliminates criminal punishment for homosexual acts does not necessarily abandon the view that homosexuality is morally wrong and socially harmful; often, abolition simply reflects the view that enforcement of such criminal laws involves unseemly intrusion into the intimate lives of citizens.

There is a problem, however, which arises when criminal sanction of homosexuality is eliminated but moral and social disapprobation of homosexuality is meant to be retained. The Court cannot be unaware of that problem; it is evident in many cities of the country, and occasionally bubbles to the surface of the news, in heated political disputes over such matters as the introduction into local schools of books teaching that homosexuality is an optional and fully acceptable "alternate life style." The problem (a problem, that is, for those who wish to retain social disapprobation of homosexuality) is that, because those who engage in homosexual conduct tend to reside in disproportionate numbers in certain communities, have high disposable income, and of course care about homosexual-rights issues much more ardently than the public at large, they possess political power much greater than their numbers, both locally and statewide. Quite understandably, they devote this political power to achieving not merely a grudging social toleration, but full social acceptance, of homosexuality. . . .

> *"No principle set forth in the Constitution, nor even any imagined by this Court in the past 200 years, prohibits what Colorado has done here."*

By the time Coloradans were asked to vote on Amendment 2, their exposure to homosexuals' quest for social endorsement was not limited to newspaper accounts of happenings in places such as New York, Los Angeles, San Francisco, and Key West. Three Colorado cities—Aspen, Boulder, and Denver—had enacted ordinances that listed "sexual orientation" as an impermissible ground for discrimination, equating the moral disapproval of homosexual conduct with racial and religious bigotry. The phenomenon had even appeared statewide: the Governor of Colorado had signed an executive order pronouncing that "in the State of Colorado we recognize the diversity in our pluralistic society and strive to bring an end to discrimination in any form," and directing state agency-heads to "ensure non-discrimination" in hiring and promotion based on, among other things, "sexual orientation." I do not mean to be critical of these legislative successes; homosexuals are as entitled to use the legal system for reinforcement of their moral sentiments as are the rest of society. But they are subject to being countered by lawful, democratic countermeasures as well.

## Making Democracy Unconstitutional

That is where Amendment 2 came in. It sought to counter both the geographic concentration and the disproportionate political power of homosexuals by (1) resolving the controversy at the statewide level, and (2) making the election a single-issue contest for both sides. It put directly, to all the citizens of the State, the question: Should homosexuality be given special protection? They answered no. The Court asserts that this most democratic of procedures is unconstitutional. Lacking any cases to establish that facially absurd proposition, it simply asserts that it must be unconstitutional, because it has never happened before.

> [Amendment 2] identifies persons by a single trait and then denies them protection across the board. The resulting disqualification of a class of persons from the right to seek specific protection from the law is unprecedented in our jurisprudence. The absence of precedent for Amendment 2 is itself instructive. . . .
>
> It is not within our constitutional tradition to enact laws of this sort. Central both to the idea of the rule of law and to our own Constitution's guarantee of equal protection is the principle that government and each of its parts remain open on impartial terms to all who seek its assistance.

As I have noted above, this is proved false every time a state law prohibiting or disfavoring certain conduct is passed, because such a law prevents the adversely affected group—whether drug addicts, or smokers, or gun owners, or motorcyclists—from changing the policy thus established in "each of [the] parts" of the State. What the Court says is even demonstrably false at the constitutional level. The Eighteenth Amendment to the Federal Constitution, for example, deprived those who drank alcohol not only of the power to alter the policy of prohibition locally or through state legislation, but even of the power to alter it through state constitutional amendment or federal legislation. The Establishment Clause of the First Amendment prevents theocrats from having their way by converting their fellow citizens at the local, state, or federal statutory level; as does the Republican Form of Government Clause prevent monarchists.

## Polygamy and Homosexuality

But there is a much closer analogy, one that involves precisely the effort by the majority of citizens to preserve its view of sexual morality statewide, against the efforts of a geographically concentrated and politically powerful minority to undermine it. The constitutions of the States of Arizona, Idaho, New Mexico, Oklahoma, and Utah to this day contain provisions stating that polygamy is "forever prohibited." Polygamists, and those who have a polygamous "orientation," have been "singled out" by these provisions for much more severe treatment than merely denial of favored status; and that treatment can only be changed by achieving amendment of the state constitutions. The Court's disposition today suggests that these provisions are unconstitutional, and that polygamy must be permitted in these States on a state-legislated, or perhaps even local-option, basis—unless, of course, polygamists for some reason have fewer constitutional rights than homosexuals. . . .

> *"The Colorado amendment does not . . . prohibit giving favored status to people who are homosexuals. . . . It prohibits favored status for homosexuality."*

I cannot say that this Court has explicitly approved any of these state constitutional provisions; but it has approved a territorial statutory provision that went even further, depriving polygamists of the ability even to achieve a constitutional amendment, by depriving them of the power to vote. In *Davis v. Beason*, (1890), Justice Stephen Field wrote for a unanimous Court:

> In our judgment, 501 of the Revised Statutes of Idaho Territory, which provides that "no person . . . who is a bigamist or polygamist or who teaches, advises, counsels, or encourages any person or persons to become bigamists or polygamists, or to commit any other crime defined by law, or to enter into what is known as plural or celestial marriage, or who is a member of any order, organization or association which teaches, advises, counsels, or encourages its members or devotees or any other persons to commit the crime of bigamy or polygamy, or any other crime defined by law . . . is permitted to vote at any election, or to hold any position or office of honor, trust, or profit within this Territory," is not open to any constitutional or legal objection.

To the extent, if any, that this opinion permits the imposition of adverse consequences upon mere abstract advocacy of polygamy, it has of course been overruled by later cases. But the proposition that polygamy can be criminalized, and those engaging in that crime deprived of the vote, remains good law. *Beason* rejected the argument that "such discrimination is a denial of the equal protection of the laws." Among the Justices joining in that rejection were the two whose views in other cases the Court treats as equal-protection lodestars—Justice John Harlan, who was to proclaim in *Plessy v. Ferguson*, (1896) (dissenting opinion), that the Constitution "neither knows nor tolerates classes among citizens," and Justice Joseph P. Bradley, who had earlier declared that "class legislation . . . [is] obnoxious to the prohibitions of the Fourteenth Amendment," *Civil Rights Cases*, (1883).

This Court cited *Beason* with approval as recently as 1993, in an opinion authored by the same Justice who writes for the Court's majority opinion [Anthony Kennedy]. That opinion said: "[A]dverse impact will not always lead to a finding of impermissible targeting. For example, a social harm may have been a legitimate concern of government for reasons quite apart from discrimination." It remains to be explained how 501 of the Idaho Revised Statutes was not an "impermissible targeting" of polygamists, but (the much more mild) Amendment 2 is an "impermissible targeting" of homosexuals. Has the Court concluded that the perceived social harm of polygamy is a "legitimate concern of government," and the perceived social harm of homosexuality is not?

*"[The U.S. Supreme Court's majority] opinion has no foundation in American constitutional law, and barely pretends to."*

I strongly suspect that the answer to the last question is yes, which leads me to the last point I wish to make: The Court, announcing that Amendment 2 "defies . . . conventional [constitutional] inquiry" and "confounds [the] normal process of judicial review," employs a constitutional theory heretofore unknown to frustrate Colorado's reasonable effort to preserve traditional American moral values. The Court's stern disapproval of "animosity" towards homosexuality might be compared with what an earlier Court (including the revered Justices Harlan and Bradley) said in *Murphy v. Ramsey*, (1885), rejecting a constitutional challenge to a United States statute that denied the franchise in federal territories to those who engaged in polygamous cohabitation:

> [C]ertainly no legislation can be supposed more wholesome and necessary in the founding of a free, self-governing commonwealth, fit to take rank as one of the co-ordinate States of the Union, than that which seeks to establish it on the basis of the idea of the family, as consisting in and springing from the union for life of one man and one woman in the holy estate of matrimony; the sure foundation of all that is stable and noble in our civilization; the best guaranty of that reverent morality which is the source of all beneficent progress in social and political improvement.

I would not myself indulge in such official praise for heterosexual monogamy, because I think it no business of the courts (as opposed to the political branches) to take sides in this culture war.

But the Court has done so, not only by inventing a novel and extravagant constitutional doctrine to take the victory away from traditional forces, but even by verbally disparaging as bigotry adherence to traditional attitudes. To suggest, for example, that this constitutional amendment springs from nothing more than "a bare . . . desire to harm a politically unpopular group," (1973), is nothing short of insulting. It is also nothing short of preposterous to call "politically unpopular" a group which enjoys enormous influence in American media and politics, and which, as the trial court here noted, though composing no more than 4% of the population had the support of 46% of the voters on Amendment 2.

When the Court takes sides in the culture wars, it tends to be with the knights rather than the villeins [serfs]—and more specifically with the Templars [London barristers], reflecting the views and values of the lawyer class from which the Court's Members are drawn. How that class feels about homosexuality will be evident to anyone who wishes to interview job applicants at virtually any of the Nation's law schools. The interviewer may refuse to offer a job because the applicant is a Republican; because he is an adulterer; because he went to the wrong prep school or belongs to the wrong country club; because he eats snails; because he is a womanizer; because she wears real-animal fur; or even because he hates the Chicago Cubs. But if the interviewer should wish not to be an associate or part-

> *"Amendment 2 is designed to prevent piecemeal deterioration of the sexual morality favored by a majority of Coloradans."*

ner of an applicant because he disapproves of the applicant's homosexuality, then he will have violated the pledge which the Association of American Law Schools requires all its member-schools to exact from job interviewers: "assurance of the employer's willingness" to hire homosexuals. This law-school view of what "prejudices" must be stamped out may be contrasted with the more plebeian attitudes that apparently still prevail in the United States Congress, which has been unresponsive to repeated attempts to extend to homosexuals the protections of federal civil rights laws, and which took the pains to exclude them specifically from the Americans With Disabilities Act of 1990.

## No Foundation in Constitutional Law

[The U.S. Supreme Court's majority] opinion has no foundation in American constitutional law, and barely pretends to. The people of Colorado have adopted an entirely reasonable provision which does not even disfavor homosexuals in any substantive sense, but merely denies them preferential treatment. Amendment 2 is designed to prevent piecemeal deterioration of the sexual morality favored by a majority of Coloradans, and is not only an appropriate means to that legitimate end, but a means that Americans have employed before. Striking it down is an act, not of judicial judgment, but of political will. I dissent.

# Bibliography

**Books**

| | |
|---|---|
| John Boswell | *Same Sex Unions in Premodern Europe*. New York: Villard, 1994. |
| John Carey, ed. | *Gays and Lesbians in the Military: Essays by Mainline Church Leaders*. Lewiston, NY: Edwin Mellen Press, 1993. |
| William N. Eskridge | *The Case for Same-Sex Marriage: From Sexual Liberty to Civilized Commitment*. New York: Free Press, 1996. |
| George Grant and Mark A. Horne | *Legislating Immorality: The Homosexual Movement Comes Out of the Closet*. Franklin, TN: Moody Press and Legacy Communications, 1993. |
| Roger Magnuson | *Are 'Gay Rights' Right?* Portland, OR: Multnomah Press, 1990. |
| Tony Marco | *Gay Rights: A Public Health Disaster and Civil Wrong*. Ft. Lauderdale, FL: Coral Ridge Ministries, 1992. |
| Brian McNaught | *Gay Issues in the Workplace*. New York: St. Martin's Press, 1993. |
| Michael Nava and Robert Dawidoff | *Created Equal: Why Gay Rights Matter to America*. New York: St. Martin's Press, 1994. |
| Ronald D. Ray | *Gays: In or Out? The U.S. Military and Homosexuals—a Sourcebook*. McLean, VA: Brassey's, 1993. |
| Andrew Sullivan | *Virtually Normal: An Argument About Homosexuality*. New York: Knopf, 1995. |
| Urvashi Vaid | *Virtual Equality: The Mainstreaming of Gay and Lesbian Liberation*. New York: Anchor Books, 1995. |
| Melissa Wells-Petry | *Exclusion: Homosexuals and the Right to Serve*. Washington, DC: Regnery Gateway, 1993. |
| Dan Woog | *School's Out: The Impact of Gay and Lesbian Issues on American Schools*. Boston: Alyson Press, 1995. |
| Steven Zeeland | *The Masculine Marine: Homoeroticism in the U.S. Marine Corps*. New York: Haworth Press, 1996. |

# Gay Rights

**Periodicals**

| | |
|---|---|
| Hadley Arkes | "Gay Marriage in 1996?" *American Enterprise*, May/June 1995. |
| Linda Bowles | "When Propaganda Cross-dresses as Science," *Conservative Chronicle*, May 29, 1996. Available from Box 29, Hampton, IA 50441. |
| Ralph deToledano | "The Fruits of the Gay-Women's Lib Revolution," *Conservative Chronicle*, April 17, 1996. |
| Elaine Donnelly | "ROTC Program Defies Gay-Exclusion Rule," *Insight*, May 27, 1996. Available from 3600 New York Ave. NE, Washington, DC 20002. |
| Randy Frame | "Seeking a Right to the Rite," *Christianity Today*, March 4, 1996. |
| Michelle Garcia | "Altared States: Same Sex Marriage and Civil Rights," *Third Force*, March/April 1996. |
| Katia Hetter | "The New Civil Rights Battle," *U.S. News & World Report*, June 3, 1996. |
| Dirk Johnson | "Gay-Rights Movement Ventures Beyond Urban America," *New York Times*, January 21, 1996. |
| David A. Kaplan and Daniel Klaidman | "A Battle, Not the War," *Newsweek*, June 3, 1996. |
| R. Cort Kirkwood | "Homosexuality as a Protected Class," *Insight*, November 13, 1995. |
| John Leo | "Civil Rights Laws Already Serve to Protect Gays," *Conservative Chronicle*, October 25, 1995. |
| Gilbert S. Maguire | "The Most Politically Significant Supreme Court Case of 1996," *American Enterprise*, January/February 1996. |
| Katha Pollitt | "Gay Marriage? Don't Say I Didn't Warn You," *Nation*, April 29, 1996. |
| Gabriel Rotello | "To Have and to Hold: The Case for Gay Marriage," *Nation*, June 24, 1996. |
| Lisa Schiffren | "Gay Marriage, an Oxymoron," *New York Times*, March 23, 1996. |
| Tony Snow | "Activists Present Society with a False Choice," *Conservative Chronicle*, April 17, 1996. |
| Joseph A. Strada | "Clinton's Army: A Catholic Soldier's Response," *Fidelity*, October 1993. Available from 206 Marquette Ave., South Bend, IN 46617. |
| Andrew Sullivan | "What You Do," *New Republic*, March 18, 1996. |
| Scott Tucker | "Panic in the Pentagon: Will Queers Demoralize the Military?" *Z Magazine*, June 1993. |
| *U.S. News & World Report* | "Should Gay Marriage Be Legal?" June 3, 1996. |

# Organizations to Contact

The editors have compiled the following list of organizations concerned with the issues debated in this book. The descriptions are derived from materials provided by the organizations themselves. All have publications or information available for interested readers. The list was compiled on the date of publication of the present volume; names, addresses, phone and fax numbers, and e-mail/internet addresses may change. Be aware that many organizations take several weeks or longer to respond to inquiries, so allow as much time as possible.

**American Civil Liberties Union (ACLU)**
132 W. 43rd St.
New York, NY 10036
(212) 944-9800
fax: (212) 359-5290
internet: http://www.aclu.org

The ACLU is the nation's oldest and largest civil liberties organization. Its Lesbian and Gay Rights/AIDS Project, started in 1986, handles litigation, education, and public policy work on behalf of gays and lesbians. The ACLU publishes the handbook *The Rights of Lesbians and Gay Men*, the briefing paper "Lesbian and Gay Rights," and the monthly newsletter *Civil Liberties Alert*.

**Canadian Lesbian and Gay Archives**
Box 639, Station A
Toronto, ON M5W 1G2
CANADA
(416) 777-2755
internet: http://www.clga.ca/archives

The archives collects and maintains information and materials relating to the gay and lesbian rights movement in Canada and elsewhere. Its collection of records and other materials documenting the stories of lesbians and gay men and their organizations in Canada is available to the public for the purpose of education and research. It also publishes an annual newsletter, *Lesbian and Gay Archivist*.

**Concerned Women for America (CWA)**
370 L'Enfant Promenade SW, Suite 800
Washington, DC 20024
(202) 488-7000
fax: (202) 488-0806

CWA works to strengthen the traditional family by applying Judeo-Christian moral standards. It opposes gay marriage and the granting of additional civil rights protections to gays and lesbians. It publishes the monthly newsmagazine *Family Voice* and various position papers on gay marriage and gays in the military.

**Family Research Council (FRC)**
700 13th St. NW, Suite 500
Washington, DC 20005
(202) 393-2100
fax: (202) 393-2134

The council is a research, resource, and educational organization that promotes the traditional family, which the council defines as a group of people bound by marriage, blood, or adoption. The council opposes gay marriage and adoption rights. It publishes numerous reports from a conservative perspective on issues affecting the family, including homosexuality. These publications include the monthly newsletter *Washington Watch* and bimonthly journal *Family Policy*.

**Family Research Institute (FRI)**
PO Box 62640
Colorado Springs, CO 80962
(303) 681-3113

FRI promotes information about sexual, family, and substance abuse issues. The institute believes that, like drug abuse and prostitution, homosexuality is a public health problem. FRI publishes the newsletter *Family Research Report* six times a year as well as the position papers "Homosexuals in the Military" and "What's Wrong With Gay Marriage?"

**Lambda Legal Defense and Education Fund, Inc.**
666 Broadway, Suite 1200
New York, NY 10012
(212) 995-8585
fax: (212) 995-2306

Lambda is a public-interest law firm committed to achieving full recognition of the civil rights of lesbians, gay men, and people with HIV/AIDS. The firm addresses a variety of areas, including equal marriage rights, the military, parenting and relationship issues, and domestic-partner benefits. It publishes the quarterly *Lambda Update* and the pamphlet *Freedom to Marry*.

**National Center for Lesbian Rights**
870 Market St., Suite 570
San Francisco, CA 94102
(415) 392-6257
fax: (415) 392-8442

The center is a public-interest law office providing legal counseling and representation for victims of sexual-orientation discrimination. Primary areas of advice include child custody and parenting, employment, housing, the military, and insurance. Among the center's publications are the handbooks *Recognizing Lesbian and Gay Families: Strategies for Obtaining Domestic Partners Benefits* and *Lesbian and Gay Parenting: A Psychological and Legal Perspective*.

**National Gay and Lesbian Task Force (NGLTF)**
2320 17th St. NW
Washington, DC 20009-2702
(202) 332-6483
fax: (202) 332-0207

NGLTF is a civil-rights advocacy organization that lobbies Congress and the White House on a range of civil rights and AIDS issues. The organization is working to make same-sex marriage legal. It publishes numerous papers and pamphlets, and the booklet *To Have and to Hold: Organizing for Our Right to Marry* and the fact sheet "Lesbian and Gay Families."

**Servicemembers Legal Defense Network (SLDN)**
PO Box 53013
Washington, DC 20009-9013
(202) 328-3244
fax: (202) 797-1635
e-mail: SLDN1@aol.com
internet: http://xq.com/sldn/

SLDN is a legal watchdog organization that represents gay, lesbian, bisexual, and heterosexual servicemembers who have been harassed within the military. It publishes "Conduct Unbecoming: The Second Annual Report on 'Don't Ask, Don't Tell, Don't Pursue' Violations."

**Traditional Values Coalition**
139 C St. SE
Washington, DC 20003
(202) 547-8570
fax: (202) 546-6403

The coalition strives to restore what the group believes are traditional moral and spiritual values in American government, schools, media, and the fiber of American society. It believes that gay rights threaten the family unit and extend civil rights beyond what the coalition considers appropriate limits. The coalition publishes the quarterly newsletter *Traditional Values Report*, as well as various information papers, one of which specifically addresses same-sex marriage.

# Index

Achtenberg, Roberta, 35, 37
adoption, by gay couples, 37, 167
Affidavit of Domestic Partnership, 21
African-Americans
  civil rights movement not analogous to
    gay rights, 164–65
  exclusion from military is analogous to
    gay ban, 150
AIDS, 110–12
  epidemic must be fought, 137
  fear of, and domestic partner insurance,
    20
Alexander the Great, 131
Amendment 2 (Colorado), 135, 137, 152
  allowed moral judgment on
    homosexuality, 167–68
  deprives gays of equal protection, 156
  did not dilute rights of gays, 169
  text of, 165
  was reasonable, 176
  see also Romer v. Evans
American Civil Liberties Union (ACLU),
  52, 143
American Medical Association, 124
American Psychiatric Association, 123–24
antidiscrimination laws
  backlash against, 144
  vs. "special" rights, 134, 139, 147
antimiscegenation laws, 143
Apple Computer, 20, 23
Aristotle, 75
Arkes, Hadley, 60, 166
Armitage, Michael, 126
Austin American-Statesman, 23

Baehr v. Lewin, 46, 51
Baker, Rosalyn, 51
Bawer, Bruce, 51
Bay Area Reporter, 162
Beckett, John, 129
Beller, Dennis, 125
Ben and Jerry's Homemade, 20

Benecke, Michelle M., 91
Berkeley, California, 21
Bible, 73, 74
Binger, Jerry, 87
Blackmun, Harry A., 146
Blair, Tony, 131
"blue" discharges, 121
Boaz, David, 25
Bogan, E. Carrington, 31
Bork, Robert, 168
Borkin, Michael, 162
Bowers v. Hardwick, 50, 82, 150, 167, 172,
  173
Bozett, Frederick W., 87
Bray, Robert, 135
Breyer, Stephen, 169
Brown, Simon, 126, 130
Brown v. Board of Education, 149, 150
Bullock, Charles, 25
Butterfield, Barbara, 26

Cameli, Mary N., 30
Cameron, Paul, 88
Cammermeyer, Margarethe, 116
Cantrell, Mark E., 100
The Capital Times, 164
Carroll, Vincent, 135
Cayetano, Benjamin, 46, 49
Chambers, Jack, 23
Cheney, Dick, 115
Clinton, Bill, 37, 40, 91, 99, 105, 117, 171
Considering Parenthood (Pies), 36
corporate benefits, for domestic partners
  companies offering, 20, 28, 45
  cost is low, 20
  purposes of, 21
  rewards immoral behavior, 24
Crawford v. Davis, 122
Created Equal (Nava and Dawidoff), 136

Dandridge v. Williams, 175
Davidson, Jerome, 51

# Index

*Davis v. Beason*, 158, 179
Dawidoff, Robert, 136
Defense of Marriage Act, 171
*Department of Agriculture v. Moreno*, 159
Diagnostic and Statistical Manual of
  Mental Disorders, 2nd ed. (DSM-II),
  123–24
domestic partnership
  businesses offering, 45
  does not confer benefits of marriage, 67
  laws conferring are needed, 34
  municipalities offering, 21, 45, 144
  same-sex vs. heterosexual, 25
Donegan, Craig, 91
Donovan, James A., 95
"Don't ask, don't tell" policy, 91, 116

Edwards, Jaki, 88
*Eisenstadt v. Baird*, 145
Emerson, Ralph Waldo, 142
employment
  benefits
    cost to companies is low, 20
    denial to heterosexual couples is
      discriminatory, 27
  discrimination
    laws protect gays from, 147
Equal Protection Clause, 145, 175
  Amendment 2 violates, 157
Evans, Anthony, 165
*Evans v. Romer*, 153, 173

*Families We Choose* (Weston), 36
family
  nontraditional
    denial of benefits to, 31
    majority of Americans live in, 141
    special status of, 30
  two-parent, is being assaulted, 38
Farah, Joseph, 27
Federation for American Immigration
  Reform, 42
*In re Fidel Armando Toboso-Alfonso*, 41
Field, Stephen, 179
*First Things*, 73
foreigners, gay and lesbian
  persecution of is well-documented, 39–40
  should not be granted asylum in U.S., 41
Fourteenth Amendment, 157
Frank, Barney, 42
Franklin, John N., 164
Freeman, Roger, 126
Freud, Sigmund, 122

Gay and Lesbian Human Rights
  Commission, 40
gay couples
  domestic-partner benefits for, 27
  rewards immoral behavior, 24
gay leaders, 26
gay parents
  can raise well-adjusted children, 69–71
  desire for children transcends sexual
    orientation, 69
  research on gay parenting is biased, 86
  support groups for, 35–36
gays and lesbians
  are promiscuous, 89, 109
  do not seek societal approval, 137
  have political clout, 163
  should be allowed to marry, 53
  should receive employment benefits, 18
    con, 23
  *see also* homosexuals
Gill, Thomas, 46
Glendon, Mary Ann, 149
Goldwater, Barry, 115
Grady, Graeme, 128
Gray, William, 42
*Griswold v. Connecticut*, 37, 145

*Harley v. Irish-American Gay, Lesbian, and
  Bisexual Group of Boston, Inc.*, 155
hate crimes, 144
Hawaii, court ruling on gay marriage in, 46,
  47, 58, 67, 72
Hays, David, 24
Hitchens, Donna, 35
homosexuality
  acquired vs. innate basis of, 133–34
  biblical injunction against, 73–74
  institutional origin of, 162
  is gender-identity problem, 85
  as mental illness, 122–23
  military policy on, 123
    is based on prejudice, 126, 129
    in NATO countries, 130
    during World War II, 121, 122
  and polygamy, 178
*Homosexuality and the Family* (Bozett), 87,
  88
homosexuals
  claim "special" rights, 134, 160
  want equal rights, 139, 147
  *see also* gays and lesbians
Human Rights Campaign Fund, 135
*Human Sexuality* (Masters, Johnson, and

Kolodny), 161

Immigration and Naturalization Service, 39, 40
individualism, 142
insurance, for domestic partners, 20
*Issues and Controversies on File*, 44

James, William, 149
John Paul II, 50
Jones, Franklin D., 121
Julius Caesar, 131

Kameny, Frank E., 135
Katzenstein, Mary, 92
Kennedy, Anthony, 152, 168, 175
*Kentucky v. Wasson*, 146
King, Martin Luther, Jr., 136
Kinsey Institute, 161
Kirkpatrick, Melanie, 47, 48
Kitchener, Lord, 131
Knight, Robert H., 83, 84
Knight, William, 47, 48, 50
Kohn, Richard H., 118
Koppelman, Andrew, 51
Korb, Lawrence, 92, 115
Koshes, Ronald J., 121
Kowalski, Sharon, 32–33
Kristol, Elizabeth, 73
Kritchevsky, Barbara, 36

Lambda Legal Defense and Education Fund, 21, 48, 52, 66
Larimer, Robert, Jr., 50
Leo, John, 47
*The Lesbian and Gay Parenting Handbook* (Martin), 85
Lesbian and Gay Rights Project, 144, 147
LeVay, Simon, 162
Levi Strauss, 20
Livingston, Mark, 130
Lott, Trent, 26
Lotus Development Corporation, 20, 22, 26, 45
*Louisiana Gas & Elec. Co. v. Coleman*, 158
*Loving v. Virginia*, 49, 145
Luddy, John, 91, 92, 93
Lustig-Prean, Duncan, 129

*The Male Couple* (McWhirter and Mattison), 89
Marco, Tony, 160
marriage

caretaking benefit of, 62, 63–64
civilizing effect of, 62–63
heterosexual
  is threatened by same-sex marriage, 76
  is undermined by giving benefits to unmarried heterosexuals, 25
  procreation as basis for, 31, 59–60
  interracial restrictions on, 68, 77, 143
purpose of, 58
same-sex
  biblical argument against, 73
  denial of is unjust, 48–49
  has always existed, 55
  is important to gays and lesbians, 136
  if legalized, should be expected of gays, 64–65
  liberal argument for, 53, 54
  national debate on, 52
  opposition to, 47–48
  provides role models for gay children, 56
  religious opposition to, 44, 50, 68, 73–74
  serves social purposes, 64
  undermines institution of marriage, 50–51
  violates natural law, 75
in secular society, 59
state-sanctioned
  could restrict benefits, 82
  gays should not seek, 80
  will not help gays, 81
traditional definition of, 67
Marshall, George C., 120
Martin, April, 69, 85
Marx, Karl, 149
The Mattachine Society, 135
Mattison, Andrew, 89
MCA, Inc., 20
McCarthy era, 144
McFeeley, Tim, 135
McNaught, Brian, 18
McWhirter, David, 89
Microsoft, 20, 26
*Military Necessity and Homosexuality* (Ray), 108
military service
  discharge of gays from, 93
  gays have served honorably in, 115, 131
  gays present medical risk in, 108
  homophobia in, 124
  policy on homosexuals in, 123
    in Britain, 126

ending ban is attack on prejudice, 57
enforcement of wastes money, 115,
130–31
no valid reason for ban, 115
social strictures supporting, 124, 125
during World War II, 121, 122
privacy is restricted in, 102–103
racial integration of, 93, 116, 120
undermines prejudice, 119
women in, 129
Mill, John Stuart, 77
Minogue, Kenneth, 76
miscegenation laws, 77
anti-, 143
Mixner, David, 140
Moberly, Elizabeth, 88
Montefiore Medical Center, 20, 26
*The Moral Sense* (Wilson), 60, 62, 72
Moskos, Charles, 94
Mountbatten, Lord, 131
*Murphy v. Ramsey*, 180

Nava, Michael, 136
Nelson, Lars-Erik, 41
*Newsweek*, 35, 162
poll on
adoption by gay parents, 52
domestic-partner benefits and gay
marriage, 48
*New York Times*, 50, 51, 168
Nunn, Robert, 130
Nunn, Sam, 97

O'Connor, Sandra Day, 169
*Of Women Born* (Rich), 36
Osburn, C. Dixon, 91
*Out* magazine, 42

Palmer, Alasdair, 126
Paniccia, Tom, 116
Pataki, George, 25, 26
Peery, J. Craig, 87
Pies, Cheri, 36
*Plessy v. Ferguson*, 152
polls
on adoption by gay parents, 52
on domestic-partner benefits and same-
sex marriage, 48
on ending military ban on gays, 96
polygamy, and homosexuality, 178
Powell, Colin, 93, 97, 150
Powell, Lewis F., 146
Prager, Dennis, 73

procreation, as basis for marriage, 51
argument against, 60–61, 67–68
Provost & Security Service, 127
*Psychogenesis* (Moberly), 88
*Public Interest*, 73

racial discrimination
in marriage laws, 68, 77, 143
in military service, 116, 120
Rauch, Jonathan, 58
Ray, Ronald D., 108
Reno, Janet, 40, 41
Rehnquist, William H., 172
Rice, Charles, 171
Rich, Adrienne, 36
Richard the Lionheart, 131
*The Rights of Gay People* (Bogan et al.), 31
*Roe v. Wade*, 145, 149, 166, 171
Romer, Roy, 153
*Romer v. Evans*, 50, 166
decision against legitimizes
homosexuality, 170–71
dissenting opinion on, 172
majority opinion on, 152
*see also* Amendment 2
Roosevelt, Eleanor, 149
Rorty, Richard, 149
Rubin, Gayle, 80

Scalia, Antonin, 169, 172
Schiffren, Lisa, 50, 51
*Sexual Disorientation* (Knight), 84
Sheldon, Louis, 137
*Shelley v. Kraemer*, 158
*Singer v. Hara*, 30
*Skinner v. Oklahoma ex rel. Williamson*,
158
sodomy laws, 137, 143
meaning of, 145–46
Solomon, A. Leiomalama, 47
Solomon, Alisa, 80
Special Investigations Bureau, 127
"special" rights
are claimed by homosexuals, 160
vs. equal rights, 134, 139
is misleading term, 147
Stanford University, 26
*Steffan v. Perry*, 175
Stonewall rebellion, 143–44
Sullivan, Andrew, 53, 75, 77
Sun Microsystems, 20
Supreme Court
on freedom to marry, 49

on marriage as civil right, 30
opinion on *Romer v. Evans*
  dissenting, 172
  majority, 152
on sodomy laws, 146

Tailhook scandal, 119
*Taking Liberties* (BBC program), 126
Thomas, Clarence, 172
Thomas Aquinas, 75
Thompson, Karen, 32–34
Torah, 74
"The Traffic in Women: Notes on the
  Political Economy of Sex" (Rubin), 80
Tuller, David, 39

"The Unmarried Woman's Right to
  Artificial Insemination" (Kritchevsky), 36
U.S. Board of Immigration Appeals, 41
U.S. Constitution, 145

*U.S. News & World Report*
  poll on adoption by gays, 52
*Virtually Normal* (Sullivan), 53, 73

*Wall Street Journal*, 135
Waterhouse, Ian, 128
Weston, Kath, 36
Whitman, Walt, 149
Will, George, 170
Williamson County (Texas), 23
Wilson, James Q., 60, 62, 72
Wilson, Pete, 25
Wolfson, Evan, 48, 49
Woodward, Sandy, 127
Worsnop, Richard L., 133
Writers Guild of America, 27

*Yick Wo v. Hopkins*, 158

Zepezauer, Frank S., 35